Management
And Culture

Robert Wang

ISBN: 9798587896512

PREFACE

The book "Management and Culture" mainly talks about the evolution of management and organization, compared with politic systems, culture and religion. When we put together things in different fields, such as technological progress, corporate development, management, and the history of world social development, we will find some interesting commonalities, if we understand further and experience cultural and social phenomena, such as ethics and religion, etc., we will have a deeper understanding, it is conducive to know management, organization, even in the development and the evolution of society.

The Western culture has three sources, Greek culture, Jewish religion and modern science. Natural philosophy, religion and science occupy a very important position in the West. After the 15th century in the Western society, the agricultural society in the late Middle Ages gradually disintegrated, many thinkers in the period of Enlightenment put forward new ideas about the economy and politics of the society. After Europe entered an industrial society in the 19th century it developed various social theories in the face of new problems, for example; traditional social theories, society divided into two major classes, the bourgeoisie and the working class. The struggle between these two classes has become the driving force for social development. In the 19th century, a surging labor movement appeared in Europe, prompting the birth of the socialist theory. Later, the socialist theory became very popular in the vast number of developing countries. At the beginning of the 20th century, the world's industrialization process was accompanied by some major inventions, such as the popularity of railways, the appearance of automobiles and airplanes which gave rise to scientific management thought. Through the practice of entrepreneurs, a vertically integrated firm was formed. In the modernized enterprises, the separation of enterprise ownership and control has appeared, the managerial class was born, and management became complex. Scientific management thought and vertically integrated firms have dominated the economic structure of the world in the 20th century.

Chinese culture is a kind of evolutionary philosophy, philosophy of life and moral philosophy. On the basis of Chinese classical philosophy, ancient Chinese society formed a bureaucratic society in politics, which lasted for thousands of years. Since the 19th century, China has gradually integrated into the process of world industrialization, traditional culture and systems are facing a huge impact. The traditional one is not very useful, but today Chinese people still live in in the spirit world which Confucianism, Taoism and Buddhism founded, it is impossible to completely get rid of the influence of tradition. Chinese have a unique view of history and society. At the beginning of the 20th century, when Chinese traditional society was undergoing transformation. Various Western social theories such as the theory of class struggle was introduced to China. At that time, some Chinese scholars doubted whether these theories could be applied to China with all kinds of wars, maintaining the unity of the country, the goal of saving the country is overwhelming. Chinese scholars have no external conditions, and no time and level to absorb, criticize, reform and innovate various theories from the West. Gradually, after experiencing various movement, China has accepted the Western natural science. The content of education and culture environment is also very different from the traditional China, Chinese can examine it's own culture.

After World War II, the Western developed countries entered the welfare society and established various social security systems. A new class – the middle class – has emerged in the society. In the field of the Western sociology, after Karl Marx, Emile Durkheim, and Max Weber, there was Talcott Parsons, Robert K.Merton, Charles Weight Mills, Peter Blau, Michel Foucault, Ralf Dahrendorf, Jurgen Habermas, Anthony Giddens and other thinkers; there have also been some new changes in management, the management method of the high tech industry represented by Silicon Valley model is different from the traditional management method. In the 1980s, China reopened the gates, developing the market economy, encouraged foreign investment, absorbed and adopted modern scientific management thoughts and the Chinese economy gradually integrated into the world economic industrial chain. Individuals are allowed to operate businesses, make investments, and have more freedom. The society also introduced many Western thoughts. In terms of cultural exchanges, it has become increasingly close with countries around the world and has gradually entered the big family of the world. The financial crisis that swept the world in 2008 seemed to herald the arrival of new management methods and new economic organizations. In fact, these new things already exist around us and increasingly affect our lives, but we have not yet understood them, as an ancient Chinese poem said, "Of Mountain Lu we cannot make out the true face, for we are lost in the heart of the very place."

The progress of society is multifaceted, including science and technology, ethics, economic systems, working methods, and many other aspects. They are also closely related to each other. This book puts forward some new view points and new ideas in a different way from the current mainstream economic and social theories. Any thoughts in the world have its own source and inheritance. Some of the ideas presented in this book are reflected in the writings of many scholars. It is limited to the condition of the times. It is impossible to fully understand many things at that time. A new set of assumptions and hypotheses cannot be perfect from the beginning. It requires a lot of experts and scholars to continuously enrich and develop, it requires mutual cooperation, inheritance and discussion among scholars. Now that the entire world has entered the era of globalization, people are coming and going closer and more frequently. The spread of the Internet has made the world smaller, and people from all countries can communicate and cooperate quickly. Society has also entered an information society from an industrialized society. In the era of digital economy, it needs more inventions and creations. Diversified cultural exchanges also help people generate new ideas and promote social progress. Just as Buddhism was introduced from India in Chinese history, the modern exchanges between the Eastern and the Western cultures have had a huge impact on the development of their respective societies. I also hope that this book can contribute to the promotion of various cultural exchanges.

CONTENTS

ACKNOWLEDGMENTS

I wish to thank my family for providing me with endless support, and I also wish to express my gratitude to the friends who put forward some comments and advices. Thanks for Benedicte du Cheyron Monroe and Elizabeth Trombley edit, proofread the English version of this book. They also provide many good suggestions to improve this book.

1 CHAPTER INTRODUCTION

Since the world entered the era of industrialization, great changes have taken place in society; people's economic production and organization have undergone tremendous development. From the initial medieval domestic system (putting-out system), the guild system, to the development of ocean trade, the shareholding system has emerged. After the industrial revolution, the factory system was invented in the 18th and 19th centuries. In the 20th century, vertically integrated firms were dominant in the economic field; in the enterprise ownership, there was the separation between the enterprise ownership and its control, and a new professional manager class appeared in the society. These changes happened mainly in Europe and later in the Americas, changes which are inseparable from the unique social, political and economic conditions of Europe and America.

In the later Middle Ages, urban autonomy began to appear in Europe. In Renaissance Italy, many city-state republics appeared, such as Venice, Genoa, Florence, etc., and they adopted the domestic system and the guild system as their mode of production. In other parts of Europe, such as Western Europe, Eastern Europe, Southern Europe and Scandinavia, similar urban handicraft and commercial developments have also occurred. After the Italian Renaissance, there was the Reformation, with the emergence of Protestantism, Anglicanism, Lutheranism, Calvinism, etc... Protestantism in the

Netherland, Germany, France, Britain and Northern Europe has achieved great development. In Britain, Protestantism became the state religion, and the Reformation was personally promoted by King Henry VIII, the original reason being the king's marriage. After the Reformation, the Church's ability to control society declined, and the citizen class developed. During that period, the age of navigation led to the discovery of the Americas and the opening of new routes. Initially Portugal and Spain carried out colonial and trade activities; later, the Netherland, Britain, France and other countries established colonies in the Americas and Asia for commercial trade contacts. In order to adapt to the new business form and colonial trade, the Netherlands and the United Kingdom established the East India Company and the West India Company, one after the other, adopted a partnership organization, issued stocks, and established stock exchanges to vigorously promote ocean trade. In the 19th century, this management method entered the industrial field; with the invention of the steam engine, the textile field has developed rapidly, and many factories have appeared. The operation of the factory is the responsibility of the factory owner and of his relatives, the number of factories is limited, and the operation is relatively simple; the factory system is the mainstream production and management method in Europe in the 19th century. During that period, the poor working environment and the lack of work and life security for the workers led to the continuous emergence of the workers' movements and the emergence of many social transformation thoughts: socialism, anarchism, cooperative movements, and so on. On the European continent, Marxism was also one of the main theories of European society during that period, and it was a method and approach to resolve social contradictions.

But in the Americas, especially in North America, there are relatively few class struggles, and the treatment of various social thoughts is completely different from the one in Europe. There, the term "socialism" does not mean advanced. This is because in the process of industrialization in the United States, unlike in Europe, the United States has developed a set of ideological systems of "scientific management", which were founded and developed by

Taylor, Fayol, Weber, Barnard, Mayo, Simon, Maslow, McGregor, Chandler and other management masters and entrepreneurs like Carnegie, Ford, Sloan, etc... continue to develop, practice and summarize. In this book, we only talk about a few typical characters, and we do not introduce many management gurus and entrepreneurs, as well as many famous management scientists Peter Drucker, Henry Mintzberg, Michael Porter, Charles Handy, Edwards Deming, Tom Peters, Peter Senge, Alvin Toffler and so on. Entrepreneurs are numerous in this piece of land in the United States, they have the courage to pioneer and innovate to provide new perspectives for business operations and development. We can mention Jack Welch, Lee Iacocca, Walt Disney, Dee Hock, Thomas Watson; in Silicon Valley, there are Robert Noyce, Gordon Moore, Andrew Grove, Louis Gerstner, Steve Jobs, Bill Gates, Paul Allen, James Clark, Jeff Bezos, Larry Ellison, Larry Page, Sergey Brin, Mark Zuckerberg et al., The emergence of the scientific management thought and entrepreneurial practices led to the formation of vertically integrated organizations.

The emergence of scientific management directly led to the phenomenon of the separation of enterprise ownership and its control, which is inseparable from the unique political and economic environment of the United States. With the promotion of railway construction, the development of the iron and steel industry, the continuous emergence of inventions such as automobiles and airplanes, the separation of enterprise ownership and control has been implanted in various industries, and basically ruled the US economic mode of production around World War II. The separation of enterprise ownership and control, scientific management, and the characteristics of vertically integrated firm are all related to each others, this is the focus of this book's analysis, which is also the mainstream of Western social and economic development in the 20th century.

The first part of this book, from chapter 2 to chapter 10, basically describes the evolution of the enterprise, the background of the times, the formation of management thought, the practice of entrepreneurs, and the development of vertically integrated firm. This part is about capitalism from birth to maturity, the phases that it goes through; the focus is to analyze the phenomenon of the separation of enterprise ownership and control, how it relates to management thought and vertically integrated organizations, etc... The latter part from Chapter 11 to Chapter 19 compares the evolution of enterprises, the origin of civilization and the evolution of ancient political systems, as there are new trends and new features in management, the chapter 14 talks about the development and influence of the computer industry. The chapter 16 and the chapter 17 describes Chinese classical thoughts, ethics and religion, new forms of work and characteristics, and the laws of market evolution in high-tech industries.

The reason for comparing the development of enterprises with the origin of civilization and the evolution of political systems in the second half of the book is mainly because these three are the same phenomenon. The emergence of scientific management and the separation of enterprise ownership and control have similar characteristics and some common features with Chinese classical thought and ancient Chinese political system. At the beginning of the organization, the scale of the enterprise was small, and it was basically owned by the family; with the expansion of the scale of the enterprise and the increase of the number of shareholders, in this case, the enterprise is owned by the family and the extended family who are going to hire professional managers for management; professional managers also own shares of the company; the ownership and control of the enterprise are separate, and persons who are not related to the family business also participate in the regular management of the company; the company which was owned by the family or extended family becomes a public company, the company's blood relationship is broken, which is similar to the country's foundation on the basis of surpassing the blood relationship. From the perspective of anthropology, the formation, development, and evolution of the enterprise is the result of a continuous decrease in blood links and a continuous strengthening of geopolitical factors. If it is viewed from the perspective of the development of the political system, it is a process from the aristocracy to the bureaucracy, professional officials have replaced feudal aristocracy, and persons who have no personal relationship with the emperor participate in the governance of the country. The various changes have taken place in the economic organization of enterprises, this evolutionary process is not accidental, there are profound social development laws behind it, which seem to be coming from three angles, the economic, national, and political aspects, different aspects, but the actual development has similar laws. The development and change of a society, or the evolution of the civilization, is a very interesting subject. The evolution of society and civilization is more complicated, including all aspects, production organizations, economic and political systems, religions, laws, humanities, science and technology, etc.; Some historical records are vague or conflicting, and the level of detail and document preservation in various countries and regions are different. Relatively speaking, the development and evolution of the enterprise is relatively simple; it has been around 500 years since the creation of enterprises until now, with complete information in various fields, many analyses and comparisons, and it is still developing and changing, and has different characteristics in various countries. For the evolution of the ownership system of enterprises, the research on the management methods of enterprises is also quite sufficient. Scientific research generally simplifies complex things and it from simple to complex, so this book first analyzes the organization of enterprises, from the perspectives of management and economics, studies such organizations as enterprises, studies the development and evolution of enterprises, and the birth and development of management thought.

Comparing the origin of the country, we know that the origin of the state and civilization has gone through three stages: clan, tribal alliance, and country. Later, when scholars joined the chiefdom between the tribal alliance and the state, they became clan, tribal alliance, chiefdom and the state in four stages. This reflects the process of property ownership from clan to private ownership. The establishment of the state and civilization goes from the clan, the tribal alliance to the chiefdom and the state. The division of labor in the business and the handicraft industry has caused people to live together, the flow of personnel has increased. The development of trade has broken the boundaries of the clan, as a result, citizens can realize their civic powers and obligations in their place of residence, and are classified according to their property.

In terms of political system, the blood relations played a very important role at the beginning. In a country ruled by nobility, the nobility is inherited, the nobility shares power with the king. From the aristocracy to the bureaucratic state, the geographical factors are more important, like in ancient China, the selection and appointment of officials was an imperial examination system, and officials had no personal relationship with the emperor. In ancient China, in the early bureaucracy, the relatives of the emperor, especially the queen's family often occupied an important position in the political life, as was very obvious in the Han Dynasty. In the Ming and Qing dynasties, the bureaucracy was very mature, the blood factors appeared less and less in the national politics. The princes of the Ming dynasty did not have real power; the princes of the Qing dynasty had real power, but after grade of the princes descended. Later, we will analyze why ancient Europe did not get rid of the consanguinity factor, while the ancient Middle East states and ancient China put more emphasis on geopolitical factors.

The development of the enterprise also follows a similar process. At the beginning, entrepreneurs and relatives controlled and managed the enterprise. With the expansion of the scale of the enterprise, the importance of blood factors decreased. After the emergence of scientific management, business talents can be trained through school, this education is completely institutionalized, professional managers have no personal relationship with the company's founders, the selection of professional managers depends more on performance. In ancient China, during the Spring and Autumn Period and the Warring States Period, various thoughts emerged, and then the Han Dynasty determined the mainstream status of Confucianism in the society. There were private schools in the local area, and there was imperial university "Guozijian" in the central government. Through education and training, professional officials were formed, the selection of professional officials is based on performance, there was an evaluation mechanism. From this, we can also see the development of the enterprise management and the changes in ownership, which have rules similar to the origin of the state and civilization, and the evolution of political systems in ancient societies. In this book, we compare the similarities and differences between the evolution of the enterprise development, the origin of civilization and the evolution of the political system in ancient societies, states; describe these interesting phenomena, give some concrete examples, list their common characteristics, and a modest spur to induce others to come forward with valuable contributions, and hope that readers can put forward better ideas and opinions.

The World War II in the 20th century directly gave birth to the computer science and industry. The technology foundation of the computer industry was semiconductors, and later integrated circuits. With the development of computer technology, in the semiconductor area, on the West coast of the United States-California, in the Silicon Valley area near San Francisco, a new management method was developed in the field of microcomputers and the Internet. The book carefully analyzes how this new model is generated and developed, which distinctive characteristics does it present, and which is its evolution process, I hope readers to analyse and to provide references. The development and changes in the computer field have processes and characteristics similar to the Western Reformation, so in this book I list a single chapter and contrast these phenomena. With the development of the computer industry, the popularity of the Internet, and the advancement of artificial intelligence technology, new changes will be made in the management methods and organizational forms of the enterprises in the future. The book also discusses these new trends and features of the management and ownership systems.

Whether it compares scientific management and modern vertically integrated firms with ancient Chinese thought and ancient political systems, or from the perspective of the development and changes of the computer industry and the process of the

Reformation, they all contain religious and cultural content; the topic of religion and culture cannot be circumvented, especially the Chinese classical thought, morality, ethics and religion. The Chinese classical thought, morality, ethics and religion are inseparable from the ancient Chinese political system, so we organize two chapters in the book to talk about classical Chinese thought, morality, ethics and religion, we can compare modern scientific management thoughts with them; the roles played in society and enterprises are similar, and they are all mainstream thoughts under certain social conditions. Chinese classical thought is broad and profound, and contains rich content, from ancient times to the present, countless masters and scholars have appeared in the inheritance and innovation of classical thought. Since modern times, as China has integrated into the world, the traditional Chinese culture has been impacted, and people have different attitudes towards traditional Chinese culture at different times; in here, I only just talk about personal experience and opinions. It must be stated here that as an author from China, I am naturally familiar with the Chinese classical thought and the Eastern philosophy, I am relatively unfamiliar with the Western culture, such as Christianity and Islam; the theme of this book is economic management, for culture and religion we analyzed and judged from the perspective of sociology, analyzing their functions and roles in society.

The last chapter of this book analyzes the market evolution process of high-tech enterprises. Now the emerging computer industry and the Internet industry have high technology content and new technologies emerge one after another frequently, in these fields, the market changes rapidly and some characteristics appear, this book also analyzes the various participants of the market, how they interact, and the laws of market evolution.

2 CHAPTER ENTERPRISE DEVELOPMENT PROCESS

1.The period of agricultural capitalism

Regarding enterprises, there are many experts and scholars discussing how such organizations are formed and evolved. Organizations such as enterprises first appeared in Europe. We can review the emergence, development and changes of the enterprises to understand how the enterprises are different from previous organization, and how have the enterprise ownership and management changed? What characteristics appear? It will help us to understand the relationship between innovation and management, and the development of society.

The enterprise changes with the development of the capitalism system. The development of capitalism can be divided into agricultural capitalism, commercial capitalism, industrial capitalism, and the information age. At different stages, the organization of the enterprise also has different forms. The enterprise is the most typical production organization of the capitalism system. It is based on wage labor and it divides the social group into two major groups: employers and workers, that is, the capital and labor. The employers are the capitalists, who have control over capital and means of production, and the workers, who are employees, sell their labor and earn wages. Employers provide the labor sites and purchase the production equipment and the machinery. Laborers concentrated on the site to work together. This work method first originated in Europe and first appeared in the textile industry and the clothing manufacturing field. Initially, the merchants bought the wool with capital, contracted it to the spinner and the weaver, and then received the finished textile, sent it to other industries to complete the garment production, and ultimately were responsible for selling the garment. At this time, the employer owns the raw materials and the products, but he does not master the entire production process. The production equipment, the loom, is owned by the individual weaver. Production is decentralized. Slowly, the production became concentrated. The employer provides the equipment and then the workplace. The factory appears. The structure of the early enterprises was very simple, most of them were owned by the family, and they were mainly concentrated in the textile field.

In the period of agricultural capitalism, the mode of production was mainly the domestic system. The remuneration paid by merchants is calculated on a piece-by-piece basis. The workers receive the processing fees on time. The domestic system prevails in Italy, France, Netherlands, the United Kingdom, and Germany. Some weavers bring their own looms, but there are no raw materials, they go to the employer and get the raw materials, some weavers rent a loom from the employer, the employer does not need to rent a factory. After the employer supplied the equipment, the employer's control was strengthened, the number of employees increased, the scale expanded, and factories appeared. The domestic system is implemented in rural areas because rural labor is cheaper than urban labor. At the same time, there were guilds in the cities. There were two types of guilds in the cities in the later Middle Ages of Europe. Merchant guilds and handicraft guilds. Merchant guilds were responsible for the purchase and sale of commodities, and handicraft guilds were responsible for manufacturing commodities. Inside the handicraft guild, there are hierarchies, masters, skilled workers and apprentices. The master owns tools, raw materials and finished products. Skilled workers are employed and do not start their own businesses. Apprentices are future workers who are learning. Guilds monitor the quality of work and control the types of work. Different industries form guilds in different industries. For instance, during the Renaissance, in Florence, there are 21 guilds, consisting of 7 large and 14 small guilds. The 7 major guilds are judges and notaries, banking, cloth industry, wool, silk, physicians and apothecaries, and furriers. Inside the guild, it is a hierarchical system. Masters can only hire a limited number of skilled workers, and wages and working hours are uniformly stipulated. There are strict boundaries between guilds. They cannot cross each other and cannot work in the field of other guilds. Merchant guilds are similar to trade associations. Merchants are middlemen of trade and employers in the domestic system.

The characteristics of the domestic system and handicraft guilds are their limited scale, the work is labor-intensive, and the production process can be divided into several stages. The labor force follows a specialized division of labor, the capital investment is very low, the production equipment is also very simple, the production process is basically uncontrollable, the efficiency is low, there is no performance monitoring, and the product quality is also uneven. These two production methods existed around the later Middle Ages. After 1600, with the rise of the factory system, these two modes of production existed longer in some regions. In addition to the textile industry, the printing industry and the hardware products industry are also another two areas where domestic system and guild systems are prevalent. Since the late 15th century, all parts of Europe have been filled with small, printing offices with a master and two or three helpers and only one printing machine. The printing industry does not have high requirements for mechanical equipment, but it is much more troublesome to operate the printing business independently ... The big book dealer is responsible for supplying paper and transportation business, becoming an employer in the domestic system and small printing houses process orders and complete tasks. The hardware products industry needs capital to purchase raw materials, to store and to sell. Merchants provide funds, supply raw materials, process orders and produce in manual workshops.

The domestic system and handicraft guilds are found in various regions of Europe, such as the United Kingdom, France, Netherland, Germany, Italy, the Baltic region, the Iberian Peninsula, Central Europe, Eastern Europe, and the Balkan Peninsula. However, the most prosperous was in Italy. Italy started as a trader like Venice and was profitable. Venice was the earliest commercial and colonial empire of history. Venice undoubtedly occupies an important position in the Renaissance Italy. Venice's economy relied mainly on overseas trade and resale trade. For instance, Venice is responsible for the distribution of woolen fabrics produced by Florence in the Middle East, at the same time it is also responsible for importing Spanish wool. The reason that Venice became the mart through which East and West were to exchange their produce was her geographical location. Venice is the seaport nearest to the center of Europe. The politics of Venice is dominated by commercial nobles, and this hereditary merchant aristocracy powerfully contributed to the economic prosperity of Venice. Someone has said, "indulgent to the subject, sumptuous in the public service, economical in the administration of the finances, equitable and impartial in the administration of justice, knowing well how to give prosperity to the arts, agriculture and commerce; beloved by the people who obeyed it."[1] But the Venetians seem to be not well described in the literary field. Like Shakespeare's play "The Merchant of Venice", the Venetians are portrayed as having been the most gainful, greedy, materialistic people of the Renaissance. Venice later became involved in the struggle for maritime hegemony with Genoa. The famous medieval European traveler Marco Polo, a Venetian businessman, came to China in the 13th century. He served in the court of the Yuan Dynasty. After returning to Venice, he was captured in the war with Genoa. With the help of his inmates, he wrote "The Travels of Marco Polo ", which recorded what he saw

---

[1] James Westfall Thompson, Economic And Social History Of Europe In The Later Middle Ages(1300-1530), (The Century Co, 1931), pp. 245

and heard, which was very influential. Many navigators in the Age of Discovery had read this book carefully. Marco Polo recorded in the book that the paper money issued by the Yuan Dynasty were the first in the world to use paper money as fiat money. The book records the production process and circulation methods of paper money. In the Yuan Dynasty, paper money were issued indiscriminately, leading to inflation.

Florence later became the leader of the wool industry and combined it with the banking industry to achieve prosperity. The famous Medici family were famous bankers at that time. Florentine merchants imported wool from the United Kingdom. Many large business firms in Florence established branches in the United Kingdom. During that period, Florentine merchants were the favored officials of the British court. Florence not only imported wool from the United Kingdom, it also imported from Spain. At that time, the Merino wool of Spain was the most famous. The Merino wool was pure in color and the fabric was soft. It is said that people who privately exported Merino from Spain before the 18th century will be convicted and sentenced to death. I remembered the story of Chinese silk. After Chinese produced silk, it exported to other countries. The silk was soft and gorgeous, the clothes made with silk were elegant and expensive, and the price was high. It was a famous luxury product. Silk revenue was an important and stable tax source of the government in the past and the technology was secret. Other countries have to spend a lot of gold and silver to buy silk. Many countries tried to produce their own silk, but they did not know how silk is produced. Some people said that it grows from trees. At that time, China also prohibited the secret of silk production to be spread, and the outflow of silkworm species was strictly prohibited. The Romans sent two monks to China and brought the silkworms back to Rome in an hollow cane. Another story is that in ancient times, a Chinese princess married in the kingdom of Khotan in the Western Regions. The king wanted to obtain Chinese silk technology, and sent an emissary to tell the princess that there was no silk in their country. The princess married over, and if she wanted to wear silk, she needed to bring the silkworms. The princess hid the silkworms in a thick hat, which was inconvenient for customs officers to check, and the silk was passed to kingdom of Khotan. It is also said that the Romans took the silkworm species from the kingdom of Khotan, so that the silk passed to Rome.

Florence not only imported wool from Spain, but also woolen fabrics. For Florentines, the West is the raw material production area, and the East is an important market for finished products. Florence sells woolen fabrics in the Eastern Market for spices, herbs, dyes, etc., like alum, and then transport these to the North.

The two forms of domestic system and handicraft guild have also appeared in ancient China. During the Ming dynasty, merchants in Jiangsu and Hangzhou, where the commodity economy was developed, also purchase cotton and other raw materials, distribute raw materials, spin in their home, and merchants purchase the finished products for resale. Or merchants buy textile machines, create machine rooms, and hire workers to do the work. This is the so-called budding period of capitalism. At the government level, there is an Imperial Textiles that controls the operations of government-owned operators, and is directly managed by the imperial household, ministry of Internal Affairs and the prince. The most typical example is Cao Xueqin, a famous novelist in the Qing Dynasty and the author of "Dream of the Red Chamber". He was born in the Cao's clan. In the Cao's clan, there were three generations and Cao's four members who have been the commissioner of Imperial Textiles in Nanjing for 60 years. The reason why Cao's family has been able to monopolize this position for so long is the close relationship between the Cao family and the emperor. Cao Yin was the grandfather of Cao Xueqin. Cao Yin was a childhood playmate and personal confident of the Kangxi Emperor. He grew up and became the commissioner of Imperial Textiles in Nanjing. He can have a close relationship with the emperor --- direct correspondence, reported every move within the jurisdiction. During the Kangxi Emperor itinerant trips South of the Nanjing region, he often lived in the Cao's family residences. The Cao family spent a lot of money because of the many receptions they gave for emperor and this was one of the reasons for the decline of the Cao family. In the Qing Dynasty, there were three Imperial Textiles in Nanjing, Suzhou, and Hangzhou, all of which belonged to the government. The three textile factories in the heyday had more than 1,800 looms, more than 7,000 artisans. The commissioner of Imperial Textiles was equivalent to the current deputy minister of the government department. The private textile industry developed well during the Qing Dynasty. The Kangxi Emperor had lifted restrictions on machine users. Private investors could own five or six hundred textile machines, and the products were also exported in large quantities.

2.The period of commercial capitalism

After the 16th century, the age of navigation, the discovery of the Americas and the opening of new routes, the ocean trade has greatly increased. European countries can bypass the Cape of Good Hope at the Southern tip of Africa and reach Asia to trade directly with India and China, or Westwards through Americas, they can also trade with the East. Silver mines have been discovered in the Americas, and the silver from the Americas can be used to pay for commodities such as spices, silk and porcelain purchased from the East. After the opening of the new route, its total trade volume is much larger than that of the Mediterranean trade. The scale of the Mediterranean trade has continued to shrink, and the status of the Italian city-state republics in world trade has declined. At that time, Italy did not achieve reunification, and the city-state republics controlled only the city and surrounding areas, fighting each other openly. Later nation-states, such as Portugal, Spain, the Netherlands, the United Kingdom and France, gradually developed, opened new routes, carried out economic system reforms, invented shareholding systems, established joint stock companies, established stock exchanges, issued stocks, adapted to the new situation of ocean trade and dominated the new pattern of world trade.

In the 17th century, the Netherlands and Britain first entered the period of commercial capitalism, during this time the main innovation of commerce was the emergence of the stock companies. During the domestic system and the handicraft guild, property rights issues were not prominent. The mode of production that appeared after the domestic system was the factory system, which is generally owned by the family. After the discovery of the Americas in the sixteenth century and the subsequent expansion of world trade, such as the spice trade, pepper trade, silk trade, etc., this trade was much larger than the previous Mediterranean trade, but the trade cycle is longer. At that time, the trade from Europe to Asia, whether it was to bypass the route from Southern Africa to India and then to Southeast Asia, or sail from Europe to the West, and then to the East through the Americas, it usually took about three years. At that time, ocean voyage was just like launching a spaceship to Mars today. It was full of various risks and uncontrollable factors, such as ocean storms, scurvy, pirate attacks and so on. However, the trade volume of ocean voyages is huge, such as the spice trade. The trade volume transferred from Venice, was 2,100 tons per year. After the opening of the new route, the trade volume suddenly increased to 7,000 tons, and the shareholding system came into being.

At that time, in Asia, in agriculture, there were pepper, cloves, nutmeg, cinnamon, cotton, tea; in the handicraft industry, there were silk and porcelain, there was a large demand for these commodities in Europe. The Moluccan Islands in Indonesia are the main producers of cloves, nutmeg kernels, and dried nutmeg skin. Pepper comes from Sumatra, Indonesia, and China is home to tea, silk and porcelain. In ancient China, the sea ban did not put an end to the export of porcelain. It reopened after the mid-Ming Dynasty, and foreign trade developed rapidly. The export of porcelain reached its peak. During that period, China produced many porcelains for export, customized porcelain according to foreign customer needs, many European nobles ordered custom porcelain with a family heraldry pattern. After the establishment of the Dutch East India Company in 1602, there were 20 million pieces of porcelain shipped from China to Europe. European royal families, nobles and other classes have purchased and collected Chinese porcelain. Today these exquisite porcelains are valuable and exhibited in many countries. British Percival David, who has collected more than 1,400 pieces of Chinese porcelain, is the world's most influential collector of Chinese cultural relics. Later he donated the collection to the David Foundation, he founded, and these collections are now exhibited at the British Museum. In the 18th century, European countries produced their own porcelain, and the peak of Chinese porcelain exports passed.

The Dutch Republic, which was established shortly after the 17th century, had just become independent from Spain and urgently needed to develop its economy. Whether with trade with Northern Europe and the Baltic Sea or trade with the Mediterranean Sea and even further trade with Asia, it stimulated the Netherlands to adopt the shareholding system first. The demand for Asian commodities was huge, and the trade with Asia was profitable. However, the demand for European commodities was not large in Asian markets at that time, so the commodities purchased in Asia must be paid for with precious metals. Due to the discovery of a large number of silver mines in the Americas, silver became the main payment currency for the ocean trade, and European merchants used silver obtained in the Americas to pay for goods purchased in Asia. The famous Manila galleon is to exchange gold and silver of the Americas for raw silk, silk and porcelain of China. China also imported crops such as corn, sweet potatoes, peanuts, tomatoes and peppers from the Americas, which provided material basis for rapid population growth during the Ming and Qing Dynasties. Among the European countries, the Netherlands first invented the joint-stock company system and created a stock exchange to share risks and raise capital. In 1602, the Netherlands established the Dutch East India Company, which is composed of six branches, which are independent of each other, and obtained the monopoly of trade in the area East of the Cape of Good Hope. The company's main shareholders were members of the city council, businessmen and officials. The company's stock was traded in the Amsterdam stock exchange and a maximum price was five times of the par value. The Dutch East India Company had 22,000 employees during its heyday, which was probably the largest company in the world at that time. This economic organization that can transfer and protect private property rights had made the Netherlands to obtain the title of "sea coachman" and also made the Netherlands the Europe's leading economy.

But soon, the country on the other side of the strait - the United Kingdom -, learned the Dutch approach and set up many joint stock trading companies and stock exchanges. The joint stock trading company obtained the trade monopoly, subject to the approval of the king. Its shareholders were mainly businessmen and officials, it attracted, surpassing individual capital and took huge risks, this business activity has also expanded into the field of colonial development. Monopoly privileges exclude businessmen other than the franchise companies. The most famous joint stock company is the British East India Company, which ruled India. The East India Company had its own army and courts, which was also a spectacle in the history of the company's development. The British East India Company assumed the political and military functions of the country, established courts, enacted laws, granted titles, built forts, mobilized troops, and went to wars. The purpose of the company is to make profit, which the function of the government is to maintain social order and coordinate various social issues. The two organizations are contradictory.

In 1857, India's First War of Independence or the Sepoy Mutiny broke out under the governance of the British East India Company. The background was ethnic opposition and religious conflict caused by colonial rule. The treatment of the British and the Indians is very different, and all classes in India are full of dissatisfaction and hatred towards the British, it led to a total outbreak of various social conflicts. The direct cause was that the East India Company issued bullets to soldiers using tallow and lard as lubricating oil, it violated the taboo of Hindus and Muslims. The war mainly took place in North India and lasted for more than one year, it ended the rule of the East India Company. In 1858, the British Parliament passed the "The Government of India Act", and the power of the East India

Company in India was transferred to the King of England.

Joint stock companies can be seen everywhere in the colonial trade. The first 13 colonies in North America were founded by joint stock companies, including the Virginia Company, the Massachusetts Gulf Colonial Company, and so on. Colonial trade was monopolized. For instance, colonial commodities can only be shipped to the United Kingdom and not to other countries. In "The Wealth of Nations", written by the classical economist Adam Smith, we can see that there is a special chapter and discussion of the colonial trade, "the tobacco in Maryland and Virginia, for example, by means of the monopoly which England enjoys of it, certainly comes cheaper to England than it can do to France, to whom England commonly sells a considerable part of it."[2] It is clear that this is a monopoly trade, and its profits are very amazing. Those who benefit from monopolizing goods are also a special class. After it said, "The monopoly of the colony trade, ... seems to have broken altogether that natural balance which would otherwise have taken place among all the different branches of British industrial."[3] The end result was that the thirteen North American colonies declared independence and established the United States.

The British East India Company also participated in the trade with China. The main product traded was tea, which was exported to the UK and other regions. The profits from the tea trade were used to pay the East India Company's management salaries and exchange tea for silver in the Americas. The famous Boston Tea Party broke out in Boston, America in 1773, throwing East India Company tea into the sea, which was the direct fuse of the American Revolutionary War. In 1833, Britain government opened up free trade to the Chinese market and cancelled the East India Company's

---

[2] Adam Smith, An Inquiry Into the Nature and Causes of the Wealth of Nations, chap 7, part 3

[3] Adam Smith, An Inquiry Into the Nature and Causes of the Wealth of Nations, chap 7, part 3

monopoly on trade with China.

By the middle of the eighteenth century and the beginning of the nineteenth century, the system of stock trading companies had entered the industrial field. At this time, the domestic system in the industrial field evolved into a factory system. The industrialization period came and the steam engine appeared.

If there is little difference between the East and the West in the forms of the domestic system, then this difference between the East and the West is obvious in the ocean trade and the overseas trade during the period of commercial capitalism. Some people say that China gradually fell behind in the 15th and 16th centuries. This makes sense, because when the West encouraged the overseas trade, signed contracts with individual navigators, and later invented joint-stock companies to share risks, China imposed sea bans. Although China has emphasized agriculture and suppressed commerce since ancient times, commerce can indeed bring huge revenue to the government. During the Song and Yuan dynasties, that is, during the 11th, 12th, 13th, and 14th centuries, the government established the overseas trading department. In the Ming Dynasty, the overseas trade was dominated by officials, it was mainly a tribute trade. The famous Zheng He's navigation, the event which took place in 1405 - 1433, mainly for political purposes, was an official event, although there was trade, but the trade was not valued, and what the nautical trip brought back was mainly some rare treasures, jewelry diamonds, rare animals, lions, ostriches, giraffes, etc., most of these were luxury goods. Because Zheng He's voyage was huge and the harvest was relatively small, it was not carried out later. In ancient China's trade with neighboring countries, Vietnam and Korea took place every three years, with Ryukyu every two years, and with Japan every ten years. Zheng He sailed from Jiangsu or Fujian and arrived in Vietnam, Cambodia, Thailand, Malaysia, Java, Sumatra, Sri Lanka, Southern India, Kolkata, Cochin, Bangladesh, Saudi Arabia, Yemen, Iran, Somalia and Kenya, etc., the navigation took various colors of silk, gauze, silver, satin, copper coins, porcelain and iron pots, etc., mainly they were used for rewards.

Private overseas trade has existed since the Tang Dynasty. In the story of the "tales from the thousand and one nights" in the ancient Arab region, the navigator Sinbad travelled to China. In the Ming Dynasty, the trade with Southeast Asia, South Asia, the Middle East and East Africa was also very developed. The goods handled were mainly spices, flowers and plants, corn, gold and silver, pearls, porcelain and hardware product. However, the private trade has not been smooth and often encountered obstacles imposed by the sea ban. The main reason for the formation of Japanese pirates in the history was that, although the Jiangsu and Zhejiang areas along the coast during the Ming Dynasty were rich, there were also many people and few farms. Many people were engaged in business or even in the overseas trade for their livelihood. This kind of activity, especially the overseas trade, can export many of the country 's handicrafts, such as silk, cotton, porcelain, iron pots and tea, etc., which was beneficial to individuals and to the country, but the Ming Dynasty did not understand, didn't care, didn't recognize and impose a sea ban on the private overseas trade. The leaders of the Japanese pirates were mostly businessmen, and most of them were merchants in Anhui, Guangdong, Fujian, and Zhejiang in China. These persons had broken away from the traditional imperial examinations to become officials, they did business, and were considered as pirates. In contrast, the famous navigator Francis Drake of Europe was the second man who completed his circumnavigation of the world after Ferdinand Magellan, he was born as a pirate and was from a pirate to a navigator, and was later knighted by the Queen of England. Today the strait between South America's Cape Horn, Chile and the South Shetland Islands of Antarctica is called the Drake Passage. The historical status and the treatment were greatly different. However, For the piracy phenomenon in ancient China, ancient government did not analyze the deep social reasons behind it, but simply arrested and eliminated it. The personal fate of the famous officials who arrested and eliminated pirates, like Hu Zongxian and Qi Jiguang was not very good, it seems to explain the problem. It was also during this period that the Western and Chinese roads diverged. At this time, Western countries vigorously promoted overseas trade, implemented mercantilist policies, promoted joint-stock companies, innovated property rights systems, set up stock exchanges, and gradually embarked on the path of capitalism. At this time, while China was unreconstructed during this period, the policy of closing the country and suppressing business restricted and hindered the development of the overseas trade and the national economy. New mode of production and new production relations were suppressed and hit. The lack of institutional innovation was a reason that China form advanced to backwardness, these historical lessons are worth pondering. It wasn't until the Opium War that Western countries used force to knock on China's door, and that the capitalism mode of production was able to develop in China.

3.The period of industrial capitalism

The joint-stock company started only in the trade field, and the risks of ocean navigation are huge. It needs a lot of capital to operate. This method gradually entered the industrial field. In the industrial manufacturing field, the joint-stock company gradually replaced the domestic system, and the joint stock operation also replaced the family ownership and the completion of this process has brought society into the period of industrial capitalism. A large number of factory systems have emerged. This period is an important period of development for capitalism. Capitalism has achieved a rapid development. Large machines, large industries, inventions and creations were emerging, and science and technology have also been increasingly valued. The emergence of new inventions, such as railway, automobiles, airplanes, electrical appliances, communications, chemicals and petroleum paved the way, and some pioneers in management appeared, they further generated scientific management thought.

In the 1760s, the reform of the political system was completed in Britain, constitutional monarchy was established, the parliament played a decisive role in the political life of the country, and the king became a symbol of the highest power but did not have real power. Under this political and social background, it provided good opportunities for the development of industrial capitalism were provided and produced the industrial revolution. First of all, in the textile field, machines replaced manpower. Why is there an industrial revolution in the textile industry first? This is because the textile industry has low capital requirements, low investment, and fast returns, which is conducive to the circulation of capital. The heart of the industrial revolution is the steam engine, which was invented by James Watt. James Watt has no academic background, was born an ordinary man. He was a Scotsman and his father was a shipbuilder. Watt worked as an apprentice in London. He collaborated with British steelmaker Matthew Boulton, who provided funding. Steam engines had existed before, but Watt has developed and perfected steam engines. Steam engines provide power, machines replace manpower. Factory systems replace domestic systems. Production equipment, energy, and production organization methods have changed. Steam power has reduced production costs, reduced the price and has expanded the market, and the scale of production has also been expanded, established various factories. The establishment of factories has created the need for leadership and management, more workers, more machines, and larger scale, this positive acceleration cycle makes the factory system go to the historical stage and become the mainstream of economic production. The emergence of the factory system also puts forward higher requirements for capital, and the expansion of factories requires more capital. The joint-stock company system can easily meet this requirement. During this period, a group of characters emerged --- the entrepreneurs. Entrepreneurs and businessmen are different. Entrepreneurs have more innovative characteristics, new organizational methods, new production equipment and new commodities. Entrepreneurs certainly need capital to buy raw materials, machinery and equipment, and hire workers. The factory system later expanded from the textile field to the railway field. Before the emergence of scientific management, the factory system has been the main production method. This period is also the main period of the activities of the famous philosopher, economist and sociologist, Karl Marx. Workers 'strikes and the destruction of machines and other social phenomena also mainly appeared in this period. The time span was from the 1760s to the early 20th century, about 100 years. During this period of ownership, a certain degree of separation of ownership and control emerged, and some pioneers of management appeared.

The factory system is the main form of industrial production after the domestic system. The field is mainly concentrated in the textile field. The investment in this field is not large. One or several families and several partners can raise enough funds to open a factory and buy equipment. Before the industrial revolution, textile machinery was relatively primitive and not so complicated. The advantage of the factory system over the domestic system is that the workers concentrate their labor in the factory, and the production process and product quality are controllable. The owner of the factory itself is an entrepreneur who is responsible for managing everything in the factory. There was no management hierarchy in the early factories. According to information, there are departments in the factory. The head of each department is a partner or a relative. There are one or two managers under the head of the department and they supervise the workers. Management is simple.

The expansion of trade has led to the discovery of new lands, the establishment of new colonies, and the cultivation of cotton on the new lands. Like the cotton plantations in the North American colonies, more raw materials have been provided, and technology has advanced. The textile industry began to mechanize, in 1765, James Hargreaves invented the Jenny spinning machine, which can release 80 yarns at a time. In 1769, Richard Arkwright invented the hydraulic spinning machine, which can spin cotton into thicker and stronger yarn. Machines were invented, and power energy became a problem again. How to drive these machines? In 1765, Watt invented the first steam engine that could be used. At the beginning, the steam engine was only used for pumping and blasting. Later, it was used to move coal and ore. The popularity of large machines laid the foundation for the development of factory systems. Work was transferred from home to the factory, the factory expanded, and thousands of workers could be hired. Someone needed to supervise their work, and he had to be trained to take care of the workers 'lives. Workers sometimes smashed machines and went on strike in order to improve working conditions, shorten working hours, work 6 days a week, one day to take a holiday. Working 8 hours a day, there were also child and female workers among the workers. The work in the factory is tedious. The same action is repeated every day. The working hours are strict. Even the time to go to the bathroom and to eat are counted. This phenomenon still exists in the contemporary era. The famous Taiwanese company Foxconn is a manufacturer of many mobile phones, including Apple's OEM. Foxconn's factory in Dongguan, Guangdong in China, is said to have 400,000 workers in a small area. So many workers work every day, work, eat and sleep, and have no entertainment, no social activities, workers are like robots. In the first half of 2010, Foxconn's factory in Guangdong had more than ten consecutive jumping events, which caused widespread concern in the society. The French telecommunications company, now called Orange Group, began the privatization process in 1997. For the purpose of competitive pressure, raising the stock price and obtaining benefits, the management began to cut costs by layoffs. France Telecom was a state-owned company before, most employees are civil servants and it is difficult to dissolve labor relations. If the managers dismissed employees and he must report to the government. In order to achieve the purpose of layoffs, the management did not make sufficient preparations, and used some informal means, called "terror management" and "workplace mental harassment", which destroyed the employees' mental health and created a deformed working atmosphere, resulting in many employees' suicide and attempt, while France Telecom's profit hit a new high. The public prosecutor's office collected evidence, and seven former executives of France Telecom, the predecessor of Orange Group, were accused in court. There are many ways to improve the profitability of an enterprise, such as organizational change, technological innovation, etc., cost reduction and layoffs are just one way. Orange Group launched Orange Bank in November

2017. It is a mobile bank that provides basic banking services, including bank accounts, locking and unlocking bank cards, remittances between accounts, personal loans and mobile payments. It is currently operating in France and Spain, and plans to provide services throughout Europe in the future.

I remember a story saying this, saying that a worker started with a meager income, but he strives to get upstream, relying on savings to become a capitalist step by step, is this story credible? Is it possible in real life? I think there is such a possibility, but the probability of realization in different countries is different. Becoming a capitalist requires capital, technology, and interpersonal relationships, etc. These need to be accumulated for a long time. For an ordinary worker who works in a factory every day, his income is wages. In addition to his daily expenses, he also needs to support his family and let his children receive an education. Is wage income enough for him to accumulate and become a capitalist? But it is undeniable that there are indeed some famous people, such as Andrew Carnegie, the steel king of the United States, who worked as a child laborer in a textile factory when he was 13 years old, and later became an entrepreneur step by step, and the founder of Ford Motor Company Henry Ford, Carnegie grew from an ordinary person step by step to an entrepreneur, a steel king, and later did so many charities, the establishment of Carnegie College, which requires the background of the times, the conditions provided by social development, and personal efforts, these are indispensable, and the personal experience of these characters will be further discussed later. From the process of Watt 's invention of the steam engine, we don't seem to see the role of government. This is another interesting topic. We will also talk about this phenomenon later. In the 18th century, Britain had completed the Reformation and the bourgeois revolution, the constitutional monarchy has been established.

During the factory system period, many pioneers appeared in management. The reason why they were pioneers was that before Frederick Winslow Taylor, the founder of scientific management,

management had not yet become a science, one that could be learned and taught in the college. Knowledge, management at that time was more accumulation of personal experience.

3 CHAPTER MANAGEMENT PIONEERS

1.Robert Owen

Before the emergence of scientific management, some management pioneers appeared. The first introduction is Robert Owen. Owen (1771-1858) is regarded as a representative-of-utopian socialism. Owen is an Englishman and a commoner. He started as an apprentice in a factory and became an entrepreneur step by step. His most famous action was to buy 1,214 hectares of land in the United States and to begin a socialist experiment. At the age of 18, Owen established his first factory in Manchester. At that time, the cotton trade developed rapidly, and the invention of the steam engine made large factories possible. Owen's first impression of management was "I looked very wisely at the men in their different departments, although I really knew nothing. But, by intensely observing everything, I maintained order and regularity throughout the establishment, which proceeded under the circumstances far better than I had anticipated."[4] Later, Owen sold the factory to a man named Drinkwater and he became the manager. From here, we can also see the emergence of the separation of corporate ownership and

---

[4] Robert Owen, The Life of Robert Owen, (London: Effingham Wilson, 1857), pp. 31-32

control. There are many examples of this. When they are inexperienced, factory owners can hire a manager. It may sometimes be incredible and should they hire their own boss? In fact, managers only receive salaries. Armand Hammer, the famous American entrepreneur and founder of Occidental Petroleum, took over the pharmaceutical company from his father when he was young. He was only a college student at Columbia Medical School. He wanted to study his university courses, and at the same time run a pharmaceutical company. He hired a general manager to manage the company, and he was just a subordinate of this general manager, and then he sold the company to this general manager. In the early days of Microsoft's development, Bill Gates was the chairman of the company and owned a large number of shares. At the same time, Bill Gates was also a vice president, responsible for managing the application software department.

Owen managed the factory successfully. Later, he established a new factory in Scotland and hired four to five hundred children. These children worked 13 hours a day, including 75 minutes for meals. He not only improved working conditions, but also perfected the surrounding villages, including streets, houses, sanitation facilities, and education systems. Owen proposed his management philosophy. The factory founded by Owen was profitable; it is said that the rate of return on investment exceeded 15%. His measures to improve working conditions were mainly to prohibit the employment of child labor with children under the age of 10, work 10 hours a day, and prohibit night work. Later these measures all became laws, and the "New Lanark Site" has also become a World Heritage Site. The success of operating the factory gave Owen the dream of transforming society. He came to the United States and purchased thousands of hectares of land and founded the "New Harmony". His blueprint is that everyone in the "New Harmony" owns half a hectare of land, is engaged in work, and has no private property. His vision was great and he believed that there is no need for the government to exist. But many persons came to the "New Harmony" and the quality of the people was uneven, some were full of Owen's dedication, and others were hard to say. At the beginning, everyone was very enthusiastic. Later, the internal division gradually split. Some people tried to obtain common property, and many people gradually left. Finally, the founder broke the project and litigated. The "New Harmony" persisted for 4 years. After several reorganizations, Owen admitted failure and returned to Britain. The land of the "New Harmony" was handed over to his son, and one of his sons later became a member of the US Congress.

2.Charles Babbage

The second pioneer of management is Charles Babbage, Babbage (1791-1871). This character may be more familiar to people engaged in computer research. It is said that he made the world's first computer. Electronic components like vacuum tube had not yet been invented, so his computer was mechanical, relatively large and heavy. Strictly speaking, Babbage invented a difference engine and an analytical engine, both of which perform mathematical equations. Babbage met Ada Lovelace, the daughter of the famous British poet, Lord Byron. She was very talented in mathematics and later became the first software programmer in history. Computers at that time did not have monitors and keyboards; so-called programming, in fact, was a series of punched cards, each row of punched or not punched represents a binary 0 or 1. The reason why Babbage is considered the inventor of the computer is because modern computers have the computing part, storage part, input and output part, and all these Babbage machines have.

Babbage was born in wealth and his father was a banker. He studied at Trinity College in Cambridge. He was interested in machine manufacturing since he was a child and made machines all his life. Although these machines were not manufactured, they were at least designed. Later generations copied his machine according to his plan. Babbage was not only interested in manufacturing machines, but also had a profound interest in management. He visited many factories in Britain and France, and carefully observed tools and machines. In 1832, he published "On the Economy of

Machinery and Manufactures". The work in the manufacturing industry and the factory can indeed be decomposed into step-by-step operations, which are calculable and determinable. Many tasks in modern factories are replaced by robots and this is the best proof. Automated workshops, assembly line operations, and even robot produced machines are seen today, Babbage was a genius from this point of view, and discovered these characteristics of modern management during the industrial revolution. He developed a "method of observing manufactories", which is similar to a research method of the production process systems. "Having been induced, during the last ten years, to visit a considerable number of workshops and factories, both in England and on the Continent, for the purpose of endeavouring to make myself acquainted with the various resources of mechanical art, I was insensibly led to apply to them those principles of generalization to which my other pursuits had naturally given rise."[5] So sometimes some people make discoveries that seem to be related to their background and education, and there seem to be the hands of fate which lead them to complete their great inventions or discoveries. The observer prepared a printed standard list about the material used, normal waste, expense, tools, price, the final market, workers, their wages, skill required, length of work cycle and son on. Babbage has developed a professional division thought of labor and believed that a complete production process requires a long learning time. If the entire process is divided into many links, the learning time required for each link is relatively short, and a worker only needs to learn one link. The time spent training workers in the entire factory can be greatly shortened, which not only saves learning time, but also saves materials needed for learning. In terms of labor, Babbage emphasized labor-management cooperation and proposed a fixed wage plus profit sharing system. The advantages are: 1. The interests of workers are directly linked to the development of the factory. 2. Every worker will urge the department to improve work and care

---

[5] Charles Babbage, On the Economy of Machinery and Manufactures, preface

about waste and mismanagement. 3. Encourage workers to improve their skills and morals, as those who perform poorly will reduce their shared profits. Workers and employers will have the same interests and prosper together. Babbage also recognized that if a company wants to survive in a competitive market, it needs originality and innovation. Many of his understandings are consistent with Taylor's ideas, which show their advanced nature. However, Babbage's machine was too advanced. It was not until World War II in the 20th century that computers were actually invented by the rapid development of electronic technology. However, this was more than 100 years later.

Comparing Owen and Babbage, you will find that these two people are very interesting. They come from different backgrounds. Owen comes from the bottom of society, while Babbage comes from the upper level of society and they have different educational backgrounds. Owen was born in poverty. He started working as a child laborer at the age of 10 and became an apprentice. Babbage was born in rich family; his father was a banker and attended a prestigious university. Owen grew up as a store manager, and later became a factory owner. After graduating from Babbage University, he became a professor of mathematics at Cambridge University. After successfully operating the factory, Owen devoted himself to transforming society, he took his four sons to the United States to develop a utopian vision. Babbage hoped to invent a kind of calculable machine, and got government funding. Owen's dream was shattered. Babbage's machine was too advanced and unsuccessful. They both contributed to management. The two men are so different and so identical. Many people think that in a capitalism society, the rich get richer, and Babbage ran out of property in order to develop computers, so the poor get poorer? Owen stepped from poverty to wealth. Sometimes society is full of contradictions, what theory can be used to explain such a rich phenomenon in society? Some people will say that you are talking about individuals and individual phenomena, in most cases, still rich people become richer, and the poor become poorer. If a society does not have the motivation to help the poor to become rich, the production cannot be consumed, then there will be economic crisis and it needs to redistribute social wealth.

3.Economic cycles and cooperatives

There are three types of economic cycles in a capitalism society. One is the business cycle, which is about 3 years. The second is the medium cycle, about 10 years. The third is the long cycle, about 60 years. Every crisis is an adjustment. There are different opinions on these three cycles. The long cycle of 60 years comes from huge technological advances, such as steam engines, railways, electrics and automobiles. The mid-cycle of 10 years is also called the Juglar cycle. It was first proposed by a French doctor, Clement Juglar. This cycle is a market cycle, because major technological innovations do not appear frequently. Regardless of technological progress, the market will experience development, prosperity, crisis and depression, just like the four seasons of the natural world, spring, summer, autumn, and winter alternate. Chinese say that spring born, summer develop, autumn harvest, and winter store, completing a cycle, the truth of the market cycle is same thing. The short cycle is also called the Kitchin cycle. It was presented by the American economist, Joseph Kitchin. The market fluctuates every 40 months. It is generally considered to be a business cycle, mainly because there is an inventory link in the production process and raw materials are prepared. Now in the society, one talks about supply chain logistics. Manufacturers need to prepare goods in advance to produce goods. However, too much inventory will cause the capital chain to be tight. Good manufacturers should try to reduce inventory as much as possible, ship as soon as possible, and withdraw funds. This process defines probably the Kitchin cycle. What I want to say here is that very few companies can exist for more than a hundred years. Most companies exist for one or two years, lasting for more than 10 years, 30 to 50 years is exceptional; the market is ruthless, the capital chain break, and the market sees depression, recession, or the emergence of new technologies, replacing the old technologies. Just like the current mobile phone network is popular, fewer and fewer people watch TV, any one of these changes in the market may cause problems for enterprises. Among the many enterprises in the computer industry, like DEC, Compaq, Nokia of the communications industry, some no longer exist, and some have transformed. Any market cycle is an adjustment and redistribution of social wealth.

When the capitalist mode of production developed from textiles to railways, energy, chemical, telecommunications and other fields, there was a serious division of the society. In the past, there were aristocrats dynasties and commoners, and in the industrial era, there were capitalists and workers. From Carnegie's story, we can see that there are indeed workers, who start from the bottom of society through their own efforts to reach higher level or near the top of society; even if they are not immensely rich, maybe they are well off or slightly rich, this phenomenon is more common in the United States than in Europe. Many workers can become shopkeepers and hotel owners after years of hard work. Relatively speaking, the conditions of European workers are worse, and it is not easy for them to climb the ladder to the upper class of society. In 19th century, an organizational structure emerged, namely the cooperative. It is said that Owen is the father of cooperatives and Western Europe is the birthplace of cooperatives. As mentioned earlier, Owen opened a new Lanark cotton mill in Scotland. The factory was profitable. He had taken some reform measures to reduce working hours and prohibit to employ child laborers under ten years old, set up factories and shops, set up public canteens, set up kindergartens and schools, set up workers' mutual aid savings association, insurance department and hospital. In New Lanark, alcoholism, police, criminal law, lawsuits, poverty relief, and charity all disappeared. Owen became famous, and later came to the United States to carry out the experiment of the New Harmony, but unfortunately failed. Owen's cooperative thought was mainly about cooperative labor. The establishment of a "labor commune", shared property, and equal rights for everyone, was difficult to achieve at that time. Another representative of the cooperative movement is Henri de Saint-Simon, he was a French nobleman. The famous sociologist Auguste Comte served as Saint-Simon's secretary for 7 years. Comte inherited many Saint-Simon's thoughts. In France, there are also famous social reform figures such as Charles Fourier, Philippe Buchez and Louis Blanc, as well as William King in England.

Cooperatives are also divided into several types, consumer cooperatives, credit cooperatives, and production cooperatives. At the moment of its birth, the cooperative mainly played a role in remedying the shortcomings of capitalism. It was in the mainstream in agricultural and rural credit, but it did not play a role in replacing the main production methods. Today, it is in Europe, North and South America, Asia and Oceania, that many cooperatives can be found, wheat cooperatives, orange cooperatives, milk cooperatives and rural credit cooperatives, etc. Some of them are well-known brands such as Sunkist oranges in North America, and its market spreads all over the world. The Fonterra Cooperative Group Limited in New Zealand is a multinational dairy cooperative operated by 15,000 local farmers and the largest cooperative in New Zealand. In some countries, like Denmark, in the agricultural field, cooperatives have become mainstream. Danish cooperatives developed from the pig and dairy industries in the late 19th century and now almost all Danish farmers have joined the cooperatives. It must be emphasized and explained that until today, the difference between cooperatives and enterprises is not too great. They all hire professional managers to manage. Large cooperatives have also formed a layer-by-layer plan management model, but the cooperatives provide cooperative members, that is, shareholders, to pay interest, but do not implement profit dividends, which is the biggest difference from enterprises. In my opinion today, after entering the industrial society, the social status of agriculture has declined, farmers engaged in agricultural work are becoming less and less important, numerous in developed countries. Cooperatives are just a form of organization to protect farmers. The way they treat farmers is more conducive to protect the interests of farmers than companies and enterprises.

4 CHAPTER THE CHARACTERISTICS OF THE PERIOD OF INDUSTRIAL CAPITALISM-THE EMERGENCE OF THE SEPARATION OF CORPORATE OWNERSHIP AND CONTROL

1.The development of stock companies in various industries

The factory system has many characteristics as it moves forward, such as labor-management tensions and separation of ownership and control. We focus on the separation of ownership and control. Some people say that the separation of ownership and control is the greatest invention of capitalism. There is some truth to this, but how did this phenomenon occur? How did it proceed?

After the invention of the steam engine, it was quickly applied to railways. The railway provided fast, reliable, regular and all-weather transportation, and the unit cost of freight was reduced. The construction of the railway requires a lot of capital, which is far greater than the capital of the textile industry. It is impossible for a single entrepreneur, family or partner to own a railway. The railway system includes locomotives, rails, roadbeds, stations, management and dispatching rooms and supporting equipment maintenance.

accept with great alacrity every suggestion for an improvement of the machinery and let the worker profit directly or indirectly from it. Twice a year honorary diplomas and cash prizes are distributed for noteworthy suggestions. In addition, employers will also grant worker a proportion of the factory's profits and offer the company's stocks to workers... In this way, the conflict between employers and workers gradually disappeared. Yes, since there are profits, and business owners share with workers, why go on strike? But the actual situation in society is not completely the case. In history, whether it is Carnegie Steel Company or Rockefeller's oil company, there have been many serious strikes. In severe cases, the government sent troops against workers, leading to bloodshed. In short, Sambat finally concluded that the United States has sufficient resources, vast unoccupied land, no nobles, democratic elections of officials, no monarchs, separation of church and state, and the people are full of vitality, and success can be achieved by struggle without being born rich. All of this is the reason why there is no socialism in the United States. They are not oppressed because they were born without oppression.[6]

Is this book by Sombart 100 years ago applicable in the United States today? I have not been to the United States, and there is no specific data, but from the news obtained from the daily news and media and frequent events around the world, we can see that the strikes that are often seen and heard around the world today are rare in the United States.

Now the workers of American large companies and large enterprises have strong trade unions, and they have become worker nobles. We can see that there may be more ethnic conflicts in the United States. There have also been protests in the United States, which seem to be more about opposing a certain policy, expressing a certain point of view, or government leaders' tidbits being exposed by the media. I think this book by Sombart is not only in the past,

---

[6] Werner Sombart, Why is there no Socialism in the United States? (The Macmillan press, 1976)

but also still applicable to the United States today. Its research methods and conclusions are also worthy of future generations to learn and respect, but I want to look at Sombart's conclusions from another angle and use another method to analyze American society.

Now there is new change of job in the society, in chapter 18 I will talk about creative work and new management model in service sector.

5 CHAPTER THE SEPARATION OF ENTERPRISE OWNERSHIP AND CONTROL

1.Background

I noticed that Sombart did not analyze the phenomenon of separation of enterprise ownership and control. His book "Why Is There No Socialism in the United States?" was published in 1906. At that time, the phenomenon of separation of ownership and control in American companies had already appeared. We can analyze the process of social development from this perspective.

After the invention of the steam engine, it was applied to the railway transportation field, which led to the emergence of railways and the large-scale popularization of railway construction, especially in the widespread application of American railways. Railway construction and operation require a lot of funds. In order to raise a lot of funds, railways need to issue bonds and stocks, this has already been analyzed. The joint-stock company system is used in many sectors from ocean trade to the textile industry, and then to the railway field. At this time, family ownership, partnership family management has been unable to meet the requirements of the times, so the separation of enterprise ownership and control began to appear on the stage of history. The development of the railway is accompanied by the development of communication technology, and the telegraph and telephone business has also adopted a management method similar to that of the railway system. The steel king, Carnegie, was initially engaged in the telegraph business, and then gradually entered the railway management. At the beginning of the 20th century, American giant companies were huge in scale. American Telegraph and Telephone Company had more wealth than 21 states. The top 15 largest companies (except banks) had total assets of US$81 billion, accounting for half of all US companies. This asset number doesn't look too big today, but it was amazing at that time. Today, the products and services provided by large companies constitute the infrastructure of industry not only in the United States but also in the world. The products and services provided by large companies occupy all aspects of people's lives. In the automotive sector, there are three major automakers in the United States, GM, Ford and Chrysler, in France there are Renault and PSA, in German there are BMW, Mercedes-Benz and Audi, and in Japan there are Honda, Toyota and Nissan. In the field of aircraft manufacturing, large aircraft manufacturers that produce plane with more than 100 seats are dominated by Boeing and Airbus; Bombardier and Embraer in the regional airliner industry take the lead. The same is true in other fields, such as the aviation service industry; in the United States there are American Airlines, United Airlines and Delta Airlines, and in Europe, there is a large airline in each country, British Airways, Air France, Lufthansa, and SAS ... in Japan there are All Nippon Airways and Japan Airlines, in Australia there is Qantas, in other emerging countries are Emirates, Singapore Airlines, etc., China has four major airlines, Air China, China Eastern Airlines, China Southern Airlines and Hainan Airlines. The same is true in the telecommunications industry. European telecom companies include Deutsche Telekom, British Telecom, Vodafone, Three UK, France Telecom; there are AT&T, T-Mobile, Verizon, Sprint in the United States, and there are three major telecom operators in China, China Mobile, China Unicom, China Telecom. There are NTT, Softbank, AU By KDDI, eMobile, WILLCOM in

Japan. In the United States, when people travel, they take the airplanes of various countries, large airplanes, either from Boeing in the United States or Airbus in Europe. The cars are produced by the three major automobile manufacturers. The mobile phones purchased are either Apple or Android. The communication service is AT&T. For housing, the aluminum needed for kitchen appliances is produced by Alcoa, the aluminum on airplanes and the aluminum on cars is also produced by Alcoa. It is now in an era of global competition. The purchase of cars may be from Japan's three major automobile companies and Germany's three major automobile companies. Household appliances, refrigerators, and washing machines may be made by Samsung, LG, and China Haier. The air conditioner may have been produced by Gree Electric in China, the meat may have come from Smithfield Foods, and the food seeds eaten may have been provided by Monsanto company. This phenomenon is almost the same in any country, with little difference. The cardboard packaging of milk and beverages is provided by Tetra Pak. In the entertainment industry, there are eight major companies in the US film industry. These large-scale companies are issuing shares and trading in financial centers around the world, New York, London, Tokyo, Paris, Shanghai, Hong Kong, Frankfurt and Singapore. By 1930, the separation of corporate ownership and control had been basically achieved. At least 78% of US corporate wealth was owned by companies. The 200 largest companies controlled at least 40% of all corporate wealth (in the United States). In various countries, large companies play a similar role. Many small companies rely on large companies to survive and provide services in the upstream and downstream industrial chains of large companies. Many small companies in society have created more employment opportunities. The issue of integration, we can put it later and further explain how large companies develop, or how large companies are related to the financial market. Compared with the step-by-step capital accumulation of family businesses, the use of proceeds for reinvestment, raising capital in the open market is undoubtedly faster and much more efficient, making the company more competitive and more smoothly putting large amounts of capital into production; the traditional family businesses cannot be compared to nowadays large companies. In reality, apart from issuing stocks, there are also mergers. Optimism about a certain technology and buying the company are also commonly seen in business now.

Companies become bigger and bigger, with more and more capital. At the same time, equity is becoming more and more diversified, especially within the largest companies. By 1930, the number of shares held by the largest shareholders of the largest companies was not at 1% of publicly issued shares, no individual holds an important proportion of shares. The top 20 largest shareholders generally only account for about 5% of the total share capital, and the total number of shares held by shareholders after 20 is even scarcer. Among the many shareholders, the directors and senior managers of the company often hold a part of the stock; in addition to the management, the other shareholders are mostly middle-income and low-income people. In modern society, especially in developed countries, the development of companies with good performance has led to the rise of stocks. Many people have made profits through this price difference by investing in stocks, but at the same time they have also brought a lot of capital to the company. The expansion of the market continuously requires a large amount of funds and continuous financing. The performance in the market is to expand the shares. Another distinctive feature of modern society is that in the past, individuals used their savings to invest in stocks. Now, due to the reform of the pension system, many countries have opened pension accounts for individuals, and the funds raised through these accounts are used in the capital market and used for stock investment.

2.Pensions bring changes in the capital market

In the nineteenth century, the European labor movement continued to develop in different countries, which caused many social problems and social conflicts. Governments of various countries have gradually paid attention to and improved the working conditions and treatment of workers. The United Kingdom issued new "English Poor Laws", "Factory Act" and a series of bills such as "Public Health Act". Germany, as an industrialized country in the later period, faced a more serious labor movement than Britain and France. The low wages of workers at the bottom of society, their health, and the end of their productive life faced serious threats. Workers engaged in organized struggles. Some upper-class people and religious leaders also called on the state to intervene and Germany promoted a relatively complete reform of the social security system, established a complete set of social security systems, and took the lead in passing a series of bills such as the "Joint Law", "Sickness Insurance Law" and "Work Injury Insurance Law" in European countries. The main objectives were to provide benefits to the working class through state taxation and social insurance, and through the states direct intervention and regulation of social redistribution to achieve the goal of eliminating and alleviating social contradictions. These measures and methods have been imitated in other countries after World War II and established the welfare state of modern society.

Beginning in the 1970s, the South American country-Chile's pension system has taken another path, a completely different path, which has attracted widespread attention from countries around the world. Its main characteristics are the capitalization of personal funds, private operations, and the government supervision, the state has withdrawn from direct intervention, and market forces dominate. The main features are: 1. Establishment of personal accounts. 2. Capitalization of pension funds. 3. Privatization management of pension funds. The role of the government is to supervise, regulate and monitor the market activities of pension fund management. Individuals pay their pensions contributions to a fixed account, and pension management companies take their pension funds to the capital market for investment activities to increase pensions. There are risks in the market, and the management of pension companies must also be monitored. This reform of the pension system started at the same time as the privatization of state-owned enterprises. After the privatization of many enterprises, their stocks were held by pension funds. Pension funds replaced the status of commercial banks in enterprises, and even pension funds became one of the most important driving forces for the development of the Chilean capital market. Pension funds enter the capital market not only in Chile, but also in the United States. The majority shareholders of many large companies are pension funds. In the modern social capital market, individual companies, bank, pensions become a company shareholder and the phenomenon is a feature different from the society of the 19th century.

Before Chile's pension reform, or in the first half of the 20th century and the 19th century, in enterprises, capitalists paid workers wages, and workers lived on wages, housing, daily expenses, food, clothing, children's education, medical care, and pension insurance and so on all rely on wages. Karl Marx analyzed that capitalists have free possession of surplus value, and this part of capital is used by enterprises to expand reproduction and continue to invest. Under Chile's social security system, personal pension insurance invests in the stock market and it is still used in corporate, finance returns to the enterprise, but through external circulation and through the management of pension funds. Investment can be combined or different companies can be selected. From this point of view, this system is more flexible and beneficial to individuals. This requires mature capital markets and good government supervision. There is cycle in the stock market.

3.Emergence of Managers

In the early stage of company development, a family or partner owns the company, and family members are in charge of management. As the company expands, capital increases, and shareholders increase, who is responsible for managing the company? We can see from the development of railway companies, along with the development of telegraph and telephone technology, railways have moved from family management to managerial management in terms of operation and management, and the emergence of professional managers. We can look specifically at how Andrew Carnegie grew up in that era.

Andrew Carnegie (1835---1919) was born in Dunfermline, Scotland. His father was a weaver. On his mother's side, his grandfather was a politician. He was the leader of the Radical Party in his area. Carnegie was greatly influenced by his mother. Carnegie's father's weaving business started well and their life was relatively ample. At that time, the population of Dunfermline was mainly composed of small manufacturers. Each family had one or more looms. The work was calculated on a piece-by-piece basis. They received the business of weaving from the big manufacturers and finished work at home, it was actually a domestic system. The invention of the steam engine brought disaster to Carnegie's family. Carnegie's father was unaware of the impending revolution and was still using the old methods to support his business. The loom he owned depreciated, and Carnegie's mother opened a small shop to maintain the family income. With the invention and improvement of the steam engine, small businesses in Dunfermline became increasingly difficult to do. Carnegie's mother had two younger sisters who worked and lived in Pittsburgh, U.S, so the Carnegie family auctioned off their looms and furniture and left Scotland to come to the United States. It was 1848, and Carnegie was only 13 years old. Carnegie also left the formal school education. The Carnegie family first came to New York, where there were many friends of Carnegie's parents, then they came to Pittsburgh from New York, and Carnegie's father started the business of weaving tablecloths in Pittsburgh. Although Carnegie was only 13 years old, he also needed to go out to work. Together with his father, he came to work in a cotton factory. The owner of this cotton factory was also a Scot. Later, another Scottish fellow needed to hire a boy with a higher salary, and Carnegie moved to work there. In 1850, the Telegraph Bureau needed a boy to be a messenger. With the help of relatives, Carnegie got the job. The messenger job was a great improvement for Carnegie. He got rid of heavy manual labor and could learn a lot of things and made a lot of friends, many of whom were Scots, all from the same poor background. Later, these friends also devoted themselves to business and became the bosses of many companies.

While Carnegie and his friends were working hard, a colonel, James Anderson, opened his library of four hundred volumes to the boys. Carnegie had the opportunity to immerse in the ocean of knowledge. Carnegie fell in love with literature. This library was very helpful to the boys, keeping them clear of low fellowship and bad habits, and proving the beneficence of the good.

In Carnegie's teenage years, although there were religious activities and some churches in Pittsburgh at that time, Carnegie's mother took no interest in these, although she also encouraged her children to attend church to worship and go to Sunday school to receive Christian education. But she taught her children to maintain for themselves a marked reserve and to discourage theological disputes. Carnegie's mother believed that many contents of the Bible were not worthy of acceptance as authoritative guides in the conduct of life. It is very interesting that Carnegie quoted Confucius' exclamation many times in his autobiography to illustrate his mother's position. "To perform the duties of this life well, troubling not about another, is the prime wisdom." Regarding music, Carnegie also quoted Confucius' exclamation, "Music, sacred tongue of God! I hear thee calling and I come."[7] Carnegie's parents had a more open-minded attitude towards religion. During the holidays, they used to entertain instead of repenting. This Puritan attitude towards work and life is somewhat similar to traditional Chinese ethics, the position for religion is not so strict. During the growth of Carnegie's youth, it was very obvious. Protestant ethics are similar to traditional Chinese ethics, but there are differences. Regarding this point, we will analyze it in detail later when we talk about traditional Chinese thought and culture. Carnegie finally said that families in the United States and England basically believed in Protestant ethics.

---

[7] Andrew Carnegie, Autobiography of Andrew Carnegie, (Houghton Mifflin, 1920), pp 45-53

They should work hard when they work, and enjoy themselves when they relax.[8]

At the Telegraph Bureau, Carnegie learned the telegraph business. At first, it was a simple delivery of telegrams, being a messenger, then distribution of telegraph, after being a telegraph operator. This period can be regarded as an apprenticeship. At the age of 17, he ended his apprenticeship and started working as an adult, and he really took up the job. Step by step, he took on different management positions at the Pennsylvania Railway Company and met Thomas A. Scott, who had a great influence on his life. Scott was the director of the Pittsburgh project of the Pennsylvania Railroad. Carnegie later became Scott's assistant and began to enter the railroad field. He followed Scott all the way up. Carnegie served as the supervisor of the Pittsburgh Railway Section and began to be in charge of a department independently. During this period, he invested in steel production companies and locomotive factories; when the railway company planned to promote Carnegie to director assistant, he left the railway company and started his own business. Carnegie worked for the Pennsylvania Railway Company for 12 years and was familiar with the railway business. The steel company he founded caught up with the good opportunity of railway development and became the king of steel. As a Scot, his origin was also very helpful for him. From the perspective of informal organization, many of his partners and assistants were all Scots, helping each other and growing up in foreign lands.

The operation and management of the railway department can be regarded as the field where the separation of ownership and control began to appear. This field is so large and has so many management positions. Many railway department managers regard their work as a lifelong career, and they work in different management positions. The railway company needs a lot of management talents, otherwise it would not be able to efficiently maintain and operate the huge

---

[8] Andrew Carnegie, Autobiography of Andrew Carnegie, (Houghton Mifflin, 1920), pp 45-53

railway traffic flow, and could not deal with so many problems, such as traffic accident handling, railway failure and operation control, passenger and freight, one-way and double track, dispatching day and night shifts, mediating workers' strikes, and dispatching vehicles. These so many management problems are difficult to handle without special training, requiring innovation in the organization.

In the second half of the 19th century, the organization of the American railway department was like this. The railway was divided into different parts according to the region. The railway was first constructed parts by parts. Each part and each section is relatively independent, and each has its own management personnel. In order to coordinate the operations of different sections, similar managers are appointed in the corresponding sections, and a headquarters is set up to supervise and coordinate the management of each section. Each section has a section director, like Carnegie, who later served as the Pittsburgh project director. A manager is responsible for railway maintenance, an engineer is responsible for the daily maintenance of locomotives, and the section supervisor is responsible for the daily dispatch of trains. The chief engineer in charge of the headquarters is also assigned in the company headquarters. The director of the company headquarters is responsible to the company's Board of directors and directors. The manager's subordinates are station attendants, train conductors, train drivers, and maintenance plant managers. Section supervisors work with higher-level departments to formulate train operation timetables. The train conductor starts the trains according to the operation timetable. The upper level of the railway company included the chairman, general manager (general supervisor) and financial supervisor. The middle level of the company was composed of the section project supervisor, transportation director and maintenance engineers; the grassroots included specific operators, train conductors, train drivers, station attendants and repair shop managers. In addition to these daily management, the company also had financial personnel, including the financial director, auditors, and bookkeepers. The general supervisor of the railway company, equivalent to the general manager of the current company, was responsible for daily railway operations, weekly and monthly locomotive conditions, and monthly daily expenses. The middle-level management personnel was responsible for the daily train operation and dispatch, and was responsible for managing the specific operators of the railway, the company's leaders could not overstep their authority. This kind of management organization was first implemented on the Pennsylvania Railway and soon expanded to other railway companies. The daily dispatch and operation of the railway companies are inseparable from the communication business-telegraph and telephone, and they were also inseparable from daily procurement. In this way, the modern accounting system and audit system were invented. The railway companies were the earliest modern industrial and commercial enterprises. The high-level, middle-level and grass-roots management structure divides the responsibilities and powers of management at different levels. The railway system invented a modern financial and auditing system to supervise and evaluate the work of the managers. These managers, including middle and top managers, were full-time managers who received salaries. There were different functional departments in the company: communication business, purchasing business, railway and locomotive maintenance business. Like Carnegie, when he went up to a level, his salary level was different, from the initial telegraph operator to the assistant of the project manager, to the project manager, in each level he had different responsibilities, these were very clear. The railway companies were undoubtedly the pioneers of modern management and had far surpassed the management level of the textile factories; they were the first step in the separation of enterprise ownership and control. In the daily management of the railway system, detailed planning, scheduling, supervision and communication appeared. This railway system was invented by a Scottish American, Daniel Craig Mccallum. He first implemented this system at the Erie Railroad Company and encountered certain setbacks. Later, the Pennsylvania Railroad Company inherited his vision. In this way, management has moved from the domestic system, partnership trade, and factory system to the door of modern scientific management, opening the door to the separation of ownership and control.

When Carnegie had the opportunity to be promoted to the head of the Pennsylvania Railroad Company, he wanted to start his own business. As an entrepreneur, not just a manager, he founded a steel company and brought the management method he learned in the railroad to the steel industry. The modern management structure, the separation of ownership and control, these systems and methods have also expanded from the railway system to the steel field, and thus to more industries. Carnegie founded a steel company and brought many friends from the railroad company as his partners. He hired many experts as the manager of the steel company. At that time, the Bessemer steelmaking method began to appear and gradually was promoted in business. Carnegie paid attention to this new technology and adopted it in his factory. He integrated various processes in the factory, increased production capacity, expanded the steel product market, implemented a set of weighing and accounting systems in the factory, and understood the cost of each process. As an entrepreneur and founder of the company, Carnegie was responsible for the company's strategic direction and business negotiations. Daily operations were delegated to his assistants. The managers he hired were responsible for the management of the factory and the handling of equipment failures at the factory site, they had to understand every process of production and to deal with production problems. The technical experts hired were the assistants of these managers, looking for and selecting high-quality iron ore. If Carnegie felt that someone in the factory had made an outstanding contribution, he would promote this person to a management position or company president and that man would hold shares. He also introduced audit work to audit the financial accounts of manufacturing companies. We can clearly see that the separation of ownership and control, the differentiation of management functions, and the introduction of supervision have enabled enterprises to develop very rapidly, to adopt new technologies and to control costs. When Carnegie first entered the steel industry, the price of rail was $100 per ton, but by 1900, the price of rail was $12 per ton. In 1868, the United States produced 85,000 tons of steel. By 1902, 9,138,000 tons of steel were produced. This period is called the system management period, from railway to manufacturing, managing large organizations, making plans, hiring workers, purchasing raw materials and machinery and equipment, financing, establishing factories, hiring managers, authorization, division of responsibilities, introducing supervision, auditing, performance evaluation, coordination and control, etc. System management is the prelude to scientific management. It is the initial separation of ownership and control. Through their own hard work, a worker can gradually go from being a grass-roots worker to a middle-level and even to top management position, from nothing to becoming an entrepreneur and a capital owner. From working as a part-timer manager to living by investment.

Just like Carnegie, after rising to a managerial position in a company or having capital to engage in investment, to establish a business, and to hire managers and workers, what else is necessary for such a person to organize and participate in strikes? Why is it necessary to participate in the labor movement? Carnegie was not just a lonely person, he had many partners, many of whom were born in poverty, Carnegie is just a typical representative of these characters. In reality, it is impossible for everyone to have the opportunity and luck of Carnegie, and it is impossible for everyone to become a capitalist. However, the constant emergence of opportunities makes it possible for anyone and anything. The degree and intensity of the labor movement was much smaller in the United States than those in Europe, and it is no surprise that the thought of the labor movement was not popular in the United States. This is what I think Sombart did not explain in his book. It is not only the level of wages, but also the smooth upward mobility of this kind of society. For individuals the opportunity is equal, it is possible for individuals to improve their own conditions through their own efforts. Now that scientific management was born in the United States and developed vigorously in the United States. The next chapter introduces the representatives of scientific management and what is the connection between scientific management thought and the separation of enterprise ownership and control.

56

6 CHAPTER THE EMERGENCE OF SCIENTIFIC MANAGEMENT

1.Frederick Winslow Taylor

The real progress in the separation of enterprise ownership and control appears after the emergence of scientific management. The reason why scientific management is called science is that this kind of management is reproducible and not limited to specific individuals. Scientific knowledge is universal and popular. Anyone can achieve it; it can be taught and can be learned in school. The knowledge of scientific management rises to theory, anyone can master it after learning, and it can be applied to management practice, so it is called scientific management. It is no longer the knowledge and skills that only a few people can master, and it is no longer a transcendent and mysterious thing that cannot be learned without authorization. The founder of scientific management was Frederick Winslow Taylor, who published "The Principles of Scientific Management" in 1911, marking the birth of scientific management. The emergence of great people always has their background and personal unique experiences. The combined effect of these two factors can produce great thought, which can be applied to the world and spread widely, and Taylor is no exception. Taylor was born in 1856 in a wealthy family in Pennsylvania, USA. His father was a lawyer and his mother was a Puritan. Taylor's early education was a classical literary education. His family also hoped that he would inherit his father's career as a lawyer. He successfully entered Harvard Law School to study law. Due to physical reasons, he dropped out of school and went to Philadelphia. After four years as an apprentice in a factory, he transferred to the Philadelphia Midvale Steel Works as a worker. Due to his hard work and outstanding performance, he was promoted to factory's chief engineer responsible for maintenance and repairs after six years. The experience of working in the steel works has benefited Taylor very superficially, he conducted management experiments and studied new management methods, which laid the foundation for his scientific management thought.

Taylor was young in the era of great railroad construction in the United States. It was also the era of rapid development in the steel industry. The so-called system management period. Management, through practice in factories, gradually can be learned. There was no school to impart knowledge of industrial and commercial management. Management did not rise to the height of science; this is also the so-called Gilded Age in the United States. The social structure of the United States is different from other countries in the world. There is no king, no feudal aristocracy, and it has a democratic system. The government has the least ability to intervene in the affairs of society. The society has freedom of publishing, association and propaganda. The company's operating behavior is mainly concerned with the market. The company developed from a joint-stock company to a monopoly, vertically integrated organization. The management methods of the company and the enterprise, purpose and means basically consider the market.

Taylor Management Thought

The benefits of employers and employees are maximized, which is achieved by improving production efficiency. Increasing productivity requires lowering costs. After the company expands its market, it will give workers higher wages and increase production per unit of time and production efficiency. In this way, a drop in single product prices will occupy more markets and expand profits.

In order to achieve the goal of increasing productivity, the key is to provide incentives to workers, promotion, raise wages, pay dividends, shorten working hours, provide a good working environment, and adopt a piece-rate wage system.

In addition, the working hours of workers must be in accordance with scientific laws, requiring fixed breaks, working frequency and length of time are regular, scientific work and rest plans, and even scientific production task plans, no doubt these are the responsibility of the manager.[9]

The key to the Taylor system is labor-management cooperation, not confrontation. This can increase corporate profits. In the past, workers went on strike and labor-management tensions were mainly due to the problem of profit distribution. Taylor's method is to increase and expand profits, which solves the problem of workers' strikes. In fact, it partially solves the problem. After increasing productivity, workers' working hours are shortened, wages are increased, and entrepreneurs have profits. After product prices fell, consumers also benefited.

Four principles of scientific management:

1.Summarize production knowledge and laws scientifically, and divide the scientific and standard operating methods of each part of the production process.

---

[9] Frederick W. Taylor, The Principles of Scientific Management, (Harper & Row, 1911)

2. Scientific selection and training of workers.

3. Combine talents with resources and work closely with workers to make work proceed as planned.

4. Reasonably distribute the work of managers and workers.[10]

As Taylor stepped into the American history, family-owned and partnership companies gradually evolved into vertically integrated and diversified corporate groups. At that time, American companies had a huge market, but there were constant labor-management conflicts, lack of management knowledge and management talents. Taylor emphasizes labor-management cooperation instead of conflict, and emphasizes win-win or even triple-win. He pioneered the use of scientific and systematic methods to study management issues, opening a new era. His research scope focuses on production operation management, with regard to management, logistics, and marketing, (personnel, and finance are not involved), but his research methods, observation experiments, and conclusions can be repeated by latecomers and others, just like natural science discoveries. This method established his position in the history of management. He took society from the era of labor-management conflict, that is, the era of emphasizing the labor movement, strikes, and even armed revolutions, and gaining power, to the era of emphasizing labor cooperation, raising workers' wages, and increasing production efficiency. Entrepreneurs gain profits. It is from focusing on the distribution of profits between labor and management, to the era of both increases in workers' wages and corporate profits.

Taylor and his students inherited and disseminated scientific management thought. Taylor's students include Carl Barth, Henry L. Gantt, Frank B. and Lillian M. Gilbreth, Harrington Emerson,

---

[10] Frederick W. Taylor, The Principles of Scientific Management, (Harper & Row, 1911)

and Morris L. Cooke. They inherited Taylor's thought, carried forward his thoughts and spread them all over the world, eased the contradiction between labor and capital tension, and expanded the research of scientific management.

So, in Europe, don't other industrialized countries produce management thought similar to Taylor? If the birth of scientific management thought alleviated class contradictions, and thus caused various social thoughts to be inadequate in the United States, then can it be said that scientific management thought is not popular in Europe and the labor movement has continued? In the 19th century, marxist doctrine was very popular in Europe, and various social transformation doctrines continued to appear. Compared with scientific management, marxist doctrine emphasized class confrontation, class conflict, and class oppression. It believed that the contradiction between capitalists and the working class was irreconcilable. Working classes can only obtain freedom and liberation if they seize power. Why this doctrine is so popular in Europe is indeed worth pondering. I think it is due to the different social structures in Europe and the United States. Sombart analyzed that European workers are not as well treated as in the United States, and their wages and living standards are worse. More importantly, I think there is limited room for workers to rise before the emergence of scientific management. The emergence of scientific management has promoted the separation of enterprise ownership and control. Many of the personnel who run and manage the company are professional salaried managers. These personnel are gradually coming up from the bottom of society. Where corporate ownership and control are not completely separated, corporate ownership and management rights are controlled by the family or partnership, the management is not open to ordinary people. Social conflicts have accumulated for a long time, and one day they will erupt. There will be strikes and protests in the streets. If the problems are not resolved, there will be continuous movements and phenomena such as worker assemblies, protests, demonstrations, and strikes.

The birth of scientific management thought occurred after 1911. Throughout the 19th century, the European industrialization process could basically shows that class antagonism was serious and the labor movement continued. Since the beginning of the 20th century, class contradictions have gradually eased. But are there scientific management thought in Europe, and how are these thoughts accepted by society? We can look at the development of European management thought.

In Europe, there are also two important management figures, Henri Fayol and Max Weber, let's talk about Fayol first.

2.Henri Fayol

Henri Fayol (1841-1925), born in a family of petty bourgeois in France, entered a public secondary school in Lyon at the age of 15, transferred to the Saint-Etienne National School of Mines at the age of 17, and obtained qualification of mining engineer. After graduating at the age of 19, he was appointed as engineer to the Commentry group of pits of the Commentry-Fourchambault Company in 1860, which is still one of the famous French metallurgical companies. From 1860 to 1872, Fayol served as a manager in the company. From 1888, at the age of 47, Fayol served as managing director of the company until his retirement at the age of 77. In 1916, Fayol published his book "Administration Industrielle et Générale". After he retired, he formed the Centre d'Etudes Administratives and devoted himself to theoretical research, exchanges and dissemination of his management experience and thoughts. He died in 1925 at the age of 85 and his was the longest life-span among the three early management figures.

"General and Industrial Management"

Fayol believed that management is human-oriented, and the objects of management are people, while the objects of technology, business, finance, security, and property are machines, raw materials, capital, etc., and management is planning, organization, coordination and control. Management capabilities can be obtained through study and training in school.

He mentions the four categories of staff work:

1. Diverse assistance afforded to the manager in current matters, correspondence, interviews, consideration and preparation of records.

2. Liaison and control.

3. Future projects, either drawing up plans or bringing them into line.

4. Development study.[11]

It may be because Fayol has held various management positions in the company, from the middle to the top, so in his writings and thoughts, all aspects of management are basically involved. Modern management is actually very complicated. In every aspect, there are many, many contents. In comparison, Fayol's work is not very maneuverable, and there are more principled things. It is not like Taylor, his work is so concise and important, you can understand it at a glance, and you can learn it quickly. What Fayol and Taylor have in common is that they both emphasize management education.

Fayol's work focuses on the principles and elements of management.

---

[11] Henri Fayol, General And Industrial Management, (Sir isaac pitman & sons, LTD, 1949), pp 63

The principles of management are:

1. Division of work
2. Authority
3. Discipline
4. Unity of command
5. Unity of direction
6. Subordination of individual interests to the general interest
7. Remuneration
8. Centralization
9. Scalar chain
10. Order
11. Equity
12. Stability of tenure of personnel
13. Initiative
14. Esprit de corps[12]

The principles of management are flexible, it is an art to make use of principles and it requires intelligence, experience, decision and sense of proportion. Management principles aim at the success of associations of individuals and at the satisfying of economic interests, it is the lighthouse fixing the bearings.[13]

The elements of management are:

1. Planning

2. Organizing

3. Command

4. Coordination

---

[12] Henri Fayol, General And Industrial Management, (Sir isaac pitman & sons, LTD, 1949), chapter 4

[13] Henri Fayol, General And Industrial Management, (Sir isaac pitman & sons, LTD, 1949), pp 42

5. Control[14]

As a manager and chief executive officer, Fayol emphasized the plan. This is different from Taylor. It seems to be very correct today. Now large enterprises have plans and the plans are very detailed. The economist Ronald Coase wrote the article "The Nature of the Firm" after thinking about the contradiction between the feasibility of large-scale enterprises, the feasibility of organizational plans and the infeasibility of the entire social plan. It can be seen that planning is a very prominent feature of modern large enterprises. The development and main viewpoints of the new institutional economics represented by Coase will be discussed later when we talk about vertical integration. About organization, Fayol thought the enterprise is similar to the body, the nervous system in particular bears close comparison with the managerial function. Nerve endings feel stimuli inside and outside the body, produce sensations that are transmitted to the brain through reflexes, the brain command through reflexes to the organs that perform the activity. The development of scientific management perfected the organization theory, found formal organization and informal organization, in chapter 8, We talk about organization theory in detail.

Fayol said, "a leader who is a good administrator but technically mediocre is generally much more useful to the enterprise than if he were a brilliant technician but a mediocre administrator."[15]

Taylor approached the study of management from the workshop and it is from the bottom to top, while Fayol approached it from the viewpoint of upper-level administration and it is from the top to down, there are different approaches. Taylor's management is easy to understand, while Fayol is comprehensive. Taylor's management is for ordinary people, and Fayol's management is for managers.

---

[14] Henri Fayol, General And Industrial Management, (Sir isaac pitman & sons, LTD, 1949), chapter 5

[15] Daniel A. Wren and Arthur G. Bedeian, The Evolution of Management Thought, (John Wiley & Sons, Sixth Edition), pp 214

Taylor's edge overwhelmed Fayol, and Fayol's lifespan surpassed Taylor. What they have in common is that they believed that management knowledge can be learned, practiced, and taught in universities and schools.

3.Max Weber

A management scholar like Fayol appeared in France, and a management scholar, Max Weber, also appeared in Germany. These three characters, Taylor (1856-1915), Fayol (1841-1925) and Weber (1864-1920), lived in the same era, at the end of the 19th century and the beginning of the 20th century. Production moved from family and partnership to large enterprises, stock company, the period of separation of corporate ownership and control. Unlike Taylor and Fayol, Weber is a scholar and sociologist, one of the three founders of sociology, and he is equal to Marx and Durkheim. Both Taylor and Fayol have practical experience in production and management, have worked in companies, and later summed up their experience to form theories. Weber is a pure scholar, a scholar who teaches and conducts research in universities. His famous work is "The Protestant Ethics and the Spirit of Capitalism", studies the relationship between religious development and social evolution. Weber observed that large enterprises that have emerged in the economic development of Germany, are different from the United States. In the United States, it appeared in the railway industry first, then the steel and communications industries, etc. In Germany, large enterprises first appeared in the chemical industry, metallurgical industry and machinery industry. Weber also noticed that bureaucracy has also emerged in large companies. Weber's great book "Economy and Society", mainly analyzes the development and changes of different parts of society, and its influence and effect on society, such as religious sociology, legal sociology, dominance sociology and so on. He analyzed the composition and types of power, and compared various social systems in different societies, Europe, China, the Middle East, India, and Africa. This book is all-encompassing, and one has to admire Weber's talent and comprehensive information. For example, according to his analysis, the typical examples of large bureaucracies that appeared in world history are: 1. Egypt, during the period of the New Kingdom; 2. the later Roman empire; 3. the Roman Catholic Church; 4. China, from the time of Shi Hwangti until the present; 5. the modern European states; 6. the large modern capitalist enterprise.[16] In "Economy and Society" Weber analyzed the bureaucracy in detail. Weber was in an era when Germany was rapidly entering industrialization. The family-based economic organization system based on blood-related factors disintegrated, and vertically integrated firm quickly emerged. Weber's writings reasonably explained these phenomena. Weber realized that bureaucratic systems have emerged in the development of modern large enterprises, but at that time such vertically integrated organizations had just appeared in developed countries in the world, and Taylor's scientific management thought had only recently appeared. Scientific management thoughts were still very imperfect, and the development of scientific management had just started, many situations were still unclear. Vertically integrated organizations were still in the process of development and improvement at that time. Scholars' understanding of the characteristics, structure, development cycle, property rights system and management methods of such organizations is far from reaching today's understanding degree. Therefore, the focus of Weber's work is to analyze various economic and political systems in agriculture and traditional society. The essence of Weber's work lies in the analysis of the sociology of domination, the types of domination and the types of power.

He analyzed three types of authority:

1. Rational legal authority

---

[16] Max Weber, Economy and Society, (University of California, 1978), pp 964

2. Traditional authority

3. Charismatic authority[17]

These three types are abstract and pure types. Any type of social authority or domination in real life is a certain degree of combination and mixing of these three types, and they are also the result of adaptation and adjustment. This also applies to the conditions of the capitalism and is suitable for various economic organizations in industrial society.[18]

Weber analyzed the bureaucracy and believed that the bureaucracy has the following principles:

1. There is the principle of official jurisdictional areas

2. The principle of office hierarchy and system that super- and subordination.

3. The management of the modern office is based upon written documents.[19]

The three elements of bureaucracy are:

---

[17] Max Weber, Economy and Society, (University of California, 1978), Volume 1, Chapter 3, pp 215

[18] Max Weber, Economy and Society, (University of California, 1978), Volume 1, Chapter 3

[19] Max Weber, Economy and Society, (University of California, 1978), pp 956-957

1. To determine the regular activities of the bureaucracy

2. Enforcement of authoritative commands and coercive means

3. Methodical provision is made for the regular and continuous fulfillment of these duties.[20]

Bureaucratic agency can constitute both a bureaucratic state and a bureaucratic enterprise. The typical bureaucratic state is ancient China, and the typical bureaucratic enterprise is a modern large vertically integrated firm. In Chapter 12, we will further analyze the characteristics of bureaucratic agency.

Weber has realized that entrepreneurs hold the most power in enterprises, similar to officials in bureaucratic countries. The occupation of the bureaucracy is a kind of regular salary, not the personal business of a certain ruler. Officials have to go through a training process, have continuous and complete work capabilities, and have a high social position. Officials are appointed by higher authorities and have a fixed or regular career path. Bureaucratic positions can sometimes be bought and sold, and bureaucratic organizations have advantages—compared to other forms of organization, their costs are the lowest.[21]

---

[20] Max Weber, Economy and Society, (University of California, 1978), pp 956

[21] Max Weber, Economy and Society, (University of California, 1978), Volume 2, Chapter 11

7 CHAPTER AUTO ERA COME

When Taylor, Fayol and Weber summarize and developed their theory, the development of the company also had new trend. An important invention appeared in society, that was the car, the car was coming. Car is undoubtedly one of the greatly inventions in the 20th century. After the stream engine invented, some persons wanted to put the steam machine on the carriage, replacing the horse. But because the steam machine was too large, this idea was not realized. After the internal combustion engine was invented, oil had become a new source of energy, the situation was different. The internal combustion engine can be miniaturized, oil is liquid, and the loading is relatively easy. Therefore, the invention follows a logical train of thought. Car this product, this invention is more complicated than any inventions prior to human being. Until now, the automotive industry is also a more complex industry, from tires, engines, gearbox to automotive design, structure, decorative interior, it has more than 10,000 parts. Today car has many new development, no driving, automatic parking berth, navigation positioning and car audio, etc.

The first person to invent the car was German engineer Carl Benz; he successfully produced a three-wheeled steam-powered car in 1885. In 1886 German engineer Gottlieb Daimler invented the world's first four-wheeled car. Soon the French company bought Daimler's blueprint and established a car manufacturer in 1889.

France produced a car with a fuel engine in 1890. Although the car was born in Europe, the automotive industry really developed in the United States, where new production methods and new management models appeared. It is not separated with one person; he is Henry Ford.

1.Henry Ford

The Ford Motor Company founded by Henry Ford is still one of the three largest automobile companies in the United States today, and it has also been very influential around the world. Henry Ford not only produced cars, but also promoted the management development of the company at that time. Today's cars generally have tens of thousands of parts. In the early days of the automotive industry, when the car was first invented, there were about 5,000 parts in Ford Model T cars, some of which were very large, and others smaller than a watch. At first, the production of a car was very similar to building a house. The parts were created in one place and the car is assembled in another place. This kind of production efficiency is naturally not high, because the workers spend their time looking for suitable parts. Ford invented the assembly line production, thereby saving working time and greatly improving productivity. The assembly line production reduces the complexity of the workers' movements to a minimum. Arranging the machines and workers in the order of work planned by themselves, the engineers designed improved conveyors, roller slides and gravity slides to ensure the continuous and regular flow of materials in the factory. The production line is first used for the assembly of the flywheel and motor, then the engine, and finally the chassis and the entire car. In the past, it took 12 hours to assemble a car. After the production line was adopted, it took only two and a half hours.

Henry Ford (1863-1947) was born on a farm in Michigan, U.S. He was from a good family and was very interested in machinery since he was a boy. When he was about 12 years old, he saw a steam car in a small town one day. He became very interested in automatic vehicles, and dreamed that one day he could also build one. Later, he realized his dream—but he built more than one. At the age of 17, Ford left school, became an apprentice in a machinery factory, became a mechanic, and entered the field of mechanical manufacturing. At that time, the popular steam car only went 12 miles per hour, was bulky, heavy, and expensive, and was mainly used on large farms for threshing grains. The structure was not complicated and consisted of a steam engine, a boiler water tank and a coal car. Ford also built steam car, but because of the inconvenience of steam car, he later abandoned these efforts. While Ford was an apprentice, the internal combustion engine had been invented. Ford took note of it, and began to study, repair and replicate this type of engine. Later, Ford got a job and became an engineer with the Edison Illuminating Company of Detroit. There he researched internal combustion engines in his spare time and eventually built his first car, which could go 20 miles per hour and seat two people. Ford was gradually promoted to chief engineer in the power company. When the Edison Illuminating Company offered him the position of company director, Ford did not accept. He did not want to interrupt the research of the car, which he saw was more promising. When he was 36 years old, he resigned. This is very similar to Carnegie. The difference is that Carnegie had already invested in the steel work and made a profit before he resigned. Carnegie did not want to be a manager anymore, but instead wanted to be an entrepreneur. But Ford did not have much in savings at that time, and what he did have was spent on automobile research. He and his partners established the Detroit Automobile Company. He was the chief engineer and made cars. At first, it was a bit unsuccessful. But later, he founded the Ford Motor Company. He was 40 years old. At Ford Motor Company, Ford built car models A, B, C, F, N, R, S, K, and finally the Model T, which developed in a huge way.

Ford adopted many methods in management. Ford's managers were all from the bottom of company. The mechanic became the work manager, and the workers could give suggestions on improving productivity and saving labor—which both improve production efficiency. Another well-known Ford measure was to raise the minimum wage to US$5/day, working eight hours a day, and later to US$6/day.

The auto industry has basically realized the separation of ownership and control. Ford Motor, General Motors, make it a practice to separate ownership vs control. The separation result in a large number of salaried managers in the firm and within it's different departments. Throughout the 1920s, small, personally-owned and family-owned companies in the United States gradually transitioned to large national companies through mergers. Managers at all levels became the main figures in economic management, such as the photographic film, tobacco and food processing industries. This has led to the development of many well-known companies, such as Kodak and American Tobacco. The common feature of these companies was to use of machines and reduce costs, and the production process became highly concentrated. Manufacturers have established large-scale sales and procurement networks. Like Ford Motors, these companies have brought huge capital returns due to their large production volume, provided the floating capital needed for business management, paid workers' wages, and purchased raw materials and parts. They did not turn to the capital market for help. The founder family and partners of the company have ownership of the company, but the regular operation of the company is managed by specialized managers. Today, the Ford Motor Company is still owned by the Ford family. During this period, marketing was the center of corporate development of these large enterprises. Production alone was not enough; sales had to be made. Large sales networks and regional centers had to be established so the company could use advertising and other marketing methods. Taylor's management thought does not include marketing. There is a Chinese saying, "Good wine is also afraid of deep alleys." The importance of publicity is self-evident. Otherwise, how would ordinary consumers know the company's products even exist?

Whether it is Kodak's cameras, or film, or various food

manufacturers, or Ford Model T cars, they all need the support of a large sales network and need to establish branches across the country to be responsible for sales and after-sales services. As Ford puts it, "A manufacturer is not through with his customer when a sale is completed. He has then only started with his customer" [22] Companies need to establish national and even global branches, with of managers, buyers and salesmen, and establish supply chains from wholesalers to retailers, so that they can sell their products in multiple cities and towns.

At first, manufacturing companies relied on full-time independent agents who were responsible for sales, and these agents received commissions. However, ordinary agents lacked basic knowledge, were unable to demonstrate and operate products, were unable to provide services and repairs, and unfortunately, also could not provide credit. Thus, many companies began to set up branches and offices in various cities. In these offices there were model operators, a mechanical engineer responsible for repairs and services, a salesperson, and a manager. Accounting was added later. The role of such an office was equivalent to a branch. It was mainly used to supervise the work of dealers, while also being responsible for credit issuance and advertising. This close contact between branch sales offices, factories, and factory purchasing departments ensured the production process from raw materials to the final product. Manufacturing equipment was now fully utilized. This is the modern supply chain link, which speeds up capital flow and reduces inventory links. Now supply chain management in every company must strive to do well, for it speeds up production, reduces costs, and thus gains an advantage in the market.

2.General Motors

Just as the Ford Motor Company was developing rapidly, another

---

[22] Henry Ford, My Life and Work, Chapter II

major American automobile company, General Motors, was also undergoing mergers and acquisitions. William Crapo Durant formed General Motors in 1908. Durant, who started from scratch, was the first American manufacturer of wagons and carriages. In 1908, Durant merged Buick and founded General Motors. Later, Oakland and Cadillac also joined the General Motors family in 1909. These companies retained their original corporate capacity and independent operation design, and General Motors became a holding company, a central organization surrounded by many independently operated satellite companies. Through a variety of means based on stock trading, from 1908 to 1910 under Durant's leadership, General Motors merged 25 companies in total, eleven of which were automobile companies, two of which were electric light companies, with the rest being parts manufacturing companies. This kind of rapid, large-scale expansion and merger activity has enabled GM to develop rapidly on the one hand, and on the other hand it also brought a host of problems. In 1910, Durant lost control of General Motors two years after founding it. In 1911, after leaving the management of General Motors, Durant and Chevrolet co-founded the Chevrolet Motor Company. Durant then regained control of General Motors through Chevrolet in 1916. This is like Steve Jobs. After leaving Apple Inc. Jobs founded NeXT, then returned to Apple Inc. through NeXT, and regained control of Apple's management.

Alfred P. Sloan (1875-1966) was born in New Haven, Connecticut, U.S. His father was a business owner. Sloan grew up in Brooklyn, New York, and when he grew up, he entered the Massachusetts Institute of Technology and obtained a degree in electrical engineering. After graduation, he joined the Hyatt Roller Bearing Company in 1895, which produced parts for automobiles. Since that time, Sloan has become associated with the automobile industry. Over time, he became the general manager of Hyatt Bearing Company. In 1916, Durant (of General Motors) founded the United Motors Company which acquired Hyatt and four other parts manufacturing companies. Sloan became president of United Motors Company and later both the vice president and a director of General

Motors. At the beginning, Sloan was only in charge of the spare parts business at General Motors. Gradually, he entered the company's accounting and auditing fields, and was responsible for purchasing the land required for the General Motors headquarters building. However, the rapid expansion and merger of General Motors led to a series of problems. There was no plan for, supervision of, or control over the varying business units' use of funds, leading to competition for the allocation of funds and consequently, rising expenditures. In 1920, an economic recession had an impact on the company's automotive business. This, coupled with loss of management, led to Durant's resignation. In his wake, DuPont initially took over as president of the company, and Sloan served as DuPont's assistant. By 1923, Mr. DuPont resigned and Sloan took over as president of General Motors.

Sloan's main contribution to General Motors was to establish a decentralized management model. Compared with the Ford Motor Company, General Motors' management method can be called a committee management and division system. Within the company, there are multiple committees---the Executive Committee, the Finance Committee, the Purchasing Committee, the Technical Committee, the Sales Committee, the Operations Committee, and the Inventory Committee. Among them, the Executive Committee is at the head of the organization and is responsible to the board of directors. The chairman of the committee serves as the company's president and Chief Executive Officer.

In labor relations, Sloan implemented a "Bonus Plan." This "Bonus Plan" provides different incentives to employees at different levels in the company. Bonuses are often linked to wages. The higher the wage, the higher the bonus. The higher the level of management positions, the more bonuses. This attracts managers work hard in the company to get promotions.

This bonus plan affords flexibility in the following way. A substantial increase in a person's wages will disrupt the entire wage system. Yet bonuses can handle this situation, rewarding employees with outstanding contributions while maintaining the stability of the wage system. Thus, a bonus plan helps the company retain senior executives.[23]

The management of General Motors is open to everyone. From the perspective of separating ownership from control, General Motors is undoubtedly a step further than the Ford Motor Company. The company's various management levels, from the middle to the top, especially the uppermost management, consists of full-time salaried managers, so later General Motors surpassed Ford and become number one in the automotive industry.

———————————————————

[23] Alfred P. Solan, My Years With General Motors, Chapter 22

8 CHAPTER RESEARCH ON ORGANIZATION THEORY

The emergence of vertically integrated firms, the separation of company ownership and control, and the emergence of a large number of full-time salaried managers in companies and enterprises have made the enterprise very large and the organization very complicated. Many scholars have gradually focused their attention on organizational research. In the first stage of management development, after the time of Taylor, Fayol and Weber, many scholars studied management from different perspectives, and in different directions. One direction is from the perspective of sociology, from the perspective of organization and decision-making, and for represents people, there are Barnard and Simon. The other direction is from the perspective of psychology (also called behavioral science); representatives of this field include Mayo, Maslow, and McGregor. First, let us talk about both management research and organization research from the perspective of sociology.

1.Chester I. Barnard

The study of organizations started with Chester I. Barnard (1886-1961). He studied at Mount Hermon School in his early years. From

1906 to 1909, Barnard studied economics at Harvard University, which he left without obtaining a degree. In 1909, he joined the American Telephone & Telegraph Company as a translator and engineer. In 1922, he was appointed assistant to the vice-president and general manager of Pennsylvania Bell Telephone Company. In 1927, he assumed the post of the first president of New Jersey Bell Telephone Company, where he worked until retirement.

Barnard was also engaged in many unpaid public activities. He was chairman of the United Service Organization Inc (USO) from 1942 to 1945, assumed the post of director-general of the Rockefeller Foundation, chairman of the National Science Foundation, an assistant to the Secretary of the Treasury, a consultant to the American representative in the United Nations Atomic Energy Committee during World War II. He was a director of a number of companies such as the New York City Board of Health, a fellow of the American Association for the Advancement of Science and of the American Academy of Arts and Sciences.

His main works include "The Functions of the Executive" published in 1938 and "Organization and Management" published ten years later. Barnard was a self-taught scholar and a very knowledgeable person. It is said that he read Vilfredo Pareto (in the original French), Max Weber (in the original German) and Alfred North Whitehead's philosophy. Whitehead was a famous British mathematician and philosopher; he wrote the philosophical work "Process and Reality".

"The Functions of the Executive"

The starting point of Barnard's research is organization—formal organization. The functions of the executive—in formal organizations—are those of control, management, supervision, and administration. These functions are exercised by top executives or anyone who is in a position of control to whatever degree. Individuals exist in a cooperative system. Personal behaviors are both physiological and social. People might cooperate and they might conflict. The function of the executive is thus to regulate conflict.

1. The object of personal cooperation is to gain greater ability, the ability of the group exceeds the ability of an individual.
2. The object of the group is different from the object of the individual; the group needs to distribute cooperative action to participants in the cooperation.
3. A change of environment will cause an adjustment of cooperation and keep balance of the various types of organizations. These adjustment processes will then become management processes, and the specialized organs are executives and executive organizations.
4. In the adjustment process, new purposes appear and old purposes are abandoned, these processes are instability.

There are psychological and social factors in systems of cooperation. [24]

Organization:

Formal organization is a system of consciously coordinated activities or forces of two or more persons.[25]

Three elements of organization:

1. Communication
2. Willingness to serve
3. Common purpose [26]

---

[24] Chester I. Barnard, The Functions of the Executive, (Harvard University Press, 1938), pp. 23-36

[25] Chester I. Barnard, The Functions of the Executive, (Harvard University Press, 1938), pp. 73

[26] Chester I. Barnard, The Functions of the Executive, (Harvard University Press, 1938), pp. 82

Barnard found that in management, there is a phenomenon he described as *informal organization*, which is indefinite and rather structureless, and has no definite subdivision. It may be regarded as a shapeless mass of quite varied densities. Informal organization creates conditions under which formal organization may arise and establishes customs, mores, folklore, institutions, social norms and ideals.[27] An important function of informal organizations is to exchange information. Barnard's informal organization thought was actually influenced by the behaviorist George Elton Mayo, and later I will talk about Mayo's thoughts.

Barnard talked about the economy of incentives, which is a fundamental subject in formal organizations.

1. Material inducements
2. Personal non-material opportunities
3. Desirable physical conditions
4. Ideal benefactions
5. Associational attractiveness
6. Adaptation of conditions to habitual methods and attitudes
7. The opportunity of enlarged participation
8. The condition of communion[28]

About decision, acts of decision are characteristic of organization behavior.

1. The occasions of decision
2. The evidences of decision

---

[27] Chester I. Barnard, The Functions of the Executive, (Harvard University Press, 1938), pp. 114-127

[28] Chester I. Barnard, The Functions of the Executive, (Harvard University Press, 1938), pp. 139-161

3.   The environment of decision[29]

The fine art of executive decision consists in not deciding questions that are not now pertinent; in not deciding prematurely; in not making decision that cannot be made effective, and in not making decisions that others should make.[30]

The executive functions: executive work is specialized work of maintaining the organization in operation.[31]

These are considered to be the three elements of management:

1. Developing and maintaining a system of communication

2. Promoting the security of the personal service

3. Formulating and defining the organization's purposes, objectives, and ends.[32]

The responsibility of an executive includes:

1.   Imply a complex morality
2.   Require a high capacity of responsibility

---

[29] Chester I. Barnard, The Functions of the Executive, (Harvard University Press, 1938), pp. 185-200

[30] Chester I. Barnard, The Functions of the Executive, (Harvard University Press, 1938), pp. 194

[31] Chester I. Barnard, The Functions of the Executive, (Harvard University Press, 1938), pp. 215

[32] Chester I. Barnard, The Functions of the Executive, (Harvard University Press, 1938), pp. 215-234

3.   Under conditions of activity[33]

Barnard emphasized that personal abilities can be cultivated. Since senior managers can be cultivated, the manager needs to pass the selection, and then they could get promotion, demotion, and dismissal of personnel. Barnard also talked about human psychological factors in his writings, but he is good at and analyzes well from an organizational perspective, that is, from a sociological perspective. Barnard's experience is similar to Fayol, and he has practical management experience and has held various management positions. He put forward the theory of organization. His style is jerky and difficult to understand. On the one hand, he insists on this method, on the other hand, it is because the articles that is easy to read, maybe it doesn't go deeply enough.

Barnard "Organization and Management"

What is leadership? Here are the four sectors of leadership behavior:

1.   The determination of objectives
2.   The manipulation of means
3.   The control of the instrumentality of action
4.   The stimulation of coordinated action

An organization is the instrument of action so far as leaders are concerned, and it is the indispensable instrumentality. So, if we talk about leadership, we need to research organization. [34]

---

[33] Chester I. Barnard, The Functions of the Executive, (Harvard University Press, 1938), pp. 272

[34] Chester I. Barnard, Organization and Management, (Harvard University Press, 1956), pp. 89

Here are five fundamental qualities or characteristics of leaders:

1. Vitality and Endurance
2. Decisiveness
3. Persuasiveness
4. Responsibility
5. Intellectual Capacity[35]

Organization can develop leader:

1. Training
2. Balance and Perspective
3. Experience[36]

As executive functions, manager may be distinguished as the maintenance of morale, the maintenance of the scheme of inducements, the maintenance of schemes of deterrents, supervision and control, inspection, education and training.

Barnard emphasized cooperation—not only the cooperation between employers and employees, but also the establishment of collaborative relationships with customers and cooperation with investors and suppliers, so that the scope of the organization's research may expand.

The following is a list of incentives applied to customer relationship:

1. Application of Inducements and Incentives to Customers
   a. Material inducements
   b. Personal non-material opportunities
   c. Desirable physical conditions
   d. Ideal benefactions

---

[35] Chester I. Barnard, Organization and Management, (Harvard University Press, 1956), pp. 93

[36] Chester I. Barnard, Organization and Management, (Harvard University Press, 1956), pp. 102

    e. Associational attractiveness
    f. Customary purchasing conditions
    g. The feeling of enlarged participation
    h. The condition of communion
2. Maintenance of schemes of deterrents
3. Supervision and control of customers
4. Inspection of customers
5. Education and training of customers[37]

Executives:

1. Continuing education
2. Superior strictly intellectual capacities
3. Understanding human relations
4. Appreciating the importance of persuasion in human affairs
5. Understanding what constitutes rational behavior toward the unknown and the unknowable.

All of the above can be trained and taught.[38]

2.Herbert A. Simon

Herbert A. Simon (1916 --- 2001) was an American management scientist, economist and computer scientist. He was very successful in management, economics, politics, computer science and he received the Nobel Prize in Economics as well as the Turing Award. In the field of management, Simon inherited Barnard's ideas, and in-depth research organization, perfect organization theory. In 1946, he published "Administrative Behavior"; later this book was reprinted multiple times and today is considered to be very influential. In his revised version of this book, Simon somewhat foresees the impact of computer development on human life and work. In the book, Simon

---

[37] Chester I. Barnard, Organization and Management, (Harvard University Press, 1956), pp. 121-123

[38] Chester I. Barnard, Organization and Management, (Harvard University Press, 1956), pp. 194

says that he was greatly influenced by Barnard—who also wrote a preface to the first edition of the book. Simon research organization theory and introduces some political concepts, for instance, authority, loyalty. In the book, Simon also introduces some economic concepts, e.g., equilibrium and efficiency. In 1978, Simon received the Nobel Prize in Economics for the ideas described in this book. In computer science, he was a pioneer in the field of artificial intelligence and cognitive science, developing with Allen Newell the Logic Theory Machine (A Complex Information Processing System). Simon had additionally been China many times and is referred to there by his Chinese name, Si Mahe.

"Administrative Behavior"

Simon emphasizes that the administrative processes are decisional processes; the book is primarily concerned with "vertical" specialization, a primary function of organization is to enforce the conformity of the individual to norms laid down by the group, or by its authority-wielding members. The core concept of organization theory is authority, hierarchy and organizational sectorization. Markets and organizations complement each other and play an effective role beneath sound infrastructure.

Simon's organization theory involves:

1. Decision-making and the execution of decisions
2. Choice and behavior
3. Value and fact in decision
4. Decision-making in the administrative process
5. Modes of organizational influence
6. The equilibrium of the organization[39]

---

[39] Herbert A. Simon, Administrative Behavior, (A Division of Simon & Schuster Inc. 1945), pp. 92-140

It is impossible for the behavior of a single, isolated individual to reach any high degree of rationality. Rational behavior, segments are not consequent, knowledge of consequences is always fragmentary, the human being never has more than a fragmentary knowledge of the conditions surrounding his action. Complete rationality is limited by a lack of knowledge. So, Simon emphasizes bounded rationality. The human being's power to observe regularities in nature of a very general sort, and to communicate with other human beings, helps him to shorten materially this learning process. In this book, Simon introduces some psychological terms, for instance habit, positive stimuli.[40]

The organizational influences on the individual are of two principal kinds:

1. Organizations and institutions permit stable expectations to be formed by each member of the groups as to the behavior of the other members under specified conditions.
2. Organizations and institutions provide the general stimuli and attention-directors that channelize the behaviors of the members of the group.[41]

These are the means that the organization may employ to influence the decisions of individual members:

1. The organization divides work among its members
2. The organization establishes standard practices
3. The organization establishes systems of authority and influence

---

[40] Herbert A. Simon, Administrative Behavior, (A Division of Simon & Schuster Inc. 1945), pp. 92-140

[41] Herbert A. Simon, Administrative Behavior, (A Division of Simon & Schuster Inc. 1945), pp. 110-111

4. The organization provides channels of communication running in all directions
5. The organization trains and indoctrinates its members[42]

The organization is a system in equilibrium which receives contributions in the form of money or effort and offers inducements in return for these contributions.

Anatomy of organization

The authority relationship, the concept of efficiency, organizational loyalties and the mechanisms of organization all influence the individual. The organization provides sufficient stimulus to the members, prompting them to make the necessary contributions to the organization, so add to complete the tasks of the organization, including material stimulation and non-material stimulation.[43]

The era of "Administrative Behavior", just after World War II, when the separation of enterprise ownership and control was completed. Professional managers dominate the economy of U.S, and professional managers have replaced figures such as Carnegie, Ford, steel king, automobile king. At the same time, society has also created a new social ethics, a new group, "the organization man", which emphasizes obedience, loyalty, discipline, efficiency, loyalty to the group and compliance with group norms. Personality, innovation and mavericks have slowly disappeared. However, in this particular place Silicon Valley, new changes have taken place in the management of the semiconductor industry, microelectronics industry, microcomputer field, software industry and Internet

---

[42] Herbert A. Simon, Administrative Behavior, (A Division of Simon & Schuster Inc. 1945), pp. 1-29

[43] Herbert A. Simon, Administrative Behavior, (A Division of Simon & Schuster Inc. 1945), pp. 305-356

industry. In Chapter 13, we analyze the new features of Silicon Valley management model.

Authority is only one of a number of forms of influence. Formal organization is division of work and authority distribution plan. There are formal and informal channels of communication. Today the biggest problem facing organizations is the effective organization of information storage and information processing, which is the decomposition of the decision-making process.

Here, I should emphasize that individual loyalty to organizational goals is good for organizational behavior, but not conducive to personal creativity. When later we talk about the Silicon Valley model, we will further analyze the relationship between organizations and individuals.

9 CHAPTER BEHAVIOR SCIENCE

Scientific management, when Barnard and Simon studied management from the perspective of organization, other scholars George Elton Mayo, Abraham Maslow and Douglas McGregor studied management from the perspective of psychology and behavioral science.

1.The Hawthorne Studies

The Hawthorne Works was a large factory complex belonging to Western Electric who produce telephone equipment. This complex had more complete entertainment facilities, a medical system and a pension system—but the productivity of the factory was not high, and the workers were very dissatisfied. In order to discover the reason, in 1924, the National Research Council organized a research team to carry out experimental research. This research is now known as the Hawthorne Studies, and it is one of the most famous studies in the history of psychology. Its findings have more important meaning for management.

The Hawthorne studies conducted a lighting experiment, a welfare experiment, interview research and group experiment. The studies originally looked into whether lighting influences productivity; it researched the relationship between performance of workers and the amount lighting in the Works. Preliminary research results showed that the fluctuation of output is not directly related to the degree of illumination within the building. The experiment thus turned to study the psychological factors of workers and found that the transformation in the welfare facilities and changes in the supervision of workers changed the attitudes of the workers toward their job and improved productivity.

Professor George Elton Mayo, a psychologist at Harvard University, visited the Hawthorne works, and then participated extensively in the research from 1928 to 1932. Using the structure interview method, he found that the changes in workers' psychological factors directly affected the productivity of the works in the Hawthorne works.

Mayo found informal organization, the function is

1. It protected them from internal indiscretions of members
2. It protected them from the outside interference of management officials

Mayo's viewpoint is to view the organization as a social system: the employees have physical needs, but they also have social needs. Formal and informal organization coexist, and both are interdependent. The manager must strive for an equilibrium between technical organization and the human one by securing economic goals. Groups in an organization are not allowed to have members with different performances. Once such high-performers appear, informal groups will treat them as traitors, alienating and isolating this member. This behavior will affect the normal operation of the entire group and functions.

The dichotomy between formal and informal organizations is very similar to the traditional Yin-Yang concept in China. Later, when we talk about the market evolution process of Silicon Valley companies, we will break this down further.

Mayo's opines that management should pay attention to

interpersonal communication—someone who commands too much attention, and who has adequate communication skills, should have a place in administrative management positions. The society should pay attention to the cooperation between people; human beings can't focus solely on technology and neglect social interpersonal relations. Mayo even suggests that this is one of the causes of war in society.

The morale theory put forward by Professor Mayo based on the results of the Hawthorne studies have given great inspiration to modern business management.

1. Management requires humanistic care
2. A manager should be a leader in human relations, and not simply a setter and supervisor
3. Coordinate informal groups in the enterprise[44]

The role of supervision from top-down management to caring supervision, the change of supervision style and the formation of an organization with a spirit of solidarity are the reasons for the increase in productivity.

Mayo pressed "the human problems of an industrial civilization", "the social problems of an industrial civilization" and "the political problem of industrial civilization"

2. Abraham Maslow

Abraham Maslow (1908---1970) was founder of humanistic psychology. Born in Brooklyn, New York, his parents were Jewish immigrants from Russia. At that time, there were many such immigrant families whose children went on to distinguish themselves—for example, Armand Hammer and Isaac Asimov. In

---

[44] George Elton Mayo, The Social Problems of an Industrial Civilization,

1934, Maslow was awarded his doctor's degree in philosophy. In 1936, Maslow joined the faculty of Brooklyn College and continued his research into psychology. In the late 1930s to the 1940s, several famous psychologists—Erich Fromm, Alfred Adler, and Max Wertheimer—escaped Nazi Germany and moved to the United States. Maslow's academic work was profoundly influenced by these psychologists.

Maslow's most famous book is "Motivation and Personality", in which Maslow establishes his theory of a hierarchy of needs. He posits five needs: physiological needs, safety needs, love and belonging needs, self-esteem needs, and self-actualization needs. The first two needs are basic, physical and biological; the last three are social needs, with self-actualization also being a need for creativity.

Here is an example of what Maslow meant by "self-actualization". Andrew Carnegie was the director of the Pittsburgh Railway Project before he founded the steel company. He was preparing to be promoted to a senior management position at the railway headquarters when he quit to start his steel company. Yet his family lived well in Pittsburgh life. They had many friends and high social status; friends respected him very much—so why would he go to start a steel company? In his own words, he no longer had to work for salary; he could make his own decisions instead of taking orders from others. Wasn't Ford the same? According to Maslow, those entrepreneurs are self-actualized people.

Thus, self-actualization is a creative work performance that transcends the self; a kind of loss of self-awareness and self-consciousness, it resolves the paradox between selfishness and selflessness. One works is introjected, subject and object are uniform.[45] Heeding the call of the heart, everyone has a mission and a task that is suitable for him (and him alone) to complete. Everyone should find their own responsibilities and jobs, and find a suitable

---

[45] Abraham H. Maslow, Maslow On Management, chapter 2

position and belongingness in this world. In Eastern cultures, specifically Chinese culture, this is called "paradic design"[46]. Maslow emphasizes this: self-actualization is hard work—it involves both a calling to service from the external, mundane world, as well as a yearning from within.

Organization will stifle creativity and innovation, according to Maslow: "Each new invention, each new discovery creates turmoil behind the lines. The people who have settled down comfortably are shaken and disturbed out of their comfort. It is clear then that any great discovery, any new invention … anything which will require a reorganization of the conquered territory will not easily be accepted… "[47]

Maslow thought formal organization would inhibit creativity, but he believed that this problem is solvable though enlightened management. With enlightened management, the company is a family and everyone becomes a partner, not an employee. Creative people are interested in change and new ideas, new direction. Maslow often quotes some examples of Blackfoot Indians. If society reaches a certain stage, it can be quite easy to earn the money necessary to meet basic needs, and these basics life can be maintained with less and less work—just like in an industrialized society, where people engaged in agricultural labor account for only 5% or less of the population. If society has come to a certain stage, high-level needs become the main needs—clothes, food, and trips, are basic needs that are easy to meet. Belonging, love, friendship, respect, and self-esteem, are higher levels needs and more important in these developed societies.

Later, Maslow published "Maslow on Management". This is a diary from the time Maslow visited "Non-linear Systems" company, a manufacturer of digital instrumentation. "Non-linear systems"

---

[46] Abraham H. Maslow, Maslow On Management, chapter 2

[47] Abraham H. Maslow, Maslow On Management, chapter 4

company implement self-management, provide employees with stock options, set up a series of management measures such as innovation vice president, etc. At that time, in 1962, they were advanced.

Non-Linear Systems was founded in 1952, by Andrew F. Kay (1919---2014). Andrew Kay found Kaypro Corporation and sold computers in the early 1980s. Kaypro had more than $120 million in revenues, briefly became the fifth-largest computer maker in the world; and in the field of portable microcomputers, it was the largest company in the world. But Kaypro's success was relatively short-lived; like many Silicon Valley companies, with the ebb and flow in market, it filed for bankruptcy in 1992, and was defunct by 2001. Kaypro's computer system used the Z80 microprocessor, and its software used the CP/M operating system, after turn to DOS operate system. In personal computer field, in hardware Intel's microprocessor is mainstream, in software Microsoft develop DOS operate system, they are core of microcomputer. CP/M exited the market, Kaypro reacted slowly to the change of personal computer market.

Thus, we can see that enlightened management resembles the enlightened politics in Chinese history and enlightened despotism in European history. Maslow absorbed many influences from Eastern culture, we can see that he researched Chinese culture.

3. Douglas McGregor

Douglas McGregor (1906---1964) was a famous behavioral scientist from the United States. He founded the theories of human work motivation and management, was one of the founders of management theory and is best known for his Theory X and Theory Y. His main writing is "The Human Side of Enterprise" (1960), and "The Professional Manager" (1967). Half a century has passed since the birth of management at the beginning of the century. The political, economic and other environments in U.S. society have changed a lot. The living conditions, education levels and political patterns of citizens have changed. McGregor looks at management from a psychological perspective; he has different views (from psychology) on organization theory in management studies. He thought that organization theory in management is still immature, and traditional organization theory has many assumptions that need to be carefully tested.

McGregor found Theory X-Y. Theory X is the theory of authority. The central principle of organization is that of direction and control through the exercise of authority. In addition to authority, there are persuasion and the professional help ("professional help" here being lawyers, doctors, engineers providing help with knowledge to influence clients). The foundation of Theory X is that group interests are higher than individual interests. Theory Y is integration; it does not deny authority, but reduces the negative influence of authority. It does not deny the rationality of authority, it only denies the practice of using authority regardless of purpose and occasion. It should be considered that Theory Y is a supplement to Theory X, including its defects. In Maslow's writings, we can see the theory of X and Y, where X includes low-level needs, while theory Y contains high-level needs. Effective prediction and control being central to the task of management, McGregor emphasizes managers' understanding of employee behavior as the key to deciding the employment relationship. He also emphasizes assessment and employee participation; managers can acquire management capabilities through training.

According to McGregor, there are four major variables in leadership:

1. The characteristics of the leader
2. The attitudes, needs, and other personal characteristics of the followers
3. The characteristics of the organization, such as its purpose, its structure, the nature of the tasks to be performed

4.   The social, economic, and political milieu[48]

Leadership is a complex relationship among these variables. The leader makes history and history makes the leader—both of them are true and they influence each other. A leader's skills and attitudes can be acquired and are not inborn characteristics of the individual.

After World War II, many management development programs and activities appeared throughout the whole Western World, it can be found in a large or medium-sized company. Skills of social interaction are also important in management. Managerial competence is created on the job, but classroom education can be used as a powerful aid to the process of management development. McGregor emphasizes respect toward the human side of enterprise, training and learning, care, participation, target setting, etc.

He describes two kinds of motivational relationships:

1.Extrinsic rewards

These include money, fringe benefits, promotion, praise, recognition, criticism, and social acceptance and rejection.

2.Intrinsic rewards

These rewards can't be directly controlled externally; for example, achievements of knowledge or skill, autonomy, self-respect, or solutions to problems.[49]

McGregor thought that it will appear new organization theory with innovation. An industrial organization is an open, organic,

---

[48] Douglas McGregor, The Human Side of Enterprise, (McGraw-Hill book), chapter 13

[49] Douglas McGregor, The Professional Manager, (McGraw-Hill book, 1967), Chapter 1

sociotechnical system; one of the majorities is that it can represent reality more fully and more adequately than the conventional picture of the formal organization. The new organization theory will include formal and informal organization.

Just as the manager should have background knowledge of management, computer technology, applied mathematics, statistics and symbolic logic, so should international industrial firms acquire additional knowledge in political science, history, anthropology, economics, philosophy and ethics. The industrial manager cannot hope to acquire detailed and systematic knowledge in all these fields, but nor can he afford to ignore this knowledge and its implications for managerial strategy and practice.

McGregor categorizes managerial styles according to one of three ways: hard, soft, and firm but fair.

McGregor also mentioned the company Non-Linear Systems in his writing. He thought the characteristic of the company was its self-regulating team. Self-regulating teams were responsible for a manager who was an expert source of help, a technical adviser, a teacher, a troubleshooter by demand of the group. The manager doesn't direct, control or discipline in the conventional sense. He doesn't set standards of performance or exert pressure for improvement. There is no relationship between self-regulating teams and conventional managerial styles.

An effective managerial team has the following qualities:

1. Understanding, mutual agreement and identification with respect to the primary task
2. Open communications
3. Mutual trust
4. Mutual support
5. Management of human differences
6. Selective use of the team
7. Appropriate member skills
8. Leadership

Leadership is a determining characteristic, and team development is more complicated than individual development.[50]

---

[50] Douglas McGregor, The Professional Manager, (McGraw-Hill book, 1967), Chapter 10

10 CHAPTER NEW INSTITUTIONAL ECONOMICS, VERTICALLY INTEGRATED ORGANIZATION AND MODERN INDUSTRIAL ENTERPRISES

1.New institutional economics, vertical integration

Today, with the emergence of large vertically integrated firms, the separation of enterprise ownership and control, a large number of professional managers appear in enterprise management; management tends to become complicated, and many scholars study management from different angles and directions. At the same time, some economists feel very curious and contradictory about the emergence of such vertically integrated firm. An economist was thinking that since there are planned and coordinated organizations in large enterprises, at the same time, some countries, such as the Soviet Union, are also using this plan to manage the entire society. Why is there such a plan in the enterprise? What type of plan is reasonable? The economist asking these questions was Ronald Coase.

Ronald Coase (1910---2013), is the longest-lived economist. Coase was born in London, U.K; when he was 18 years old, he attended the London School of Economics and received a bachelor of commerce degree. When he was about to graduate from college, Coase received the Sir Ernest Cassel Travelling Scholarship. He decided to visit the United States and studied vertical and lateral integration in industry. At that time, there was a problem in Coase's mind, there were factories in Europe and America, at the same time a planned economy appeared in the Soviet Union, the economic system would be run as one big factory. How did one reconcile the impossibility of running Russia as one big factory with the existence of factories in the western world? With this question, Coase came to the United States. During his time in the United States, Coase attended very few classes, most of his time was spent in visiting business and industrial plants. Coase visited Ford Motor Company, some steel works and department stores. During his time in the United States, Coase's ideas about vertically integrated organization gradually became clear. In 1937, Coase wrote "The Nature of the Firm", he pioneered new institutional (transaction cost) economics and was the first among Western economists to think about the vertically integrated firm. The article "The Nature of the Firm" was met with a cold reception for a while after publication, I think the main reason is that World War II broke out. In World War II, the economic system of the Soviet Union effectively carried out national war mobilization, created tremendous energy, and achieved victory in the war, indicating that the economic system of the Soviet Union has its superiority. After World War II, Western developed countries followed the planned economic system of the Soviet Union, strengthened the government, implemented nationalization of enterprises, and established a welfare state. At the same time, Keynes's ideas were widely recognized in the Western world. The government invested in the construction of various public infrastructure, established personal medical insurance, improved the state-funded social security system, and planned and regulated the social economy. After World War II, the vertically integrated firms continued to develop and improve, the management thought continued to enrich, and the role of the vertically integrated firm in social life became more and more important. The tradition of

Western countries doesn't emphasize the role of the government, the main focus of discussion in Western society is the relationship between the government and the market, the main concern of economics is the price issue, so this article "The Nature of the Firm" received a cold reception. Since the 1970s and 1980s, more and more economists have begun to study the problem of industrial organization, and the number of citations of the article "The Nature of the Firm" has gradually increased.

In the late 1970s and early 1980s, Western developed countries experienced a "stagflation" of economic development. On the one hand, the socioeconomic development was stagnant, on the other hand, there was inflation in society. So Western developed countries began to focus on the research on the vertically integrated firm and promoted neoliberalism economic policies. Several sectors of the economy were fully or partially deregulated, these sectors included airlines, trucking, railroads, telecommunications, cable television and electric utility, etc. These fields were previously dominated by vertically integrated organizations. How to deregulate the fields is a problem faced by economists in industrial organizations. They need to study the internal composition, property rights, transaction costs, and long-term contracts of the vertically integrated organizations. In this context, many scholars have further deepened Coase's thinking and the developed new institutional economics. Some scholars, such as Oliver Williamson, has published "Markets and Hierarchies" and "The Economic Institutions of Capitalism". Later Coase received the Nobel Memorial Prize in Economic Sciences in 1991, Williamson received the Nobel Memorial Prize in Economic Sciences in 2009. Coase wrote a book "How China Became Capitalist" co-authored with Ning Wang, he explained the change of China society. Coase put forward the concept of a market place of ideas, the hope to put forward new ideas for the development of enterprises; his idea needs to be carefully studied. Before, economics mainly analyzed prices, and there was no organization content; economists often think that organization research is a category of management science, the defect is compensated by the emergence of the new institutional economics. Simon said "the key idea of new institutional economics is to regard most organizational phenomena as simply another kind of market behavior, of market interaction between employees and their employers... the new institutional economics tries to explain how organizations operate by analyzing the employment contract and other explicit or implied contracts that individuals have with organizations."[51]

Some people say that Coase's thinking is privatization, because the reforms carried out by many countries in the world, including China, in the 1980s were a departure from planned economy, an re-advocacy of free market dominance, and the privatization of many industries, such as energy, water treatment, railway, electricity, telecommunications and postal services, etc. A World famous think tank, the Club of Rome, published a book "Limits to privatization", the book is based on a large number of examples and makes an objective and critical review and summary of global privatization; it is a good book. Everything has a good side and a bad side, there are pros and cons, just like Yin and Yang. The privatization has succeeded in some fields but not in others, the privatization of certain types of companies has succeeded in some countries and failed in others. If we look at the development of the personal computer field from the perspective of privatization, then the emergence of many software and hardware companies is the result of privatization, and privatization is conducive to the development of innovation, this problem will be further analyzed later. We can't simply say that privatization is good or bad, nor can we simply use the concept of privatization to look at many things. From the perspective of the origin of civilization, the disintegration of the clan and the creation of the private ownership was inevitable for historical development. During the period of clans and tribes, property is public. With the development of the business and the economy, the people is intermixed, and the emergence of common management institutions, the state has emerged and the property became private, this is also in line with the privatization process.

---

[51] Herbert A. Simon, Administrative Behavior, Fourth Edition, chapter 1

Coase's "The Nature of the Firm" was published in 1937. At that time, the size of enterprises was already very large. Planning, decision-making, execution, etc., the functional departments within the enterprise were also differentiated, and many functional departments appeared. In the 1930s, the enterprises of the United States have basically established a professional managerial system. The company has become vertically integrated and diversified. Such an organization is dominated by managers and management is open to everyone. In history, it never has seen such a large, well-organized industrial organization.

The main purpose of vertical integration is to save transaction costs. The cost of this kind of administrative order is lower than the cost of contract transactions, and it is more efficient. Vertical integration is further divided into forward integration, lateral integration and backward integration, which are directed to cover distribution, components and basic materials, it provides complex products and services.

Meanwhile, some scholars have studied the phenomenon of separation of enterprise ownership and control. In 1932, Adolf A. Berle and Gardiner C. Means published "the modern corporation & private property" book, which presented the classical agency theory problem. The ownership system of vertically integrated firm is the separation of enterprise ownership and control. The transaction cost theory and the agency theory study the same things, but they have different research perspectives.

The commonalities of transaction cost theory and agency theory:

1. **Managerial discretion**
   The concerns of them are same, both transaction cost theory and agency theory work out of substantially identical behavioral assumptions.
2. **Efficient contracting**
   Incomplete contracting in its entirety
3. **Endogenous Board of directors**

The Board of directors is an endogenous control instrument.[52]

The differences of transaction cost theory and agency theory:

1. **Unit of analysis**
   transaction cost theory regards the transaction as the basic unit of analysis
   agency theory the individual agent is the elementary unit of analysis
2. **Agency costs/transactions costs**
   transaction cost theory: expected costs
   agency theory: ex post costs
3. **Organizational concern**
   transaction cost theory: it settles dispute through administrative arrangements within the organization.
   agency theory: it is little concerned with dispute resolution.[53]

Williamson thinks bureaucracy is not in the category of economics, but in the field of sociology.

Enterprise strategy in transaction cost economics:

1. **Pricing**
   Final product, intermediate product (squeeze)
2. **Product development**
   Research and development, introduction
3. **Marketing**
   Advertising, other promotion, testing
4. **Investment**
   Plant location, integration, asset attributes
5. **Government**

---

[52] Oliver E. Williamson, The Mechanisms of Governance, (Oxford University, 1996), pp. 173-175

[53] Oliver E. Williamson, The Mechanisms of Governance, (Oxford University, 1996), pp. 175-177

Standards, contracting, trade policy, litigation
6. Other
    Wage, taxes[54]

2.The development and perfection of modern vertically integrated firm

Vertical integrations are directed to cover distribution forward, to cover components lateral, and to cover basic materials backward. It appears in sales department, procurement and transportation department, which integrates production, sales and procurement processes. In the past, railway companies, telegraph companies, sales companies and financial companies all performed only a single function. The modern vertically integrated firms perform multiple functions and need more full-time managers in their operations. Managers also need to deal with diversified work, planning and coordination.

This versatile vertically integrated firm has gradually become the most influential institution in the United States economy, and surpass railway companies in scale, complexity and diversity. The methods and procedures for managing such enterprises have laid the foundation for the modern enterprise management.

In early modern companies like Ford and Kodak, family partners controlled the business, and full-time salaried managers were responsible for day-to-day operations. Major long-term decisions, investment, allocation of funds, managerial recruitment and other issues remained concentrated in the hands of a few owners. Such enterprises were all capital-intensive.

---

[54] Oliver E. Williamson, The Mechanisms of Governance, (Oxford University, 1996), pp. 296-297

In that era, production equipment was not difficult to obtain, the price was not expensive, and patents were no a barrier. The pioneering enterprises first often gained an advantage and occupied a leading position in the market, but what is the disadvantage of competitor enterprises? The most imposing barrier of entry in these industries was the organization the pioneers had built to produce and sell, a competitor had to create a national and often global organization of managers, buyers, and salesmen. The pioneering enterprises did not build a huge sales network from the beginning, cash flow generated by high volume was used to establish the sales network. The competitor had to set up another same sizable competing network from the beginning, but at this time the volume of sales is not high, which increases the difficulty of the competitor, and the pioneers form an oligopoly. In the United States, this phenomenon appeared in the manufacture of sewing machines, agricultural machinery, office machines, cigarettes, matches, breakfast cereals, canned milk, soup, roll film and Kodak cameras, fresh meat processing, petroleum trusts, aluminum, cotton oil, linseed oil, sugar and paper making, glass, machine manufacturing and other industries are all reflected.

Two ways of vertically integrated firm:

1. the addition of sales and procurement agencies

2. integration by way of merger

This process of financing resulted in a significant difference in the relationship of owners and managers. The firms that initially became large through internal expansion continued to have the stock ownership closely held by the founder, a few associates, and their families; top executives in the central office were nearly always major stockholders or personally close to such stockholders, the early Ford is a typical representative. The new mergers spread the ownership of capital stock and the ownership began to disperse, top executives became salaried managers who held only a small amount of the total stocks and had little personal acquaintance with the scattered owners, GM is a typical representative.

The separation of ownership and control first appeared in the United States in business firms other than the railroad and the telegraph. In the 1880s and 1890s, the vertically integrated organizations began to appear, from the early 20th century to World War I, a large number of vertically integrated organizations appeared. In the 1920s, it was a period of adjustment after mergers, successful mergers enterprises were established and unsuccessful enterprises were eliminated.

The earliest family companies hired a large number of professional managers in middle management. The founders were responsible for the high-level management. The middle managers coordinated, supervised and evaluated the various functions and activities, as well as coordinated the work between various departments and other departments. The middle managers work includes coordination, smooth flow from suppliers of raw material to consumers, invented and perfected ways to expand markets and to speed up the processes of production and distribution, and developed techniques to advertise, marketing, place warehouses, purchase, store, and move huge stocks of raw and semi-finished materials. The procurement, sales and production processes have basically been mechanized. The largest part of the general company is the sales department, with offices and branches in the country and even around the world; the headquarters has sales department, production department, purchasing department, collection department, as well as order and shipping department, accounting and audit department.

Competition between these enterprises was ultimately between their managers and organizations, the success of a firm depended primarily on the caliber of its managerial hierarchy. Like the competition between Ford and General Motors, Ford initially had an advantage and had a large share of the market. One type of car, Ford Model T has always dominated the company. GM, through management innovation, adopted business division system and there were professional managers at all level of the enterprise. In the automotive market, there are Cadillac in high end market, Buick in mid end market and Chevrolet in low end market. Compared to Ford's, the product line of GM is more abundant.

3.Top management

In the vertically integrated firm developed through the merger, the top and middle management are controlled by full-time salaried supervisors, the owner of enterprise no longer manages the company, and promotes and appoints managers who have no or only a small number of stocks as supervisors. Top managers establish a unified accounting and statistical supervision system to assess the performance of managers. The owner does not participate in management, and a few of the managers have a large number of voting shares. Typically, Standard Oil created the administrative structure that came to be called the functional holding company form, and had a functionally departmentalized structure.

General Motors used committees

Standard Oil, GM all set up formal committees. By 1917, in Standard Oil, Rockefellers no longer even sat on the Board of directors and were simply receiving their dividends and voting at the annual meetings. Du Pont has become a managerial enterprise, before it was a preeminent family firm. The family continues to enjoy a substantial share of the company's profits. Du Ponts no longer manage and make significant industrial decisions.

During World War I, vertically integrated firms and modern enterprises with the separation of ownership and control were basically established, although there were still some defects.

GM's organizational form has become a standard model for other companies to transform their organizations, it is a typical managerial enterprise, a vertically integrated organization, and the most complete representative of the separation of ownership and control. Like in GM, the creation of a general office consisting of general executives and a large financial and advisory staff and with the calibration of product flow and from day-to-day operating activities to forecasted demand, the basic organizational structure and administrative procedures of the modern industrial enterprise were virtually completed.

By the middle of the 20th century, professionally oriented, salaried career managers were the men who had taken charge of the large multi-unit enterprises dominating the critical sectors of the American economy. During the 1960s, the conglomerate appeared on the American business scene. The conglomerate expanded entirely by the acquisition of existing enterprises and it often did so in totally unrelated fields. Conglomerates tended to purchase relatively small enterprises in industries that were not yet oligopolies and provided small enterprises with new administrative and operational techniques.

Alfred D. Chandler said "at the beginning of this century, the American economic system still included elements of financial and family capitalism. Managerial capitalism was not yet fully dominant… Nevertheless, members of the entrepreneurial family rarely became active in top management unless they, themselves, were trained as professional managers… In only a few of the large American business enterprises did family members continue to participate for more than two generations in the management of the companies they owned…These families remain the primary beneficiaries of managerial capitalism, but they are no longer involved in the operation of its central institution. By mid-twentieth century, few had any direct say in the decisions concerning current flows and future allocations so essential to the operation of the American economy…Thus by the 1950s, the managerial firm had become the standard form of modern business enterprise in major sectors of the American economy. In those sectors where modern multi-unit enterprises had come to dominate, managerial capitalism had gained ascendancy over family and financial capitalism."[55]

4. The emergence of modern business education and business schools

After Taylor became famous, Harvard University invited him to give lectures. Taylor's students like Barth, Gantt, Gilbreths, Emerson and Cooke also went to the University of Chicago, and to Harvard University to give lectures or set up consulting companies.

The famous Wharton School of the University of Pennsylvania was established in 1881, it is the first undergraduate business school in the Unites States, its founder is Joseph Wharton. Wharton started business through Bethlehem Steel company, Taylor conducted the experiment of scientific management in Bethlehem Steel company. Later the University of Chicago and the University of California, Berkeley, also established business schools. Harvard University established the Graduate School of business, conferring a Master of Science degree in business, today it is the Master of Business Administration (MBA), becoming the world's most famous business education and research center; Harvard Business School was established in 1908; from 1909, every winter, Taylor taught at Harvard University until 1914. Other university founded a school of management, and Yale University established the School of Management in 1976. In Europe, business schools in the United Kingdom were only established in British universities in the 1960s. at the beginning, some old universities, such as Oxford and Cambridge, did not look at this kind of business education, rational thinking and science spirit are the pursuit of prestigious universities, they trained scholars like Newton, Darwin, Russell, Whitehead, Locke, Bacon,

---

[55] Alfred D. Chandler, The Visible Hand, (Harvard University, 1977), pp 491-493

Spencer, Babbage, Toynbee, Tolkien, Hawking... but later universities like the University of Manchester and the University of London gained rapid development with business schools, and those old universities have changed their self aims and established business schools.

Since scientific management can be learned and taught by anyone, like scientific knowledge, it is the most natural thing to conduct theoretical study and research in universities. At the same time, there are managers who are responsible for coordination in the society. Because of the coordination of product development processes, sales have become more and more complicated. The managers of large industrial enterprises have gradually become professionals. Many professional associations and professional publications have appeared, such as the "Accounting Association", "Journal of Accountancy", as well as marketing association, management association... Universities and colleges began to teach professional courses, such as financial accounting and cost accounting. In the early business schools, teachers taught about factory management. As Taylor and his students spread scientific management thought; the main content taught by the business school was engineering and industrial management. From that period until now, there is a debate: Is management a science or an art? Because the object of management is people, not cold things. Taylor's management thought has neglected the human factor to some extent, and treated humans as a machine. The content gradually taught by the business school has increased economics, accounting, finance, marketing, business law, logistics, statistics, physical environment, ethics, production, personnel and labor, etc.

Harvard's business school uses the case method for teaching, a method which continues until today. The method is to bring actual enterprise development cases into the classroom, analyze the problems encountered by the enterprise, require students to discuss and analyze, and write a report. With the support of business education, a large number of business talents who accept scientific management thought can be cultivated and can gain further education. Full-time professional managers gradually penetrate into all fields of industry. It can be said that without the emergence of the scientific management thought and without the popularization of business education, there will not be a new class of professional managers, and there will be no separation of ownership and control. It should be said that the emergence of the scientific management thought, the popularization of business education, the emergence of professional managers and the separation of ownership and control, these phenomena are complementary and interactive. Just like discussing the question of which came first, chicken or egg? the occurrence of these phenomena is a process of gradual development and gradual improvement.

Now not only in North America, in Europe, various countries and major universities all over the world have business schools, and spread similar business education theories, as long as they are engaged in industry and commerce, the theory of scientific management, is applicable. Different countries have different historical development paths due to different social systems, and the business environment will not be exactly the same. Some government interventions are less important and some governments intervene more in business. The degree of acceptance of scientific management thought is different in different countries. Each country should absorb and adjust the scientific management thought according to its own history, moral concepts, and management methods in order to better play the role of scientific management thought.

5.China Public-private partnership

In the early 1950s, China's new regime had just been established, and it carried out the socialist transformation of the national industry and commerce, that is, from the initial purchase and distribution of enterprise products, to processing orders, and finally adopting a public-private partnership policy for enterprises. The ownership of the enterprise is nationalized, the capitalist may become manager, retains the company's shares, and regularly pays the capitalist dividends. This process continued until 1966. From the perspective of the separation of enterprises ownership and control, it seems that it is reasonable. Western manufacturing companies have basically established a professional manager system after World War II, managers control the enterprise, and the management of enterprises are in the hands of managers. Is China's public-private partnership policy historically correct? After 1980s, why did China's reform and opening up allow private enterprises to develop again? I think in today's society, private companies and family businesses still exist widely in the world. In many industries and fields, family business occupies an important position, such as retail, pharmaceuticals, food processing and manufacturing, industrial manufacturing, hotels, tourism, real estate, etc., Like Ford Motor Company, Walmart Inc, Hilton Inc, Auchan Group, Dassault Aircraft Company, Toyota Motor Corporation, Honda Motor Company, Samsung Group, Hyundai Group... Many of these family companies' professional managers control companies, like Ford Motor Company hired Boeing Vice President Mulally as President and CEO of Ford Motor Company. In the field of large-scale manufacturing, the advantages of vertical integration are very obvious. In the field of large-scale manufacturing, the demand for creativity, management and capital makes the separation of enterprise ownership and control more advantageous, especially in the fields of telecommunications, transportation, energy, chemical industry, aviation and aerospace, sometimes the power of a country is not enough, and it is necessary to integrate various resources. However, the problem of China's public-private partnership policy was that some small and medium-sized enterprises were engaged in public-private partnerships. Later, the society even denied the existence of the market, relying solely on administrative power and went to the extreme. Managers themselves constitute also a market, a talent market, managers can flow between enterprises, and promote the activation of informal organizations between enterprises. This is not available in public-private partnerships. According to the understanding of Yin-Yang theory, a lone Yin is not born, solitary Yang does not develop. The education of professional managers is an important support for the vertically integrated firm. In the 1950s, although there was some business education in China, there were not many business schools. The education of the business schools was not promoted and popularized until China reform and opening up. In the 1980s, many universities in China established business schools or management schools, introduced Western textbooks, and offered courses in business management.

After the public-private partnership, the enterprise became a public institution affiliated to the government department and did not really face the market. The person in charge of the enterprise was the same as the official of the government agency. This person was mainly responsible to his superiors. Innovation of the enterprise and upgrading of equipment became secondary factors. In order to maintain stability, government agencies are also reluctant to have new ideas and new initiatives brought by leaders of company. The companies controlled by the managers of Western companies are mainly oriented to the market, and the government has limited power in society. This is a big difference between the two. Of course, it is not easy to innovate after the vertically integrated organization becomes larger. The company's management levels increase, with layer-by-layer reporting and level-by-level authority. In this case, information transmission and communication will have many problems or may become difficult, if there is too much emphasis on authority, it will inhibit creativity, it is similar regardless whether in Western developed countries or in developing countries, but in the societies, there are markets and, in the firm, there are internal markets, people are more free and have more creativity.

11 CHAPTER THE DEVELOPMENT OF THE ENTERPRISE AND THE ORIGINS OF CIVILIZATION

There is a similar process between the development and evolution of the enterprise and the origin of civilization. The origin of civilization has moved from clan, tribal alliance, and chiefdom to the state; It has broken the original clan system step by step, and the property has changed from clan sharing to private ownership; To establish a city and a political system and to form a state. The state is established beyond blood relationship. After the emergence of the scientific management, the separation of enterprises ownership and control, the emergence of the vertically integrated firm, the ownership of the enterprise has changed from the family ownership to public ownership, person own shares, it reflects exactly the process of moving from blood links to geography factor. Here it is a brief introduction to the origin of the country and civilization, which allows us to look at the process of the enterprise development and evolution from another perspective.

1.Origins of the state and civilization

The origin of civilization in the world can be traced back to about 4,000 BC. Generally speaking, there were four major ancient civilizations and regions, and someone said there were six major civilizations: the Mesopotamian civilization in the Middle East, the ancient Egyptian civilization, the ancient Indian civilization and the ancient Chinese civilization. Other experts believe that the ancient Indian civilizations of Central and South America should also be regarded as two ancient civilizations. These ancient civilizations, their origins and formation have some common characteristics. The original anthropologists like Lewis Henry. Morgan, through comparing the origins of ancient Greek and Roman civilizations in Europe and the Indian civilizations of the Americas, drew the conclusion that the human society has gone from obscurant, barbarism to civilization, it has experienced three stage from the clan, tribal alliances to the state. The change in these three stages is that the property has changed from a clan to a private one. The clan system has disintegrated, and then appeared the class; After the tribal alliance, a political society was based on geography and property, the tribal alliance chief has become king. Friedrich Engels wrote "The Origin of the Family, Private Property and the State" and analyzed the process of the origin of civilization from an economic perspective, comparing the clan of the Iroquois of the North American Indian tribes, as well as clans and states of Greeks, Romans and Germans.

The origin of the state and civilization is characterized by the emergence of written language, cities and political systems. This is the three elements of the formation of the state; some scholars believe that the factor of bronze should be considered, and it becomes the four elements. The invention of written language can make mankind inherit knowledge; the city keeps mankind away from caves, in city the division of work of the agriculture, the handicraft industry and business emerged; the political system makes rules and laws to mediate social conflicts; in the West, bronze is used in the manufacture and production of tools, but in the East, China, the manufacture of bronzes is mainly reflected in rituals and weapons. In the clan society and tribal alliance society, the people are basically equal, at that time, the level of productivity is not high, there is not much common wealth. When it comes to the state, it is different, there is class and class differentiation, property is private, and people are not equal, the state is a social regime established beyond the blood relationship.

Later scholars like Elman R. Service and Morton. Fried thought that the transition from tribe to country is a process, and there should be a stage in the middle, a chiefdom society or a hierarchical society. The chiefdom is a preliminary inequality, the chieftain has political power in his hands, he can control and distribute wealth. However, during the chiefdom period, the system was not formal, there were no perfect administrative and political institutions, and the inheritance of power did not form a formal system, there was no religion. This process is very complicated, the emergence of civilization is the change of the whole society, including economic, political, religious, scientific, cultural and other aspects. Anthropologists have concluded that these characteristics are common and can be found in many areas, but each region has some different features.

The clan and tribal society are basically a small society. Morgen said the number of persons in a clan is estimated to be about 100 to 1000, it is equivalent to a natural village today. There is a village chief in a village, but everyone else is basically equal, one organization is not big, the same is true in the company; basic equality is not absolute equality, everyone has similar conditions. In this kind of equal society also there is authority, it may be like a consultant, it has a unique charm but does not have much practical power; it is similar to the glamorous leadership, that Max Weber said, has power by his experience, personal influence. In the period of the chiefdom, the population increased, the chiefdom society was bigger and more complicated than the tribal society and the role of authority rose. However, there was no standardized system. It should be said that the original legal authority appeared and more traditionally led, this is similar to the traditional leader that Weber said. It should be said that this period is a mixed period, relying on both personal ability and influence, and on traditional habits. When the country emerged into a civilized society, the law was created, at this time, the society was advanced than the tribe.

Friedrich Engels wrote, "the sea trade in the Aegean was captured from the Phoenicians... through the sale and purchase of land and the progressive division of labour between agriculture and handicraft, trade, and shipping, it was inevitable that the members of the different gentes, phratries, and tribes very soon became intermixed... the smooth functioning of the organs of the gentile constitution was thus thrown ...the principal change which it made was to set up a central authority in Athens – that is, part of the affairs hitherto administered by the tribes independently were declared common affairs and entrusted to the common council sitting in Athens... hence arose a common Athenian civil law which stood above the legal customs of the tribes and gentes. The Athenian citizen as such acquired definite rights and a new protection in law even on territory which was not that of his tribe. The first step had been taken toward undermining the gentile constitution"[56]

Individuals not only survive in his tribal area, but also can survive in other areas, and the flow of people has greatly increased. There was the division of labour between the commercial and handicraft industries. The state has a coercive function, some scholars say that this is violence, but the state also has a mediation function, not everything is solved through violence. The customs, beliefs, and lifestyles of various tribes may be inconsistent, if people live together, how to deal with these contradictions? There may be things that are banned in one tribe, but allowed in another tribe, so that a regulatory body that overrides traditional customs and habits is required, and the law and the original government are created.

In the process of the transition from the chiefdom to the state, there is still a phenomenon that is often seen. In the beginning, one of many chiefdoms is strong; after conquering other chiefdoms, the aristocrats of the original chiefdom are often appointed to serve in the local government and the central government. In order to maintain the new situation, and break the original bloodline-based

---

[56] Friedrich Engels, The Origin of the Family, Private Property and the State, (Pathfinder Press, 1972), chapter 5, pp 109-110

structure of the chiefdom, or the identity and society formed on the basis of blood relationship, a new political structure based on geography is established; in the new political structure, the appointment of officials is based on the principle of loyalty, thus it initially establishes a bureaucratic society, but this approach is very different in different regions and different countries. In the aristocratic countries, the new aristocrats replaced the original feudal aristocracy, and in the bureaucratic state, the new bureaucrats replaced the original tribal leaders.

2.The Chinese ancient civilization

As a region where ancient civilizations were born, China has a long history of about 5,000 years. However, from an academic point of view, from the perspective of the three elements of civilization: written language, city and the political system, the well-documented history starts from 2000 BC, China entered the era of civilization and formed the state. Compared with the ancient civilization of Egypt, which was born in 3100 BC; the two rivers civilizations in the Middle East were born in 3000 BC; the ancient Indian civilization was born in 2500 BC. The time of the beginning of the Chinese civilization is later than the first three civilizations. I think this is mainly because China's geographical environment; in the land of China, there are sea in the East, a Gobi Desert in the North, Pamirs in the West, and Qinghai-Tibet Plateau in the Southwest, it forms a large and independent area, and it is not so easy to contact the outside world, especially before the economy was backward and productivity was not developed. The development of the commercial and commodity economy has led to the mixing of personnel in various departments, it led to the emergence of cross-clan, cross-tribal management institutions, and then it formed a state. It can be seen that the development of commerce and trade plays an important role in the formation of the state. Ancient civilizations, two river basins, Egypt and later Minoans civilizations, Mycenae civilizations, are all on the Mediterranean coast, where traffic is developed, which is conducive to the development of commercial trade. There are many islands in the Mediterranean region that form land bridges, where there are many connections between civilizations, it is conducive to exchanges between people in various regions. Like the ancient Greeks, Cretan's Minoans, born in 2500 BC, invented the written language, established the city-state, inherited from the ancient civilization of Egypt, and later influenced the Greek Mycenae civilization. Therefore, Mesopotamia and Egypt in the Middle East took the lead in entering the stage of civilization. The Indus Valley is adjacent to the Middle East; according to modern research, some of the ancient Indians migrated from the Middle East and the Mediterranean. In ancient times, places like China, although there is vast hinterland, but surrounded by mountains and seas; if people want to communicate with the Middle East and even India, to the West, they need to cross the Pamirs and deserts; to the Southwest, they need to cross the Himalayas, to the South, they need to sail to Southeast Asia, cross the Straits of Malacca, and then head West to India and the Middle East. In the history of China, until the Han Dynasty, about the second century BC and the first century AD, on the road and the sea, and there are large-scale exchanges with other regions; at this time, China's national civilization has long been established.

At present, the ancient civilizations of China, from the point of view of the written language, can be traced back to the Shang Dynasty in 1600 BC in accordance with modern archaeological discoveries; the main reason is to find the written language at that time---Oracle bone script; if from the point of view of bronze, it can be traced back to the Xia Dynasty around 2000 BC, various types of bronzes were discovered during that period. In recent years, Chinese scholars have traced the civilization to a farther period through the astronomical phenomena recorded in ancient books and archaeological discoveries. For example, in some areas are found ancient cities and ruins, large altars, and a variety of carefully polished jade artifacts, it can be expected to have more archaeological discoveries in the future and prove that ancient China had a longer civilization.

According to historical records and modern archaeological discoveries, in China the first civilized state began about 2070 BC, the Xia Dynasty, and later the Shang Dynasty and the Zhou Dynasty. These three dynasties have lasted a total of 1800 years. In comparison, after the Zhou Dynasty, from when Qin Shihuang unified China to now, it is only 2200 years. These three dynasties, Xia, Shang, Zhou, were three dynasties and three nationalities. Xia Dynasty first formed the state, established the city and etiquette system, followed by Shang, and later Zhou, they all went through a similar establishment process of the state. The Xia and Zhou nationalities came from the West and had a kinship relationship; the Shang nationality came from the East. At that time, the Eastern and Western regions were mainly competing. After the Qin Dynasty unified China, the Northern grassland tribes and the Central Plains farming civilization had different modes of economic production and the struggle between the two cultures continued for another 2000 years.

At the beginning, the Xia Dynasty gained the dominant position among the tribal alliances by leading the construction of large-scale water conservancy projects. It initially established a unified state, mainly based on blood organizations and completed the transition from the chiefdom to the country. After 470 years or so, the rule was overthrown by the Shang Dynasty. The Shang tribes contacted the surrounding tribes to form an alliance, overthrew the Xia, and established the Shang Dynasty. The politics and religion of the Shang Dynasty were relatively complete, they were still dominated by blood groups, but the geographical factors were greatly strengthened. The rule of the Shang Dynasty lasted for about 550 years and it was overthrown by the Zhou Dynasty. The Zhou Dynasty, with the relationship with the Xia, created the patriarchal system and the ritual and music system, it established many states, the geographical factors were strengthened more than the Shang Dynasty. Later the Zhou Dynasty experienced a chaotic situation in each region, it is known as the Spring and Autumn Period and the Warring States Period. During this period, the ancient Chinese thoughts were born and enriched, and many thinkers were active, it is the same time as ancient Greek philosophy. The development of this period broke the limitations of blood organizations, and the people flowed fully, the final result is the emergence of a bureaucratic society. The ancient Chinese broke the bloodline organization mainly from a political perspective, which is very different from the Western society, and will be mentioned later. During the Spring and Autumn Period and the Warring States period, wars and mergers between various countries continued. In order to compete and improve strength of the state, countries introduced various policies to absorb various talents, and the flow of personnel was greatly strengthened. Compared with the West, there were business factors in breaking the blood organization, but political factors were more important.

Although the three dynasties, Xia, Shang, and Zhou became three countries, the areas they directly ruled were not large. There were many other countries outside them. The Xia, the Shang, and the Zhou were personal union of these countries, they formed a national union with neighbouring countries. They often have contradictions with neighbouring countries, how to deal with these contradictions? In addition to war, there are other methods. For instance, during the Shang Dynasty, the neighbouring countries needed to take positions in the central government and help the Central Plains dynasty to rule; neighbouring countries also often obeyed the arrangements of the central dynasty and stabilized the regional situation. During the Zhou Dynasty, the relatives of the king were further sent into neighbouring countries for management, the world was a family. In the late Zhou Dynasty, the thoughts of the philosophers were born. In the Qin and Han dynasties, feudalism was abolished and centralization was founded. In fact, the central dynasty was a bureaucrat, the state employed professional bureaucrats.

The ancient Chinese civilization has not a single origin, now scholars believe that there were six or seven areas of origin in the ancient Chinese civilization. The maps of today are the Northern, Shandong province, Northwest, Jiangsu province and Zhejiang province, Jiangxi province and Hunan province, and Sichuan basins, they had characteristics and established exchanges. These areas are basically distributed in the middle and lower reaches of the two rivers, the Yellow River and the Yangtze River. At the beginning, the development of the Yellow River Basin is faster, which is mainly related to the cooperation of water conservancy management; the Xia, the Shang and the Zhou, the three ethnic groups also acted mainly in the Yellow River Basin. These regions also experienced a similar process from clan, tribal alliances to chiefdoms and state. The time that they entered the civilized era was inconsistent, early and late, and later this development of civilization has been staged continuously in Chinese history, like the Northern grassland tribe, Xiongnu, Donghu, Rouran, Xianbei, Turkic, Uyghur, Khitan, Jurchen, Tangut, Mongolia, bod chen po of the Qinghai-Tibet Plateau, Nanzhao and Dali of Yunnan, they constantly experienced a similar process, from the clan, the tribal alliance, to the chiefdom and the state, as if the historical drama repeated itself and repeated itself again.

After the fall of the Xia Dynasty, the Shang dynasty rose. The royal family of the Xia Dynasty no longer enjoyed privileges, they ran away and ran to remote areas, the Zhou nationality, who was related to the Xia nationality, also stayed in those undeveloped areas for 400-500 years. After the Shang Dynasty was over, the Zhou Dynasty rose, and the royal family of the Shang Dynasty also lost their privileges, some led the tribe to other areas, one noble man of the Shang dynasty led the tribe to the Korean peninsula and established a new state. China's great thinker and educator--- Confucius is also a descendant of the Shang nation. Similarly, in the end, after the Zhou Dynasty, it was Qin Empire, its tribe came from the Shang nationality and was a part of the Shang nationality, it rose after the decline of the Zhou Dynasty and unified China in the end of the Warring States, they established an unprecedented unified empire. The process can be seen that the Western and the Eastern peoples in the Yellow River Basin have alternately established the country and become the personal union of many countries. Finally, a unified multi-ethnic country has been established and the original ethnic group has been integrated into the Han nationality. The Qin dynasty had a great influence, the subsequent Han dynasty continued the various systems of the Qin dynasty. Now in some countries, China is still called Qin, in English, "China" this word is related to Qin dynasty; like Russian, China is called Kntan, which was the result of the influence of Khitan on Western grassland tribes at that time. This process is long and painful, the bureaucratic system eliminated the nobility and rely on moral and ethical basis. This bureaucratic system was from the Qing Dynasty about 221 BC to the last dynasty of the Qing dynasty - 1911.

3.Differences between Eastern and Western civilizations

The three elements of civilization, or four elements--- written language, cities, ceremonial systems and bronzes, are different in these respects. In general, the West is biased towards the economy, while the East is more political. In the West, the creation of written language is for production technology and commercial trade. The priests of the temple create hieroglyphs to record various assets and accounts, while in the ancient Chinese written language serve politics and religion, the contents of the oracles bone script in the Shang Dynasty, most of them are about the ruler asking God for divination. Cities, in the West, have become the centres of trade exchanges and handicraft workshops, and urban autonomy has occurred until the Middle Ages. In China, cities have always been the residence of officials. Bronze is used in the West to manufacture production tools. In China, there are few bronze production tools, the manufacture of bronzes is mainly embodied in rituals and weapons.

Etiquette system and religion, in any region, political system and religion are closely related, but there are differences in various regions. In China, due to the emergence of moral and ethical philosophy, later the bureaucrats were invented, religion have fallen into a less important position. In contrast to the West, due to the continuation of aristocratic rule and the imperfection of bureaucracy, religion has occupied an important position in political life. Now in Egypt, the Middle East and India, religion is still important in society. During the Spring and Autumn Period of China and before, when the country had a major event, the king asked help from God, but in the Warring States and later, various thoughts replaced divination, and politicians, military personnel and diplomats became the core of the stage, humanistic thoughts replaced religion. Like "I Ching", it is considered to be the head of the Confucian classics. In the Qin Dynasty, when Qin Shi Huang burned many thinkers' books, including Confucian classics, but he considered "I Ching" to be a book of divination and did not pay attention. It indicated that by the late Warring States period, the development of knowledge reduced the status of religion.

In the Chinese history, there has never been a country like the European countries, such as Spain, the Holy Roman Empire, England and Scotland, formed by the merger of marriage or inheritance, and there has never been a federal state like Switzerland. China is not a nation-state like Europe, Lucian Pye described China as a "civilization-state, pretending to be a (nation-) state." In the history of China, the descendants of emperors of dynasties can continue to be emperors and princes, but officials come from all regions, and in each dynasty, it is the case. There have been splits in Chinese history and there were various independent kingdoms; however, after a certain kingdom is strong, it will unify through force. After reunification, there will be many factions and many vassals state. There is a law in the field of biology called recapitulation law, also known as biogenetic law, which means that the history of ontogeny is a simple and rapid re-enactment of the history of system development. If society is regarded as an organism, the formation process of any country will be repeated in the process of clan, tribal alliance, chiefdom, and state. The dynasties and countries in Chinese history are from clans and tribes to chiefdoms and state, the process constantly repeated. The clan and tribal alliances are mainly composed of blood relations, the chiefdoms and state are composed of geographical and property relations. Because the organization expands, engaging in business and dividing the class with property relations is conducive to breaking the traditional blood ties and facilitating the formation of the state and civilization.

The development and evolution of the enterprise repeats the process of state creation. Home business is equivalent to clan, and later family business is equivalent to tribal alliance. When it reaches the stage of chiefdom and state, it is similar to the modern vertically integrated firm. The blood factors are declining, with professional managers and officials bureaucratic enterprise and bureaucratic state are established. Privatization is similar to public shareholding, both management and insiders of enterprise can hold stocks of company. The class is divided by property and geography because of mixed population, the emergence of division of labour in agriculture, handicrafts and business. Public ownership is the division of functions in enterprise. As we mentioned in chapter 10, the enterprise employs a variety of talents from various professions and needs to establish offices, branches and sales departments in various regions and countries. In order to stabilize and encourage managers, enterprise needs to give shares to managers. After the enterprise grows and develops, it merges with other enterprises. In order to consolidate and develop the products of the merged enterprise and continues to occupy the market, the new enterprise continues to appoint the managers of the merged enterprise to take up management positions. These practices are the same as the procession that after the states' conquest by the tribal alliance and chiefdom, it appoints the nobles of the conquered tribes and chiefdom.

12 CHAPTER THE DEVELOPMENT OF THE ENTERPRISE AND THE EVOLUTION OF THE POLITICAL SYSTEM

This book mainly presents management and economics. So far, we have talked about the stages of capitalism development, the pioneers of business management, and the three iconic figures of scientific management, Taylor, Fayol and Weber. After the organizational research direction and the behavioral science research direction in the development of science management appeared. they introduced the practice of entrepreneurs, the separation of enterprises ownership and control, and the formation and characteristics of the vertically integrated firm. The second half of the book turns to the cultural content. In this chapter, we analyze the political system. Why in here do we analyze the political system? Is it not irrelevant to the subject of this book? Through the following discussion, we will find two seemingly different aspects, but they have very similar characteristics. This was also mentioned when we talked about Weber. It is the problem of the bureaucratic state and the bureaucratic enterprise. The typical bureaucratic state is ancient in the Chinese society and the typical bureaucratic enterprise is a modern vertically integration firm, both have many similar characteristics. For instance, the bureaucratic state relies on traditional moral and ethical thoughts, and the bureaucratic enterprises rely on modern scientific management thoughts. Moral and ethical thoughts are used to deal with interpersonal relationships, such as the relationship between superior and subordinate persons, and the people around. The scientific management aims mainly to save expenses of enterprises, to accelerate capital turnover, to reduce costs, etc.; in a bureaucratic state, the emperor or king owns the country and can be hereditary, but the administrative officials have considerable powers. The daily management tasks of the state are the responsibility of officials. In bureaucratic enterprises, the separation of enterprise ownership and control appears, as well as professional managers. The top and middle management of enterprises is in the hands of professional managers. The commonalities of the ancient Chinese society and the modern vertically integrated firm are that there is a typical bureaucratic class, educated by classical moral and ethical thought, and scientific management theory. The bureaucratic class can be promoted step by step, they have status and privileges. The professional managers correspond to the ancient officials, the general manager is equivalent to the prime minister. Officials and managers in bureaucracies are trained, appointed by higher authorities, they have high social status, and privileges.

Bureaucratic institutions, vertically integrated organizations, which evolved from family organizations, have advantages over family organizations; especially in the construction of large-scale projects, the bureaucratic institutions have the characteristics of a strong mobilization ability and high organizational efficiency, this is undoubted. But history always moves forward, nothing will be flawless and perfect. Bureaucratic institutions and vertically integrated organizations also have their shortcomings. Will this type of organizations continue to evolve and develop? Which new features will appear? Which new types of organizations will appear? These issues are very interesting. To clarify these issues, we need to analyze the vertically integrated organization and bureaucracy from various angles, and compare its own characteristics from other angles.

1.The source and structure of the bureaucracy

Some scholars have analyzed that the Chinese bureaucratic system originated from the implementation of a large-scale water conservancy project in ancient times, which created the need for coordination of large-scale human resources. The earliest water conservancy projects can be traced back to the Great Flood of Gun-Yu among the origins of the Chinese civilization. In Chinese history, the governance of the Yellow River Basin has many times and also has the construction of canals, such as the Jing-Hang Grand Canal, which connects the transport of the South and the North. These large-scale water conservancy projects promoted the emergence and improvement of the bureaucratic system. The ancient Chinese political system and the present political system can be divided into three levels. The top is the central government, the middle is local government, such as province, and the grassroots are counties, towns. Nowadays in every country, the political system is similar in its class division, and can be divided into three levels, the top, the middle and the grassroots. The education in ancient China was open to all social strata, people studied the classic books of Confucianism. There were private schools at the grassroots and the Imperial College at the top. After passing the imperial examinations, ordinary people in the society at first could go to local governments and take up certain junior positions, such as county magistrates, and then, if they passed the performance of evaluations, they could get promoted in different positions of government. Officials could take up the middle position, such as the chief executive of a big city. At last, they could be appointed to the top government position, such as governors and ministers of the central government, and even secretary of the emperor and the prime ministers.

The scientific management comes from the popularization of American railways. The first part of this book analyze that the construction and management of railway are the enlightenment era of scientific management, it is called the systematic management period. The large-scale construction and management of railway require huge funds, as it appeared with the decentralization of shareholders and the full-time professional managers in companies. The management of the entire railway company can be divided into three levels, the top, the middle and the grassroots. The top of railway company is the chairman, general manager and financial supervisor. The middle is the section project supervisor, transportation director and maintenance engineer. The grassroots are the specific operators. The transfer of management from the railway sector to the steel manufacturing enterprises prompted the birth of the scientific management. Taylor practiced his management theory in the steel manufacturing company. The scientific management is universal. In business school, the knowledge of scientific management is taught. Anyone can enter a business school to learn the management knowledge after passing the exam. After graduation, they can go to the company to take up positions, such as grassroots managers. Perhaps they were trained in different positions in the company. In some company, there is evaluations of performance. Through evaluation, the managers can be gradually promoted, and further take up the middle management positions, such as department manager or branch manager. Later they may be moved to senior management position and become senior leader and general manager.

The evolution and development of society are very complicated. This chapter only describes the similarities and differences of the political system of different regions in ancient society. At the same time, modern vertically integrated firms are huge and complicated. Modern enterprises can be divided into many departments according to their functions, design, research, production, operation, marketing, sale, audit, finance, law, public relations, human resources. The enterprise is also divided into different branches or business departments according to professional functions or different product types. The management of enterprise involves the flow of people, finances and materials, and needs to handle relationship with customers, government, upstream and downstream enterprises, etc., In this chapter, we analyze and compare the similarities between bureaucratic enterprises and bureaucratic countries, and cite examples.

2.The Noble system and bureaucracy

The political systems of various countries in the ancient world can be roughly divided into two types: aristocracy or feudal system, and bureaucratic system. Some regions have only developed aristocracy, for instance, Europe. but China, has further developed the bureaucratic system. The bureaucracy is a more advanced system than the aristocracy, which emphasizes more geographical factors. The ancient country was a dynasty country and a family controlled the state, which was similar in many regions. Kings and emperors were hereditary, but the composition of officials was very different. In medieval Europe, a nation-state was formed. It was the nobles who maintained the daily management of the country, and the nobles were very powerful in the political life. The Wars of the Roses in the United Kingdom was a struggle between nobles. In French history, the various dynasties were full of struggles between kings and nobles. Like the Fronde in the 17th century. The emperor of the Holy Roman Empire was elected by Princes-electors, namely the great nobles and archbishops. None of the states have developed a complete bureaucracy. There was also aristocratic rule in Chinese history. This period was about during the Shang and Zhou dynasties (11th century BC-3rd century BC). At that time, the feudalism was established and many principalities appeared. However, after the Qin dynasty unified China, it changed and became a bureaucratic country, also called a centralized country. The status of aristocracy has declined, and the status of professional bureaucrats has risen. After selection, training, and assessment, officials can take up position in local and central governments.

This kind of politics in China is also called civilian politics. Ordinary people who pass the imperial examination and the subsequent assessments can be gradually promoted in the government. In the end, they can even be a prime minister, "he has only one over him and millions under him" he becomes second leader and only the emperor has more power than him in the politics of the state. However, it cannot be simply said that ancient China has been a bureaucracy since the Qin Dynasty (221 BC-207 BC) and that there was no aristocracy. It was a long process for bureaucracy to replace aristocracy. After the establishment of a bureaucratic society in the Qin Dynasty, because at that time the technique was not developed, paper was invented in the Eastern Han Dynasty (25 AC-220 AC). It was not easy for ordinary people to obtain books. Although official positions can no longer be hereditary, knowledge is actually monopolized, and through factors such as teacher-student relations, some aristocratic families have formed a disguised monopoly in society. It was a deformed aristocracy that lasted until the Northern and Southern Dynasties (420 AC – 589 AC). In the Sui and Tang Dynasties (581 AC – 907 AC), the imperial examination system was invented and the aristocracy gradually weakened. Many civilians were selected as officials, and even more and more senior officials. The Tang Dynasty was a period of transition from a mixture of aristocracy and bureaucracy to a complete bureaucracy. In the Song Dynasty (960 AC – 1279 AC), printing was invented, knowledge was further popularized, and bureaucracy was completely established in social politics. This can be reflected in some cultural phenomena. Compared with China, ancient Japan was a hierarchical society and an aristocratic society. Some cultural phenomena in Japan today, such as the tea ceremony, illustrates this hierarchical society; the tea ceremony culture originated in China. The nobles in the Tang Dynasty were very particular about drinking tea, drinking tea has a detailed process, beautiful utensils, delicate cooking methods and rigorous rituals. Tea and tea culture spread to Japan during the Tang Dynasty in China. The tea ceremony was preserved and passed down in Japan; today in Japan, the tea ceremony is still very popular, but this tea ceremony has disappeared in China. The tea ceremony etiquette is complicated and requires special learning. In ordinary families, there is no time and economic conditions to learn such things. In aristocratic society, nobles can have the conditions and time to learn, so this tea ceremony gradually disappeared in China. Another example is Chinese esoteric Buddhism in the history of Chinese Buddhism. During the Tang Dynasty, it was introduced into China from India and was called Chinese Esoteric Buddhism, and then it was introduced to Japan and called Shingon Buddhism. Today, Shingon Buddhism is preserved in Japan, but Chinese Esoteric Buddhism disappeared in China. Now the Tantric Buddhism in Chinese Buddhism was later introduced from Tibet. The Chinese Esoteric

Buddhism also requires cumbersome etiquette and is not suitable for a civilian society like China.

The politics in the Middle East is a slave politic. Ordinary people in Christian areas were selected as slaves to Sudan. After training, they could hold official positions, and could also be promoted to Vizir, which is equivalent to the prime minister, similar to the ancient Chinese politics. But the problem is that, in ancient Europe, aristocracy politics, which rely on blood relation, gave birth to modern capitalism. This is indeed worth thinking, what factors played an important role in the generation of capitalism? For example, overseas trade, urban development, and Renaissance, Reformation and so on. The evolution of this ancient political system from aristocracy to bureaucracy is very similar to the development process of modern enterprises from family ownership to mass ownership, the separation of ownership and control, and the emergence of professional managers. They all reflect the transition from blood factor to geography factor. There are many similar phenomena in the two types of things, let us give two examples to illustrate.

3.Zheng He's navigation and Columbus's navigation

We know that in the Ming Dynasty (1368-1644), the ancient China political system was very mature, various rules and regulations were perfect, such as imperial examinations, cabinet system, and so on. In the early Ming Dynasty, a Chinese mariner Zheng He has led the fleet and arrived in South East Asia, South Asia, Middle East and East Africa, it is not far from Cape of good hope. Zheng He's navigation activity total includes 7 trips, from 1405 --- 1433. His fleet was a large-scale voyage fleet, a special mixed fleet at sea, it included more than 200 ship of different purposes and different functions; at most the soldiers were about 27,000; the scale is grand, the organization is tight. So many people had sailed for many times, long-term and today the cost is huge. At that time, in technology and economy China had more strength and opportunities to find new route, but unfortunately, because of the old system and thought, self-consciousness conservative, Zheng He didn't find the route to the Europe, didn't find the Americas, he just navigated along at that time mature route, from China to the Southeast Asia, South Asia, Middle East, East Africa, the route has a trade history of thousands of years(in 5th century AD, this route had existed). Because of the political purpose of Zheng He's navigation was more important and it was the official event, although there were trade, but trade was not valued. Each navigation consumed huge amounts, harvesting benefits were small, the things they bring back in nautical activity were only rare items or goods, jewelry and exotic animals, like giraffe, the most cargo was luxury. Later there were no more similar activities, even navigation data were officially destroyed by the government. If the original Zheng He found the Cape of good hope, bypassing Africa, and thus reached Europe, Zheng He's fleet would have dominated Europe; after about 100 years the Spanish Armada, had more than 100 battleships, more than 3,000 door cannons, tens thousands of soldiers, the two fleet were same scale. Even if later Zheng He and his fleet could have navigated to Europe, but because of the far distance, huge amount spent, such activity will not be lasting. In the history of China, Ming dynasty had a mature system, but in this period, there was no business freedom; ordinary people could not be free to sea trade. The foreign trade was only official trade --- tribute trade; their political significance is much larger than the economy, expenditure is greater than return, the government has forbidden private trade. When the social population grew, the land was not sufficient, developing commerce and trade is a very normal solution, if it only considers the political side, for consolidating its regime and keeping social stability, the government restricted private trade and private businesses, even banned it. The system of the Ming dynasty was mature, but the idea was retrograde and conservative, the policy was closed and restricted business, it constrained and prevented overseas trade and the development of the national economy, at that time China started to be left behind.

The age of discovery, in 1492, Columbus found the Americas, the age of navigation arrived at the climax. Columbus was born in Genoa, Italy, and when he was young, he came to Portugal and became a navigator. At that time, Portugal and Spain in the Iberian Peninsula had navigation activities; Portugal's strategic direction was along the African continent to the South, and later found Cape of good hope, bypassing the African continent, to arrive in India. Columbus proposed distinctive scheme, he thought he should sail to the West and can reach Japan and China, because he believed the earth is round. At first Columbus was frustrated in Portugal, later he came to Spain and continued to implement his program, but he was there as a foreigner and when he came to publicize his idea, it was difficult, as he was neither nobility, nor bureaucracy, normal people didn't believe him. In addition, at that time, there was controversy over spherical earth, and gravitational scientific explanation produced after many years; Copernicus, the "On the Revolutions of Heavenly Spheres" was published in 1543, and Newton wrote the book and described gravity, "The Mathematical Principles of Natural Philosophy" published in 1687. Another reason is that some experts thought that the route envisaged by Columbus was too short, and sometimes experts are also right, but at that time no one knew the existence of America. Hypotheses are always imperfect before they become scientific truths, such as Alfred Wegener's continental drift theory, Nicolaus Copernicus's heliocentrism and so on.

In Spain, Columbus initially also had difficulty until 1492; Spain finally agreed to funded Columbus's West navigation and discovery. After a negotiated consultation, they signed the "Santa Fe agreement ", which awarded the explorers and adventurers to the corresponding honor, terms of reference and interests. There are: 1. It promises Columbus to be Admiral of the Ocean Sea. 2. It appoints Columbus as viceroy and governor of lands that he may discover. 3. Columbus shall have 1/10 of all gold, gems, spices or other merchandise produced or obtained by trade within those domains, tax free. 4. Columbus shall have the right to invest in one eighth of any ship going thither. 5. These offices and emoluments will be enjoyed by his heirs and successors forever.[57]

Maybe some adventure is leading, other adventure is secondary. Some adventure have great result, other adventure have little result. leadership and subordinate negotiate, consult and grant the power and benefits for the explorer, this way is more valuable and has more significance than the adventure itself. One side has knowledge and experience, the other side has substance, economic and organization strength, the two sides equally cooperate and share interest. This method is an exchange and a division of labor. One side proposes an idea while the other side provides material guarantee. In this way, it is very good for institutions and individual. The upper-and-subordinate relationship in the bureaucracy is unequal. It is difficult for subordinates to come up with novel, unique and distinctive ideas, especially risky assumptions. Zheng He's risk is not the unknown route, but the person in strange land. Zheng He is unlikely to propose a new route, he is just an official, henchman of the emperor. What he did was in accordance with the instructions of the emperor. The relationship between Zheng He and the emperor was not equal. At that time, in Spain the bureaucracy was immature, it had just completed its reunification. Through marriage, the kingdoms of Castile and the kingdom of Aragon were merged to achieve reunification. The Catholic monarchs of Spain, king and queen, were ruling Spain. Columbus was not an official and he was a navigator. Columbus proposed a new idea, wanted to engage in expeditions and get profits in return. This activity is a kind of adventure and a new thing. Columbus's plan is novel and unique, it may succeed or fail and there was uncertainty. Both sides sign a contract which stipulates the right and obligations of each side and it is somewhat similar to commercial cooperation.

Later some countries and explorers signed similar agreements, this adventure had found North and South America and the other regions of the world. Columbus's West navigation didn't find the

---

[57] Samuel Eliot Morison, Christopher Columbus, (Mariner. Little, Brown and Company, 1955), pp 31

way to China, didn't find quantities of gold, but coincidentally found the Americas, the results is far greater than what was expected. After the vast lands of North and South America became Spanish colonies, until now, the official language of most countries in Central and South America is Spanish. Scientific discovery is usually in this way, incidental discoveries cause great results.

There are differences between the marine activity of Europe and China, it reflects the cultural, political and economic huge difference. Columbus's navigation cost not too much, a total of 3 vessels, a total of 90 people, the main purpose was to explore and look for land, gold. Columbus was Italian, but he got the support of the Spanish government, Zheng He is the Ming Emperor's confidant, and he is an official of the government. " Santa Fe agreement" in China is inconceivable; today it is also impossible, in China there is no contractual relationship similar to the West. Imperial power is higher, the Chinese society is a big bureaucratic institution, a vertically integrated government; subordinate should unconditionally perform a superior's command; there is almost no equality and agreements, holding notary and notarization, are fundamentally unimaginable. Subordinates are unlikely to fight for their own rights through similar business negotiations. The first thing that subordinates present is loyalty, and whether they have innovative ideas is not important. It is simple to see Columbus's West navigation as some a capital venture, Zheng He's navigation more like the task of leadership.

Columbus's navigation is out of the ordinary and the result of Columbus's deliberation and careful consideration. As long as the king and queen of Spain agreed, and the queen played a major role, it can be implemented. The bureaucracy has a sound management system and many management levels. Innovative ideas are difficult to quickly achieve because of the many levels of reporting. In Chinese history, there is no document that anyone proposed a plan to sail Eastward. In history, there were many trades between China and Japan, Korea and Ryukyu. There is such a record in ancient Chinese history that during the Southern and Northern Dynasties, about 5th century, a monk named Hui Shen sailed Eastward and once reached a place called Fusang state. Now some scholars believe that Fusang is Mexico. Some scholars point out that some cultural features of indigenous peoples of the Americas, like totem, jade worship, are close to the ancient Chinese culture.

4.Analysis of the enterprise development process

When a society and organization is in the early stage of development, the size is small, the level is not high, everyone's position is in relative equality, the organization is also vibrant and it may be good at absorbing and admitting different ideas and advice, at that time because there is not much benefit, there is not great difference, and little emphasis on interpersonal relations. The authority of the organization may recognize everyone in the organization. During this period, family-owned company is main form of management. In anthropology, this period is equivalent to the period of clan and tribal alliance. With the development of organization, the size become larger, management is gradually reasonable, bureaucratization will inevitably appear. The company introduces professional managers and forms vertically integrated organization. In organization of the same size, the bureaucratic cost is the lowest. Some extent of bureaucratization is reasonable, it is able to perform policies, but when organization is in the late stage of development, the size becomes large, there are many complex levels and many different departments of functions, bureaucratization becomes a serious problem, decisions taking becomes slow, there are many levels in this management mechanism, any change becomes very difficult; then if you want to develop in organization, you must comply with the original interest pattern and depend on people you know; for the managers of the institutions, it is difficult to listen to any innovative ideas and constructive opinion. One reason is they do not hear, another reason is they do not want to hear. This period management of organization is good, order is stable, there are strict levels and significant differences, but the organization lacks vitality, conservatism becomes mainstream, new behavior and new idea want to break the existing order and need to make great efforts; they will affect the original interest; in organization there are various interest groups, they have their own interests range, then people in the organization maybe prefer to maintain current interest, so the way of the most insurance and the most secure is to do nothing.

After the bureaucracy has grown and matured, there is still a prominent problem and this is how to treat the role of authority. There are many authorities in an organization. Bureaucratic organizations, like ancient Chinese government and the modern vertically integrated firms, have many departments. The authority of the central government is the emperor and the prime minister. The authority of the department was the minister. The authority of local government is the prefect of district or the governor. The authority of the modern enterprises is the chairman and general manager, and the authority of the business department is the department manager. The larger the organization, the greater the responsibility of authority and the higher the requirements for authority. The premise of the traditional organization theory is that leadership can be cultivated. Through learning and training, authority has higher knowledge, personal ability, and moral level than others. This is an ideal situation... People need to learn and grow, and maybe make various mistakes; it is also normal and no one is always right. But if there are problems from official or manager of an enterprise, there are not just personal problems, they will involve the entire organization led by an authority. If the development of the institution meets a problem, how to treat the authority of the institution? In traditional bureaucratic institutions, officials and managers are appointed by their superiors, so officials and managers are only responsible to the superiors. If there are problems with officials and managers, they can only be appointed and removed by their superiors. Ideally, the higher the level of authority in the organization, the higher the level of ability, intelligence, and morality. In reality, usually, officials and managers of vertically integrated organization can not appoint persons who have kinship with authority, they will appoint persons who are familiar with authority. So these relationships like classmate relationship, regional relations, and friendships among each others, these relationships are more important. These factors are likely to affect the appointment and dismissal of officials and managers. This is what the saying goes, "somebody has an influential supporter" and "officials protect each others" These phenomena are common in Chinese history and modern times.

The problem of vertically integrated organization perhaps is, even if an official or manager is not able to fill a position, even if the bureaucratic organization has an evaluation mechanism, the official or manager can still hold a certain position for a long time. Such officials and managers have a negative impact on the organization. The improvement of the vertically integrated firm over family enterprises lies in the diversification of managers in the enterprise, which prevents family members with insufficient capabilities from controlling the enterprise. The bureaucratic institution that is more advanced than the family organizations, and the vertically integrated firm under various complex situations, due to their own mechanism and structure, even if the enterprise has achieved the separation of ownership and control, even if there is no blood relationship between managers at all levels, even if the managers has a high level of academic literacy and scientific management, as well as various selection and inspection mechanisms, bureaucratic institutions will encounter the phenomenon that if the authority does not match the position, it is difficult for the organization to adjust the authority. In here, "not match" include the overall evaluation of personal ethics, knowledge level and real ability.

The vertically integrated organizations, the bureaucratic institutions are highly efficient. Under the influence of the administrative power, the transaction costs are very low. The internal contradictions within the organization can be resolved through coordination. However, the problems exist while the organization has high efficiency, the organization suppresses innovation, criticism and disagreements. There is a question how to deal with innovation, criticism, and challenge? How to allow the organization to maintain the existing order at the same time the organization is able to accommodate innovation and criticism. In

Chapter 9 we talk about McGregor, McGregor believed that the existing organization theory was not perfect, and the new organization theory containing creativity will emerge. After the current vertically integrated organization is mature and stable, the mentality of authority will change and authority is accustomed to issuing commands, for authority it is not easy to tolerate various criticisms. Humans are not machines, they always have various emotions and opinions, and authority is also human. Organizations can use morality to restrain authority, they can hope that authority can tolerate criticism and dissenting opinions, but moral restraint is not mandatory, and authority may listen or not. It is not as coercive as institutional restraint, while the character of vertically integrated organizations is subordinates obey superiors and superiors order subordinates.

When there are inconsistencies with tradition in the organization, personal criticism, or even challenges to authority, then what happen? Since authority holds power, authority has an unequal relationship with subordinates. When a person in charge feels that criticism, innovation, and challenge are inconsistent with his own interests, his status is shaken, and his influence is weakened, as an authority, he will naturally use his own power and administrative means to deal with criticism and challenges and suppress innovation. Montesquieu wrote in "The Spirit of laws", "But constant experience shows us that every man invested with power is apt to abuse it, and to carry his authority as far as it will go."[58] I think this sentence is also very appropriate when analyzing vertically integrated firm. Authority can obtain huge benefits through status, treatment, and rent-seeking. Criticism, innovation and challenges often will shake these benefits. An authority is also a representative of an interest group. In order to protect the interests of himself and the group, he will also suppress criticism, innovation and challenges. This situation is also common in enterprises and in society. Criticism and challenge of authority, even if the object of criticism and challenge may only be

---

[58] Montesquieu, Charles de Secondat, baron de, The Spirit of laws, book 11, chapter 4

the authority of a certain department, due to this model of vertically integrated organizations and the bureaucratic institutions, authority can only be judged, appointed and removed by superiors, so all levels of authority will interact with each others to maintain their respective status and interests. Even if there is no relationship between the various levels of authority mentioned above, in order to maintain their own status and interests, the entire management is unlikely to allow various criticisms and challenges to exist. If the object of criticisms and challenges is the whole organization, the responsibility of authority is to keep order.

If the external environment and the external market change, at the same time, in the organization no one is willing to take risk and perform a surgical operation for the organization, break their interests range and restructure the organization, then the final result is that the organization will likely be rebuild instead of tinkering; in Chinese history, many dynasties faced similar problems and difficulties at the end of their development. Now in the market, many companies and organizations fall down, like Kodak company, Nokia, Sun company and more.

The bureaucracy is in conflict with innovation. The bureaucracy, as Maslow said, is the people who have settled down comfortably, and are shaken and disturbed out of their comfort, so the bureaucracy is resistant to the new things. In addition, when the bureaucracy considers problems, the starting point is not entirely the value of new things. Unlike market exchanges, if both parties find that the value is appropriate in the market, they can exchange value. My understanding is that a large-scale organization has developed to a certain level and scale, it has a complex structure and a lot of things to deal with. Many things in a vertically integrated firm need to be decided by the leader. A leader actually does not have enough energy to cover everything. In this case, if internal labor markets can be achieved, many things can be handled quickly, efficiency will be improved, and be resolved by the market, avoiding the interference of many complicated factors, and not needing to make decisions by the high leader. However, this approach will bringing some changes in management, the bureaucracy has formed many layers of the management hierarchy. The higher the management level and the higher the status, the more privileges and rent-seeking opportunities will be enjoyed. If the internal labor markets are achieved, the management level will be reduced, the scale of management will be reduced too, privileges reduced, and rent-seeking opportunities lost. Some managers may not be willing to see the reduction of their own power and the loss of their privileged status, so this kind of marketization may not be easy to achieve. In the transformation of real enterprises, we rarely see the managers of enterprises in their heyday daring to operate on the enterprises themselves. At this time, as long as the managers maintain the situation, the enterprises will have no problems. As long as the enterprises perform well in the market, the income of enterprises is not affected, there will be no manager asking to change the company. Only when the market changes and the company is affected, the company may make some changes. If the company can't sustain it, then it needs to replace the managers to save the company. Apple was about to be acquired by other companies before Steve Jobs returned; when IBM was faced with difficulties, Louis V. Gerstner was hired.

The development of enterprises is regular, and the process of enterprise development is similar to ancient dynasties. Like in ancient China, after the traditional ethics thoughts had matured in the Spring and Autumn and Warring States period, the Qin Dynasty established a centralized country, which we call in here a bureaucratic country, and the development of dynasties is very common. The cycle of dynasties is about 200 years. All dynasties since the Qin Dynasty have basically adopted professional officials, similar to the professional manager system of the modern vertically integrated firm. The development process of every dynasty has basically gone through different stages: The dynasty is founded, dynasty flourishes, reaching its peak, the path winds along mountain ridges, and problems increase, internal and external troubles, dynasty demise. In China, society and politics dominate. Politically, there is a very regular pattern: be honest and upright, enlightened despotism, a time of national peace and order, corruption, buying and selling officials, and the collapse of the dynasty. After the management thought and the system of modern enterprises are mature, the development of the enterprise and the evolution of the market are also very regular. It is very similar to the development process of the ancient dynasty; it can be explained in the same way. The stage and process of the development of the enterprise can be analyzed and be compared with the ancient Chinese dynasty history. Ancient Chinese dynasty and modern enterprises, top managers are center, all levels of management are appointed by superior leaders, and managers are trained by relevant educational institutions, a perfect management selection mechanism has been formed within the organization.

When a new enterprise is just founded and it has small size, there are few decision-making levels, few things to deal with, and no mature bureaucracy. Leaders of the enterprise have multiple roles, are energetic and can do everything by themselves. In addition, the leaders face market competition and the pressure of the enterprise survival, they must go forward with their all strength and devote themselves. As long as new ideas and new products can bring benefits, profits, and markets for the enterprise, they will be valued, implemented as soon as possible, fully developed and improved, and customers' opinions valued. They dare to take risks and be tolerant of failure. The founder of company needs spirit, creativity and foreseeability, and will dedicate themselves to company. With the maturity and development of the company and the expansion of the product sales, the company has gradually found its feet in the market, and management has also become formal. With the perfect functional department and the employment of professional managers, various regulations and systems have been gradually established to clarify the responsibilities of each department. With the professional managers, the company develops well, at the same time, the professional managers get good treatment and career. When the enterprise further develops, the quality and function of company product is gradually perfect, the company occupy a monopoly position in the market, at this time, the company's products in the market share to maximize. The enterprise reaches its peak of development and has a large scale, numerous departments, perfect management, sound system, and multiple decision-making levels. During this period, Enterprises engaged in micro-innovation of existing products can maintain and consolidate their market position. The management is satisfied with expanding the market of existing products and lacks strong motivation to develop new disruptive products. The development of new disruptive products, on the one hand, new technologies have unknown market risks, on the other hand, companies need to re-allocate resources in product design, technology research, manufacturing, marketing, after-sales service and other links, which will trigger companies instability. Habits will become the model of corporate management at this time. Following the old fashioned, established conventions, and inheriting the original model will become the dominant thinking in the company. Since the products have been successful in the market and the company has obtained a monopoly position, why does the company need to change?

After the peak period, the motivation of the company extension has weakened, but the scales of the company needs to be maintained; companies will have various problems, these problems were previously covered up by the rapid growth of the company. They can also be explained by the Chinese Yin-Yang theory. During the development period of the company, the Yang is better than the Yin. The rapid growth of the company and the increase of sales make the negative factors less important. When the company is in decline, Yin is better than Yang. Negative factors in the company gradually dominate, and Yin and Yang are transformed into each other. Now the management of the company, the managers are appointed by superiors, only the affirmation of authority in the organization has the ultimate value, many staffs in the company need to obey the authority. The creativity of an enterprise is in the hands of managers at all levels, especially the top management. During the period of enterprise growth, the scale of the enterprise is small, when the management faces various problems, the enterprise pays more attention to creativity, and creativity is easy to display; after the enterprise has passed the peak period, after hard work, the product has succeeded in the market, and there is no urgent need for creativity, maintaining the current scale of the enterprise requires a lot of energy from managers.

When the company expands to a certain scale and the managers have not made breakthroughs in disruptive innovation, for the managers in this period, from personal rationality, the safest way is not to take risks. If a manager wants a smooth promotion in a company, it is best to say nothing, maintain the status quo and avoid risks. During this period, the corporate management emphasized form more than reality, and customers became less and less important. Disruptive innovation is difficult to achieve in this period, mainly due to two reasons. One is that there are ideological constraints, individuals in the enterprise do not dare to have creative thinking for their own interests; the other is the management style, the management model of the separation of enterprise ownership and control, and the allocation of various resources in the enterprise cannot meet the requirements of disruptive innovation. If the market change, the company continues to develop, the situation will deteriorate further, and the leaders of the company will easily lose their way at this time. Even some leaders can use their position to seek rent and satisfy their private interests. Things that can be handled quickly will be delayed for a long time. Even if new things are beneficial to both parties, organizations and individuals, many new things will be difficult to achieve, and face many obstacles. Even if some managers know it, they have to take into account all kinds of feelings factor in the huge management. For the sake of relationship, especially in the vertically integrated organization, administrative forces dominate, and various complex factors are at work. In the later stages of the development of the vertically integrated firm, when manager considers problems, the starting point is not only market factors and technical factors, but also human factors. Emotional factors play a major role. Managers usually compare treatment, qualifications, personal connections, and relationships. Many factions have formed, and they are fighting each other, jealous people fighting with both open and secret means. Even if the management clearly knows many things that are not good for the company, they can only maintain the status quo. This situation continues until the market change, the company fails in the market, goes bankrupt, or is acquired.

So, the mature system did not lead to the discovery of the Americas, but the immature system discovered South and North America, later many lands and islands in the world. This is an example of political system. Let's look at an example of corporate management. This example is very close to us.

5.General Motors and Toyota Motor

General Motors Corporation, we analyzed in previous chapters, is a typical modern enterprise, in which the separation of ownership and control is thorough, and it is a typical representative of the vertically integrated firm. The manager of GM has a deep understanding of the car industry, GM managers are professionals and have many knowledge and experience of business, they are very clever for management, but they failed. Someone says if a enterprise is big enough?, the enterprise can't fail, " What's good for General Motors is good for the country ", General Motors is "Phoenix Nirvana, Born of Fire". General Motors as the United States and the world's largest car manufacturing company, has the most financial and technical strength and should first successfully develop new acceptable electric cars in market; before, they have indeed developed electric cars, but later they interrupted their research. In 1996 General Motors launched EV1 electric cars, they have a compound body and use lead-acid (later NiMH) battery; a two-seater car, they are a pioneer of electric car, but they were expensive and difficult to sale; only 1,200 units were produced, then GM rent EV1 to customers at a low price, because in EV1, General Motors spent huge funds and returns were rare, later they stop renting EV1, and finally even destroyed EV1. Some information said that General Motors in the EV1 project lost more than $ 1 billion. In the 2008 financial crisis, General Motors suffered a huge loss in its most profitable pickup car, even if the company made money in the Chevrolet small car, but it was also difficult to compensate that huge vulnerability. At that time General Motors just showed the latest hybrid cars Volt in the 2007 Detroit North American International Auto Show; product maturity, market reaction conditions, the customer satisfaction are unknown. When the financial crisis came, GM is fundamentally unprepared, it is too late to prepare again, and General Motors under pressure was forced to a bankruptcy reorganization. In Japan, Toyota Motor Corporation developed the Toyota Prius. After several product iterations, it finally found its feet in the market. Toyota Prius became the world's first mass-produced hybrid vehicle.

The reason why Spain passed the Columbus's plan was mainly the agreement of the Queen. Although the experts of the committee did not agree with Columbus's plan, the Queen had a good impression on Columbus and believed that he was sincere and serious. At the same time, some ministers said that the risk of Columbus's plan was small and the gain will be big, those experts often do not know much. GM did not continue to develop electric vehicles, mainly because the Board of directors failed to support this project. The Board of directors believed that it was not worth investing resources in a project that will lose money; no one knew that there would be a financial crisis in 2008, just like in ancient society, no one knew at the time of Columbus that there is America in oceans between Europe and China. In Toyota Motor Corporation, the Toyota family runs the company, selects the top leaders, and appoints family members as CEOs of the company. They think that the company could develop a hybrid car with 300 million US dollars a year and that is not a big problem, it is just advertising. In comparison, car companies spend billions of dollars on traditional global advertising. Just as the Queen of Spain considered the plan of Columbus and the risk as not high, so Toyota developed the Prius and Columbus received funding. Obviously, countries and companies with an immature bureaucracy often dare to take risks, while organizations with well-established bureaucracies are hesitant to take risks.

From a commercial point of view, Columbus's navigation was a disruptive innovation, while Zheng He's navigation was a micro-innovation. Columbus's navigation was a nautical activity which the mainland cannot see for more than a month, while Zheng He's voyage is only along the mature, existing overseas trade routes that are not far from the mainland, they were greatly different.

GM's development of electric vehicles and Zheng He's navigation activity have many similar characteristics. A large-scale organization, with complete management and mature systems. The management has transitioned from kinship factors to geographic factors. It hires professional officials and professional managers; they are well trained and have more experience. The company invest in and engage in new activities or research new products at this time. In the beginning the organization spent huge funds, they have some return, but the return is insuffisant, later the activity stopped, the data and products were destroyed, and at last other companies made more significant discoveries and better products. It indicates, in a new field, that the organization that is making a great discovery is often not those agencies with most substance and economic strength. Like Columbus's navigation, replacing the administrative order in the bureaucracy with the market and contract is conducive to innovation. Later, it will explain that replacing the traditional management method of the vertically integrated firm with long-term contracts has already been carried in the electric power industry in some countries.

In here, the focus of the discussion is the problem of an excessive bureaucracy. Whether it is Columbus's sailing activities or Toyota Motor Corporation, there is a mechanism. The three ships led by Columbus constitute a small organization. In each ship, there were a captain, helmsman, navigator, doctor, sailor and other crews who perform different tasks. The ships led by Columbus form an organization belonging to the Spanish government. Columbus is responsible for the exploration, the coordination and management of the three ships. All personnel on the three ships must obey Columbus's commands, plans and arrangements, while the Spanish government is responsible for providing ships and logistics supplies. Obviously, the management of the three ships is similar to that of 200 ships, but they are very different. For example, the more than 200 ships of Zheng He, including various personnel, have a more complex structure than Columbus's ships, including combatants and non-combatant personnel. The management of more than 20,000 people is completely different from the management of more than 90 people. In order to accomplish the same task together, the coordination and management of 20,000 people are more complicated. The fleet led by Zheng He and the Ming Dynasty government also constitute a large organization.

Bureaucratic institutions have huge advantages; at the same time, it is superior to other forms of organization. Just like a sophisticated machine, it can complete complex tasks. Zheng He's navigation activities and modern vertically integrated firm are typical examples. In modern enterprises, technology research and development, product design, manufacturing, advertising, sales and service, a complete set of systems, coordinated to turn the product from an idea into a reality, and hand it to the customer. A car has tens of thousands of parts, an airplane has millions of parts. About the quality, price, service life, and economy of the goods, in these aspects, an enterprise cannot make smooth manufacturing and production without strong management and coordination capabilities. This cannot be denied. It has been analyzed in the previous chapter about the vertically integrated firm, but society always needs to develop, and history needs to advance.

The smaller the organization, the more flexible, and the larger the bureaucracy, the less conducive to innovation. The bureaucracy first emphasizes loyalty. In modern society and countries, there are many bureaucracies. In bureaucracies, government agencies and large enterprises, people are straight, they have stable incomes, and various benefits. Individuals also have a status in society, subsidies, welfare housing, and official vehicles, free travel abroad, various gray income... These good conditions are beneficial for attracting talents. But if the external environment and the market change and the organization needs to adjust and adapt, can people in the organization come up with innovative ideas? Can they take a risk and invest in a new plan? Can they successfully research new products accepted by the market? Can the organization complete the transformation?

In the 1980s, Western society raised the banner of liberalism again, and privatized in many fields. In chapter 10, we talk about the new institutional economics and the deregulation of many sectors. In the electric power industry, the traditional power generation, transmission and distribution are integrated. After deregulation, a power market will be formed, the transmission system will be opened, power transactions will be realized on the grid, and power distributors and retailers will appear. Users can freely choose power suppliers. In the power consumption departments and power generation departments, long-term contracts can be signed to achieve marketization within the electric power industry. This pattern is very similar to the development of the microcomputer market. The hardware and software of microcomputers have been marketed. The integration pattern of hardware and software development previously led by IBM evolved into many independent chip manufacturers, mainboard manufacturers, host manufacturers, system software development companies and application software development companies, etc. They all make corresponding decisions based on market changes, develop corresponding products, and constantly upgrade products, adopt new technologies, and occupy the market, so that they will not be eliminated by the market, instead of the pattern which the traditional administrative force dominates and the vertically integrated firm monopolizes market, those factors outside of management naturally have no role. Therefore, technical factors and market factors play a leading role in the development of enterprises. In the future reform of the electric power industry, the concept of "plug and play" is proposed, which means that in the future development of smart grids, the popularization and utilization of various new energy sources, such as wind energy, solar energy, etc., can be achieved in various forms of power generation. This is also a practical application in the field of copying microcomputers. In microcomputers, there are many peripheral slots in the structure of microcomputers. Users can develop external boards for various applications, insert them into the microcomputer, and design hardware circuits according to the standards and specifications of hardware and software, code software drivers and application programs. The computer realizes the combination of generalization and specialization. To apply the computer to a certain field, you only need to purchase the computer host and then develop the corresponding peripheral hardware and software. The peripheral board can do "Plug and play".

In chapter 14, we will analyze the new changes in the semiconductor industry, the computer industry, the Internet industry and the Silicon Valley management. In Chapter 18, we will discuss the creative field, the service industry and the future social work methods and characteristics. Will there be a brand-new stage in the development of enterprises in the future? In the new stage, a completely different way of business operation and management will appear. The new way of business management can be conducive to innovation and better respond to the change of market.

To think about and study the similarities between the management, ownership system of the vertically integrated firm and ancient bureaucratic countries, it is necessary to understand the characteristics of the political systems of various countries and regions in ancient society, to understand the differences between bureaucratic countries and aristocratic countries, and their different development trajectories, it also require a comparative understanding of the background and conditions for the birth of capitalism.

13 CHAPTER POLITICAL SYSTEMS IN VARIOUS REGIONS

1.Introduction of political systems

The development of enterprise organizational forms in European society are indeed related to the European social systems, especially the urban systems. Compared with other countries and regions, Asia, Africa, scientific management and modern business operations have not been developed. For example, in ancient China, it was also related to the ancient Chinese political system. The ancient Chinese political system was mainly based on administrative management. Officials occupied a dominant position and undoubtedly limited the further development of industry and commerce. The bureaucratic class was in conflict with the industrial and commercial class. Here we can analyze the political systems of different countries and regions, and analyze why the modern industry and commerce have developed only in Europe and America.

Political system generally refers to how a country organizes government and state institutions, how to manage society, how to deal with the relationship between central government and local governments, how to choose and select officials, who participate in state management, etc. Due to the differences of the development trajectory of history in different regions and different countries, the development path is different, and it evolves in different political systems. It is better to review the political systems of various regions and countries. Because there are many differences between countries, different countries in the same region, their political system also differs. The same country has different political systems during different periods, so in here we just review the political systems of various regions, countries in this period, before the countries entered the capitalism period. During this period (from the fifteenth to the seventeenth centuries), the political systems of most countries were relatively mature, representative, and have many things in common.

Studying this period, from the fifteenth to the seventeenth centuries, we mainly research the political systems in East Asia, South Asia, the Middle East, North Africa and Europe. Before the age of navigation, South and North Americas were not discovered, they were not known by other places, and there was less exchange and less civilization, so they were not included in the analysis. All of the above regions have formed a complete social system, including political system, economic system, religion, culture, etc., and it can also be divided into Buddhist cultural areas, Islamic cultural areas and Christian cultural areas. The Buddhist cultural areas generally include East Asia, North Asia, part of Southeast Asia and parts of South Asia; the Islamic cultural district roughly includes the Middle East, North Africa, parts of South Asia and some Southeast Asian countries, and the Christian Cultural areas mainly includes all of Europe.

The political systems in these regions are different and each has their own feature. We can look at the political systems in various regions from the perspective of administration and justice; after we will also analyze the urban systems in each region.

2.The ancient China political system

The ancient Chinese political system has also undergone an evolutionary process from kinship relationship to geographic relationship. After the emergence of the country, in Xia Dynasty, there was a political system. Since there are not many documents recorded in the Xia Dynasty and Shang Dynasty, we do not know much about them. In the Zhou Dynasty, ritual and musical Instruments were created. From Zhou Dynasty to Qin Shihuang unified China; in this period, there are relatively complete documents. This period reflects the continuous decline of blood factors and the continuous strengthening of geographical factors.

The Zhou Dynasty established the patriarchal system and granted titles and territories to the noble and meritorious statesman. Compared with the Shang Dynasty, the geographical factors were greatly strengthened. Within the vassal states, the blood factor was still very important; the politics within the vassal states were basically ruled by the nobility. In the Spring and Autumn Period, it is particularly obvious that the senior officials of Chu State were basically nobles. In the Jin state and Lu state, senior officials were nobles, and these nobles were also hereditary. It was not until Qin Shihuang established the Qin Dynasty in 221 BC that feudalism was abolished and a bureaucratic system was established. Compared with the West, the mature political system in ancient China is the least feudalized. This system is a political system dominated by administrative methods. It has evolved and been implemented for nearly two thousand years. So far, it still influences Chinese society. With regard to the composition and development of the ancient Chinese political systems, there are several outstanding features.

Civilian politics

China political system is a kind of civilian regime. The selection and appointment of officials is relatively fair. They are selected according to individual abilities and ethical standards. Later, the imperial examinations system was relatively objective. Officials did not see their parentage, they only looked at performance; correspondingly the central government has established a mechanism for assessing and appraising officials. Populism does not lie in the fact that officials are civilians, many dynasties were also established by civilians. In a dynasty, the emperor was hereditary and officials were not hereditary. Modern Chinese characters like Chiang Kai-shek and Mao Zedong also came from civilian origins.

Focus on administrative means

The ancient China political system focused on administrative means and judicial means. It does not mean that there was no law in ancient China; but compared with ancient Europe and Islamic regions, the ancient China society was more administrative. In the ancient China local government, the administration and the judiciary were not separate. Local officials were both executive heads and judges, presiding over the cases. The Government had long formed a bureaucratic system, this was a very fine political system. The central government was divided into six departments according to their functions: The Board of Civil Office, the Board of Revenue, the Board of Rites, the Board of War, the Board of Punishments, and the Board of Works. They were responsible for staff management, accounts and servitude, etiquette education, military defense, public security criminals, industrial and commercial water conservancy, etc.; there were many division-level institutions under various departments, and later the central government had also developed a cabinet mechanism. There were special performance assessments for officials at all levels, and there were special supervisory institutions. The selection of officials was through the imperial examinations, and there was a distinction between local officials and central officials. This administrative system was quite perfect in ancient China.

Emphasize on morality

Ancient china society formed an ideology with Confucianism as the official religion, paying attention to moral, ethics and interpersonal relationships, ignoring natural science and engineering technology; Confucianism is also the basis of the imperial examination and of the system of official selection. Confucianism and the administrative management complement and rely on each other. In ancient China, there was a set of methods for dealing with local affairs; local administrative power, financial power and military power were separated, and local governments only had administrative power. In terms of local government, a provincial system has been established, and the provincial governor was appointed by the central government. Such a place was not easy to form a separatist force and could safeguard the unity of the country.

In Asia, among the countries neighboring China, especially the East Asian countries, ancient Japan and China have different political systems. Although Japan has studied China in history, Japan has not adopted the Chinese imperial examination system. In ancient Japan, the feudal system is similar to Europe, the social hierarchy is distinct, social mobility is difficult, and the samurai class grasps political power. However, after entering the modern society, Japan integrates the commercial class into the political system, the samurai class transformed into the capitalist class, and quickly enters the capitalist society. At the same time, China has formed a stark contrast.

3.Political system in the Islamic region

The Mesopotamia of the Middle East and North Africa are one of the birthplaces of the ancient civilizations of human society. It has a long history and then declined and later the Roman Empire controlled these areas. After the fall of the Roman Empire, in the 7th century, Islam rose in the Arabian Peninsula and formed the caliphate system. Islam spread from the Arabian Peninsula to the Middle East, Central Asia, Africa, Southeast Asia and South Asia. In the history of the Middle East, there were the Umayyad dynasty and the Abbasid dynasty. In the end, the Ottoman Empire was formed and its forces were extended to the Southeast of Europe. The political system of the Ottoman Empire has two characteristics.

A centralized political system

The emperor of the Ottoman Empire is called the Sultan. Under the Sultan, there is a minister called the Vizier, which is equivalent to the prime minister. However, the Vizier not only controls the state's administrative organs, but also has the military command and possesses military power. In the beginning, this position was hereditary, most of them have a background of Tujue origins, and later Christians from different ethnic groups took over the Vizier position. The local administrative region of the Ottoman Empire is called Sanjak (meaning the flag); after the conquest of the Balkan Peninsula, the province was established. The governor of the province was called Pasha and was directly controlled by the Sultan. The Pasha was appointed and removed by the Sultan. There were a number of different Sanjaks under the provinces; a Sanjak includes military fiefs whose leader is called Sipahi and the chief of Sanjak is regularly rotated to ensure the Sultan's control over local affairs. There are also many fiefs outside the province, their lord is hereditary, relatively autonomous, most of them are Christian aristocrats.

Slave politics

As early as the Abbasid period, there were many slaves who served as high-ranking officials and local governor, as well as in the Egyptian Mamluk dynasty. Most of the slaves of the Ottoman Empire came from the recruitment of Christian subjects in the empire. The empire recruited men between the ages of 8 and 20 to serve as slaves of the Sultan. The slaves entered the court school, received education and training, some of them with good condition entered the Sultanese court and then entered the official career and were appointed with heavy responsibilities; other joined the Sultan imperial guard troop of about 1,000 people each year.

"Becoming a slave of the Sultan means honor and privilege". The bureaucrats from slavery possess considerable personal property and prominent social status, the Sultan is their absolute master. This system weakens the Ottoman tribal tradition and strengthens the political control of the Sultan. The bureaucrats of slavery played a pivotal role in maintaining the centralization of the empire and overcoming local centrifugal tendencies. This kind of system that does not look at the parentage and measures the individual by merits is somewhat similar to the China imperial examination. A slave was born in an ordinary family, educated and trained, step by step became an official and even became a national minister, as a Vizier, has privileges.

Slavery politics is based on an educational system. There is a royal college in the court, the students study Islamic theology and jurisprudence, learn more about secular knowledge, humanities, history and mathematics, as well as sports training and archery, wrestling, swordsmanship, spears and polo. After graduating from school, he began to acquire low-level military and administrative positions, and gradually upgraded to serve as Pasha and Vizier. The slavery politics began in the military field and later expanded into the administrative field. The Vizier, the governor of the province, the landlord, the tax collector, and the administrative officials at all levels, all the administrative officials of the empire and most of the officers were from the "Slave House."

The Ottoman empire also has aristocrats, military aristocrats, who enjoy a fief. The Ottoman empire's land system is different from Europe. The military fief is small, not hereditary, and the land is state-owned; therefore, the Ottoman empire does not have nobles who have land. In the Ottoman empire, Islam mastered justice and education, possessed fief. The Kadi judge presiding over the courts, enforcing laws, arbitral proceedings, collecting war materials, recruiting troops, securing traffic and road safety, supervising market transactions, and the Kadi judge participated in daily affairs and management of the empire. The Islamic law is much more perfect than the Chinese law, and Islamic judges are also very important officials of the country. In general, the administrative system in the Islamic region is similar to China, and the judicial system is somewhat similar to Europe.

4.European political system

Between the fourteenth and fifteenth centuries, we assist to the rise of the nation-state in the late Middle Ages in Europe; at that time, there were three orders: the nobility, the church and the burghers class in society; only the aristocrats and churches can participate in politics; these levels have been maintained until the French Revolution. After the commercial recovery, the urban development, the Renaissance, the Reformation, the scientific revolution, and enlightenment, the European society was ready to enter the capitalist era, and the burghers class was becoming more and more important in society. The characteristics of the European political system are:

Aristocratic politics

Aristocrats occupy an important position in European social and political life, they possess fief and it can be hereditary. Aristocratic lords can have their own military and justice jurisdiction, so it is easy for them to form a local separatist force. Because there is no bureaucratic system like the East, especially like China, the daily administration of government depends on the nobility and the church. The nobility is very powerful and sometimes able to restrict the royal power, like the "the Great Charter" in British history, and some countries also form "Nobles' Democracy".

Judicial administration

Europe is greatly influenced by the Roman law. Judges play an important role in political life. Because there is no bureaucratic system, before becoming a capitalist society, the centralization of the nation-state is mainly dependent on the country gentlemen and the local dignitaries who limit the power of the nobility. However, this centralization is very different from China centralization. The centralization of power in European history is the centralization of the judiciary, the magistrates in various regions are appointed by the king. In the United Kingdom, they are called the "gentry invasion" and the justice of the peace has mastered the judiciary, not the administrative power; the administration of the justice of the peace has the nature of the "Kadi Justice". The exercise of power is negative and is very different from the exercise of positive power. Negative power exercise can only be exercised after a case is filed, and the object and scope of the power coverage is much smaller. As for the exercise of positive power, there is a sentence in China, "if you don't care about politics, politics will care about you." There is an old sentence, "Kings have long arms, all the lands and people belong to the emperor."

Europe has developed public and private laws. Some people say that the Chinese law is mainly the criminal law. In 2020, China just has a complete civil code. China laws are more of a top-down, maintaining the norms of the social order, but lacking horizontal and non-affiliated civil law. Compared with the maturity of the China administrative management, China legal system is not mature. In comparison, the Western legal system is perfect, and administrative management is relatively lacking. Europe has formed "the king is under the law", and in China it always says, "officials are the law"

The biggest difference between West and East in the development is that Western society lacks a bureaucratic class or a bureaucratic group. It also can be said that in ancient Europe the blood factor was important. The Ottoman Empire is similar to ancient China in that it has a set of official selection mechanisms and a mature bureaucratic mechanism to achieve social control and management; the slavery politics of the Ottoman Empire include a system similar to the China imperial examination system. Many officials in slave politics came from Christian areas, while in ancient China the imperial examinations opened to people from all the provinces and regions of the state, and the grassland tribes implemented a different system. Officials are loyal to the monarchs and dynasties. After becoming officials, they have the privileges and status. The officials in ancient China were nominally prohibited to engage in business and they could benefit from their power and status. Although in these countries, there are also commercial activities, even more developed, they have not developed like those Western set of complete business systems including banks, securities, stocks, and factories, but these are developed in a place where officials are weak. The modern country is essentially a society dominated by industry and commerce, which was first developed from Europe. The country in the Middle East and the China dynasties are typical agricultural societies.

The composition of a modern state is very different from a traditional society in terms of who represents the country, and how to organize the state institution. As a general view, modern country emphasizes judicial power, legislative power, there is also strong administrative power, but officials who hold administrative power are elected, their terms of office are limited and their rights are supervised. The bureaucratic politics and the civil service system formed the basis of the Western capitalism society and this is inconsistent with the traditional Eastern bureaucracy, it is based on the modern enterprise system. Political system and the economic foundation are different. The transition from judicial governance to democratic electoral system requires a mature merchant class; from the Western experience, the mature merchants class must be cultivated in a centralized government and monarchy. They need to have a mature ideology, like the philosophy of Locke, Hobbes, Montesquieu, Rousseau, Tocqueville, etc. The merchant class entered the government management, implemented the representative government, organized the separation of the three powers and restricted the power of the summit.

The officials of the ancient agricultural society were opposed to the spirit of capitalism. Officials relied on gradual promotion and on receiving wages. The ideal situation was honest and upright, but it was difficult to attain. Many officials relied on rent-seeking, which led to corruption, these officials could become rich in fact. They were hateful and resentful if other person could get wealth though business, although they could make a fortune through corruption. When a class can survive on the market, they don't have to rely on officials; officials have lost a lot of rent-seeking space, which many officials do not want to see. This situation is the same as the situation where professional managers dominate in vertically integrated firm.

Now many developing countries are gradually guiding and controlling the economy and establishing state-owned enterprises because there is no mature merchant class there. However, those people who have power are inclined easily to collude with the merchant class, forming an official business group, also known as bureaucratic capital; they use power to seek rent for profit, because in these countries, the bureaucratic class has a longer history than the merchant class, this bureaucratic capital can easily block the upward way for the underlying people. Because business is a way for ordinary people to develop, ordinary people do not have to seek kinship with leaders, don't need bribery, they only engage in commodity production and exchange and can improve their own conditions.

In the feudal dynasty, no matter whether it was the Middle East, Africa, India, or China, the traditional order provided an upward space for the underlying people through slave politics or the imperial examination system. The bureaucracy was relatively fair, but the society is complex, there were many informal factors, such as superior and subordinate relations, fellowship, teacher-student relationship, and nepotism. Individual promotion often depends not only on performance but also on various relationships.

In the development of ancient Europe states, a new order has emerged (the later middle ages). Through the commercial development, individuals rely on the commodity production and exchange. Individuals can concentrate their energy on business and focus on the invention of products. In this way, science and technology have been developed. Compared with the traditional agricultural society, the industrial and commercial society is more conducive to the advancement of science and technology.

We can see many interesting phenomena. In the past dynasty countries and the ancient society, the dynasty had a cycle of domination. In the late dynasty, it was necessary to change the dynasty and establish a new dynasty. Like the dynasty cycle in ancient China, each dynasty is about two more hundred years old. The Tang Dynasty is 289 years, the Ming Dynasty is 276 years, and the Qing Dynasty is 267 years, these cycles all appeared when the bureaucracy matured.

5.Urban system

The city is one of the three elements of the state and civilization. In history, cities exist after countries became civilized, but in different regions, the development of cities in different countries has different paths and different characteristics. The commonality of cities around the world is that at first there is a fortress, and then there is a market. No matter whether in Asia, the Middle East, Africa, India, China or Europe, these two characteristics are shared, but European cities have developed a number of different characteristics - urban autonomy, which is characterized by the unique structure of the European society, the aristocratic politics and the absence of administrative power.

The European cities are characterized by self-government and have a juridical person autonomous organization, it is called the city commune. In the East, in the Middle East, India, Africa and China, there is no such feature. In China, the city is always the residence of the administrative officials and the place of administrative institution, the city has more political meaning.

The European cities are the home of the burghers class and the merchant class relative to the nobility. The nobility has the fief and the city is just a source of tax for them. Both Western and Eastern cities have merchants and artisans' guilds, but only in the West, was formed the urban burghers class. The urban citizens seize the power of the city and break the shackles of the lords, it is the biggest feature of Western cities and it is different from other cities in the world. There is an old saying in Europe that "the air of the city makes people free." The Western cities form a civil association, they are legally autonomous and have their own courts, which are unique to the European cities. I think it is the lack of a perfect bureaucracy in the European society and the lack of administrative officials which allowed the cities to develop. Relative to the Middle East, China, India and Africa, the European society does not have a strong control over the city. The European rulers often faced the challenges of the feudal aristocracy, so they preferred to develop the city as the place of opposition to the feudal aristocracy--- the burghers class. This kind of autonomous city first appeared in Italy and formed a city-state. Its development is also divided into two stages. One is the aristocratic city which is represented by Venice, mainly monopolizing overseas trade and doing business with the East. The aristocrats of Venice depended on the income of land property; they monopolized the politics of the city. The rights of urban communes were concentrated in the hands of the aristocracy. The word "people" is relatively aristocracy (people is from popolo and mean non-noble).

In other parts of Europe, cities have also gained financial autonomy. The king regards the city as a tax object, the city guild governs the city, the king issues a charter, the city is granted legal rights, and the right to elect its chief executive. It is different from Italy, there is the representative of the city who is a member of the National Assembly, representing the interests of the city, thus avoiding a city-state like Italy. Later, Florence developed a low-profit wool textile industry, broke the control of aristocracy and established a civilian city, this is the second stage. The nobility is excluded from the commune administration, there are seven major guilds in Florence, judges and notaries, bankers and so on; there are also fourteen small guilds, and finally the banker Medici family dominates the politics of Florence.

The European autonomous city has these characteristic:

1. Political autonomy, sending representatives to the national legislature

2. City has its own laws, different from the laws of other parts of the country, laws are suitable for the development of industry and commerce

3. Political independence, with its own judicial and independent institutions

4. Independent finance

5. Market rights and independent urban economic policies, the right to control the markets and adjust economic policies

The urban law abolished the individual slave status and the enslavement of the land; the local governor must be elected by the burghers class and must be members of the commune.

The development of Western cities disintegrated the feudal society. The development of the city relied on the food supply of the village, the city provided goods and industrial products, they were exchanged in the market. This is the circulation of commodities. Later, the city came to the forefront in contrast with the power of the countryside and the city dominated the countryside, industry and commerce are no longer subordinate to agriculture, but in turn dominated agriculture. The development of the commodity economy and the urban economy has changed the natural economy relying solely on land. Under natural economic conditions, land is fundamental, a person can only rely on land to survive. After the rise of the commodity economy, a person no longer relies solely on land, he relies on production exchange and commodity circulation; this can make a person rich and break the bond of the land for a person. The industry and commerce have become the main activities of the society. Today in developed countries, less than 5% of the people are engaged in agriculture, and the urban population accounts for more than 80% of the total population.

The modern capitalist society restricts the administrative power of the administrative officials, avoiding the rent-seeking by officials and for the merchant class, it opens the way through smooth business. The democratic electoral system, the representative government, and the separation of powers are all used to restrict the administrative power of officials. In countries outside Europe, because of the mature bureaucracy in these countries, the bureaucrats will naturally resist the Western political system. In addition, Western philosophy is a kind of foreign thought when it reaches other regions. There is a process of acceptance and absorption of foreign thought in any region. In Chinese history, Buddhism was introduced to China, and it took hundreds of years to evolve and appeared as a native Chinese Buddhism-Zen Buddhism. In politics, the developing countries rashly accept the separation of powers, the parliamentary system; there will be problems, the rule of law is imperfect, the market mechanism is not perfect, the merchant class is immature, if the ethnic issues are not handled well, it will easily lead to local separatism and division, the society become turbulent. Industrialization outside Europe took another industrialization path. In economy, it found state-owned enterprises and the leadership of enterprises are also state bureaucrats, thus avoiding conflicts and incorporating the original political system. However, this system also encounters problems, the bureaucratic system led to institutional rigidity, social development was slow or even stagnant. The enterprises need innovation, officials and innovation have conflicts; innovation is not the primary task of officials. The bureaucratic group became a vested interest group and a resistance of reform.

6.Education and Imperial Examination in ancient China

In Chapter 10, we talked about modern business education, the earliest Wharton School in the United States, and the famous MBA education of Harvard University. Modern business education is based on scientific management thought, and also includes many business knowledge such as finance, research and development, marketing, accounting, etc. The modern vertically integrated firm and the modern business education supplement each other. Professional managers who receive business education and training are employed in enterprises. The separation of enterprise ownership and control is more thorough. In the ancient Chinese society, there was an education system and an imperial examination system, which were compatible with the political system. In the mature period of the bureaucracy in ancient China, officials at all levels in the government were basically trained by the education system and selected by the imperial examination system. In here, we introduce the ancient Chinese education and imperial examination system, which can be compared with the modern commercial education system.

The education system in ancient China developed earlier than the imperial examination system, and the main content of education was moral education. There were two forms of education: government-run school and private school. According to historical records, government-run schools existed during the Shang and Zhou dynasties, which was the early stage of Chinese civilization. The real development was in the Han Dynasty (2nd century BC), when Confucianism was established as the country's mainstream ideology, and government-run education used the Confucian classics books as textbooks. The country's highest institution was called "Tai Xue", and in the Sui and Tang Dynasties, as well as during the Song, Yuan, Ming, and Qing periods, it was called "Guo Zi Jian"; it has administrative functions, similar to today's Ministry of Education and imperial college. Private education, called "academy", is independent of the government-run education and was a supplement to the government-run education, the content of both educations was the same.

The imperial examination system is a unique invention and creation of the ancient Chinese society; it even affected the civil servant system of modern Western countries. Until now, the imperial examination system has a great influence in China. The form of the imperial examination initially contained many contents, such as countermeasures to major current political issues at that time, including poems, articles; it can creatively write, mainly literature, and is an assessment of familiarity with the classics. With the development of history, the examination content later concentrated on Confucius' works and the interpretations of later generations, and it became rigid; even the content and format of writing were strictly regulated, and independent thinking was not allowed. The imperial examination is open to the whole society, except for certain low-level occupations. An ordinary civilian, after years of study and education, who once passed the imperial examination, could be directly appointed as an official, enjoy various privileges and status, and become part of the ruling class. This relatively fair method of selecting officials is very important to ordinary people in society. It can be said that the imperial examination system played a huge role in promoting the flow of upper and lower classes in the ancient Chinese society. However, as China entered the modern world and gradually entered an industrial society, the imperial examination system was not compatible with social development when the society developed technology and trade. It was abolished in 1905 after 1300 years of implementation.

The imperial examination system was established and developed during the Sui and Tang Dynasties, about 6th to 9th centuries. It is a sign of the maturity of all aspects of the ancient Chinese society. During this period, the classical education and political system have been relatively perfect. As mentioned earlier, the political system in the Sui and Tang dynasties of China was a system where bureaucracy and aristocracy coexisted. The role of the imperial examination system was to make the bureaucracy dominate social politics. After the Sui and Tang dynasties, the political system was basically bureaucracy, and aristocracy disappeared.

When a society makes no significant progress in productivity and technology for a long period of time, emphasizing morality, popularizing education, selecting talents through imperial examinations, and breaking the limitations of blood factors, this society can indeed effectively maintain social stability and maintain the rule of a dynasty; its ethics can weaken the opposition situation of different religions and sects; the development of education and imperial examinations can promote the flow of the upper and lower classes of the society, and discourage the aristocracy. The ancient Chinese education system, the imperial examination system and the bureaucracy together constituted the ancient Chinese talent system. But at the same time, we must also see that these three systems all focus on ethics. The knowledge learned is ethics, the content of examinations is also ethics, and the selection and evaluation mechanism of officials also focuses on ethics. As a result, in ancient China, talents were attracted to a separate field—the moral field. Science and technology were not valued, could not be combined with business, and were restrained by government ideology. People engaged in scientific, technological inventions and creations, and industry and commerce have no status or development in that society, which affects the progress of science, technology, and business exchanges; this is an important reason why Chinese society has stagnated in modern times and lags behind the times. The imperial examination system does not encourage creation, nor can it create new wealth. It is only conducive to the distribution of wealth, the flow of social personnel, and is conducive to breaking aristocratic politics. The number of the management class in a society is limited, and it is impossible to expand unlimitedly. With no obvious changes in productivity, the social economy is always an agricultural economy, and social wealth mainly depends on the land economy; the continuous expansion of the officials will inevitably lead to the end of the dynasty. The imperial examination system revealed its limitations. Therefore, when the Chinese society further developed into an industrial society, it needed to develop trade, industry and commerce, and needed more technological inventions and creations; it needed to create more social wealth, the imperial examination system and its related political systems were very unsuitable for the development of science and technology, did not adapt to the progress of industrialization and it placed too much emphasis on morality. In the end, the imperial examination system was eliminated by the times.

Regarding morality, ethics, technological invention and creation, the two are related. Emphasis on one aspect is not good enough. Confucianism emphasizes "Golden Mean", while Confucius speaks of "the middle way", maintaining balance and opposing extremes. Buddhism also emphasizes the "the middle way" and avoid leaning to either side. After six years of asceticism, Shakyamuni received the shepherdess' benevolence, changed to the middle way and created Buddhism. The best explanation of the relationship between the two is the Chinese Taoist thought. The classic Taoist thought works "Tao Te Ching" explains the importance and role of ethics in social development. The principles described are not only conducive to social development and progress, they are also conducive to personal self-cultivation and physical and mental health.

There should be no bias towards both moral, ethics and technological invention and creation, and one should not be attached to either aspect. We can see that in modern society, those famous scientists, inventors and entrepreneurs have no low moral quality; they also have a high pursuit of faith and knowledge. Like Carnegie, who, although he did not receive a complete education and was mainly engaged in industry and technology as an adult, but he was familiar with Confucius' works. When Carnegie wrote his biography, he still remembered that Colonel Anderson opened his library to boys in his childhood. The ocean of knowledge and the palace of imagination can keep Carnegie and his friends away from bad friends and vices. Carnegie later donated more than 2500 public libraries around the world, and founded Carnegie University and the Carnegie Charitable Foundation. Carnegie Mellon University is at the forefront of the academic field of computer science; Herbert Simon's academic and research career was mainly spent at Carnegie Mellon University. I remember that Einstein once wrote an article that said that there are three types of people engaged in scientific research. The first type is for utilitarian purposes; the second type is for hobbies; and the third type is for their duty. There are similar sayings in China, called utilitarian life, game life, and Taoist life, three different realms. I think those who can make major scientific discoveries and outstanding inventions, and those who have made achievements in their careers, have done hard work to gain the favor of the muse and make them appreciated. These efforts and achievements need to be realized in a society that allows and encourages the development of science and technology.

Humans are the intelligent part of the universe, they are high-level creatures with a rational spirit and can think, not low-level creatures that compete for food, territory, and mating objects in the forest and grassland. In a society, if individuals rely on animal methods, rely on "The Law of the Jungle" to earn and snatch daily necessities and material wealth, and then climb to the upper strata of society, it can only show that the society has not evolved well enough, and the level of the individual is still very low. Under the imperial examination system, ordinary individuals do not need to snatch for survival like primitive people in primitive society and animals in nature, nor do they need to work in manors all day long like slaves to obtain the materials needed for a basic life. Individuals only need to study, learn about ethics, and take the imperial examinations; it is possible to improve oneself, thereby entering the upper strata of society, enjoying social status, being respected by others, and meeting people's high-level needs. In modern industrialized society; in business education, individuals learn scientific management thought in schools, and then they can work in enterprises and become professional managers. They may become senior managers of enterprises, serve in government positions, or start their own businesses, enjoying higher wages, stocks, various benefits and social status; it also meets the individual's high-level needs and self-actualization needs. As a politician, school education is only a part of life, and there are more things to learn in society. In the process of industrialization, there are many successful entrepreneurs who have not received a complete business education, these is beyond the scope of this book.

The ancient Chinese imperial examination system and the modern commercial education system were adapted to different social development stages in different societies, were in line with people's rational spirit, were more reasonable and fairer, and were systems that were conducive to social mobility.

14 CHAPTER THE SILICON VALLEY MODE

1. The development path of Silicon Valley

Since the 1960s, with the development of the vertically integrated firm, scientific management has matured and improved in all fields of society and commerce, and the separation of enterprise ownership and control has become more thorough. Managerial capitalism has found its feet in the United States and all over the world. In one field, some changes have quietly appeared, and a unique enterprise management method has gradually developed. Let's talk about this new trend, which, to this day, is still developing and evolving. It has not yet matured to its final state.

This new management method first appeared on the west coast of the United States, in California---Silicon Valley. This new method made its first appearance in the semiconductor field. Its development process can be roughly divided into three stages:

1. The late 1950s to the early 1970s (the era of the semiconductor industry)

2. The 1970s through the 1980s (the era of the microcomputer industry)

3. The 1990s till present (the Internet age)

In the 1940s, the invention of the transistor brought new breakthroughs to the development of the semiconductor industry. In 1947, William Shockley, Walter Houser Brattain, and John Bardeen of Bell Labs in the United States developed a transistor to replace the bulky and power-consuming electronic tube. In 1956, they won the Nobel Prize in Physics for their joint invention of the transistor. Shockley's hometown was in California, and Frederick Terman, the dean of Stanford University at that time, was very interested in attracting the emerging electronics industry to the California Bay Area. He strongly persuaded Shockley to establish a new laboratory near Stanford University. Shockley did so, and developed advanced transistors and other electronic components. Shockley recruited eight physicists and engineers from the eastern United States. Five of these eight physicists and engineers had doctor degrees in physics and had graduated from prestigious universities, such as Massachusetts Institute of Technology, California Institute of Technology, Oxford University and Geneva University. The three engineers also had strong professional backgrounds. Because of Shockley's great reputation, these eight men joined Shockley's laboratory in the spring of 1956.

Shockley was a successful scientist, but he was an unqualified manager. Shockley's tough management method made his assistants, physicists and engineers, unite against him. Shockley had a fierce temper and often threatened employees with immediate termination. He also got publicly angry over trivial matters and used a polygraph to perform a polygraph.

The eight assistants decided to leave Shockley to find another job, but there was a problem. They needed to be hired by a company because they were all scientists and engineers, didn't understand management, and had no capital. At that time in California, the silicon semiconductor industry was an emerging field with a small market, and many companies and enterprises did not know the eight men well. To solve this dilemma, they consulted a small investment bank in New York, in the hope that this bank could connect them with a company willing to hire them. At the same time, they also hoped to establish a research institute in the San Francisco Peninsula. Two financial professionals, Arthur Rock and Alfred Coyle, were very interested in the eight men and helped connect them with a company willing to invest in their skills—Fairchild Camera and Instrument, on Long Island, New York. At the same time, the two financiers suggested the eight men set up their own companies instead of waiting to be hired. This was an unusual suggestion, because setting up a business at that time required capital and talent who understood operation and management. In the traditional way of starting a business, if one feel that there is market in a certain area and in a certain field.

There is a lot to founding a business—including dealing with assets and mortgages, obtaining loans, contacting companies upstream and downstream, getting customers and cornering markets, hiring employees. But these eight men had neither the capital nor the know-how to do so. For Fairchild Camera and Instrument, entering the emerging field of transistors required a large number of professionals, huge capital investment, and research and development. The company saw that these eight physicists and engineers had already mastered all the manufacturing processes and did not need to start from scratch. Thus, mutual cooperation between Fairchild and these eight men would save a lot of capital and costs. Both parties had complementary advantages and needed each other. An alliance between Fairchild and these eight men was only natural. So, Fairchild Camera and Instrument raised funds to establish a new company with them in joint ownership—Fairchild Semiconductor. This new company was established on October 1957, with accompanying managers, sales executives, salesmen, and manufacturing and control engineers hired from the outside.

In the 1960s, Fairchild Semiconductor led the development of the semiconductor industry. The semiconductor industry developed rapidly, and later invented integrated circuits. There were more and more new opportunities. Fairchild Semiconductor was conservative in the follow-up development of technology. Later, many engineers developed independently from Fairchild, e.g., Intel, AMD, Amelco, National Semiconductor, and Edex. Indeed, Fairchild seemed to become a school dedicated to cultivating Silicon Valley entrepreneurs.

Those same eight physicists and engineers later left Fairchild because their development strategy was inconsistent with the company's. Someone founded new companies, and someone entered the field of venture capital. Among them were two men, Robert Noyce and Gordon Moore, and they founded Intel Corporation in 1968. In the early days of Intel's establishment, a Japanese company came to Intel in search of a customized calculator chip. Intel was not very interested in creating this customized product at the beginning, but they needed to establish a customer base, so Intel found an engineer - Marcian Hoff - to see if he could fulfill and standardize such a chip, and then sell it to other clients. Hoff thought about it for a while, and later designed the central processing unit (CPU). This was a major invention. With the CPU, coupled with the random access memory (RAM), the core of the microcomputer was formed, and it led to the microcomputer revolution. This invention also laid the foundation for Intel to become the core of microcomputer industry hardware in the 1980s.

In the 1970s, the invention of integrated circuits and CPUs brought huge technological advances. Due to these advances, the appearance of microcomputers was already inevitable. During this time, several more characters arose to lead the computer industry to profound changes. If the 1960s was the world of semiconductors, then the 1970s was the field of microcomputers. Intel created the 8080 microprocessor chip, plus some peripheral chips, anyone can make a microcomputer. At that time, many computer fans and circuit enthusiasts did it. An engineer named Henry Edward Roberts founded Micro Instrumentation and Telemetry Systems (MITS) and hired two men to write software for him. These men were Bill Gates and Paul Allen, who went on to found Microsoft. At the same time,

Steve Jobs and his partner Steve Wozniak found venture capitalists and established Apple Inc. to produce Apple computers. Apple computers sold well in the market; Apple computers did not use Intel's 8080 chips, but Motorola's 6502 chips.

All of this happened in the mid- to late 1970s. At that time, the microcomputer market did exist; however, microcomputers were still relatively primitive at that time. There was no human-computer graphical interface such as we have today. These microcomputers were produced by little-known men, and the buying customers were mainly computer enthusiasts. In the computer field at that time, IBM was No.1. IBM's management found that these young men were very successful, IBM didn't feel good about it and wanted to enter the microcomputer market. IBM had strong technical strength and many scientific researchers and engineers, so it set up an internal R&D team to develop IBM's microcomputer.

By the 1980s, IBM's microcomputer hardware used Intel's 8088 chip, with the software in cooperation with Microsoft - which was responsible for the development of operating systems and application software. After IBM's microcomputer products were introduced to the market, they were immediately successful. What they hadn't foreseen was that their technology had opened a door to a new world, and what was to follow far exceeded their expectations.

IBM entered the field of microcomputers according to a traditional vertical integration model. At that time, IBM's focus was still on mainframe computers, while the software and hardware of the mainframe computer are all controlled by IBM itself, not independent. Although IBM's microcomputers achieved great success in the market in the early stage, the microcomputer hardware and software were all products of other companies. The reason owed partly to an ongoing antitrust investigation and lawsuit by the US Department of Justice, and partly to the product development cycle. In the end, IBM still wants to put the software and hardware production system of the microcomputer under their control. They proposed a closed system in the development of subsequent microcomputers. As a result, this path was unworkable, the market formed a new open standard and the system of microcomputer was from closed to open. At the same time, IBM's management made a series of bad business and technical decisions. IBM did not have an advantage in the microcomputer market and was gradually going downhill. Although they once led the way, IBM finally withdrew from the personal computer market.

At the same time, many new compatible companies had been established on the market. Intel chips were used in the hardware and Microsoft operating systems were used in the software. Any new company can produce the best-selling computers on the market. The market has become a structure with Intel and Microsoft as the core. This open architecture almost monopolizes the market. It is not a monopoly of the market by a company, but a standard, a standard with Intel and Microsoft as the core, monopolize the market. Correspondingly, the market is flooded with all kinds of compatible computers, their software and hardware are similar, the competition is product quality and internal management of the company, like Dell, which is ahead of other companies in tailoring products for consumers and supply chain management. At the end of the 1980s, IBM fell into a huge loss, and it took several years to ease off. It hired a managerial figure, Louis V. Gerstner Jr, to carry out a service transformation, from the previous manufacturing-centered transformation to service is the center. In the 1980s, the development of microcomputers was rapid, with CPUs from 8086, 80286, 80386, 80486, 80586... constantly innovating, with higher performance and faster speed. In software, a variety of database software, image and graphics processing, word processing, financial table software, anti-virus software, and game software continue to appear, and many software companies have emerged, such as Oracle, Informix, Sybase, Adobe, lotus, VisiCalc, Autodesk, McAfee... The human-machine interface developed from a character format to a graphical interface. Apple Inc first set a precedent for the development of Macintosh computers, and then Microsoft's Windows system. They all originated from the interpersonal interaction developed by Xerox Palo Alto Research Center, unfortunately Xerox did not commercialize the research results and missed this great opportunity.

With the rise of the Internet in the 1990s, a new era began, and a multitude of new Internet companies appeared. First it was Netscape and Yahoo, then Amazon, Google, eBay, Facebook, Instagram, and Twitter. From simple Internet yellow pages, corporate websites, to search engines, social media, and e-commerce, the Internet connects people all over the world. The richness and depth of information has greatly increased, and things that were previously unimaginable can now be readily achieved. For example, free communication is now available anywhere in the world, as long as there is a connection to the network. Anyone can publish video, audio, text, and images on the Internet—just as though they owned their own media. In the past, it would have been prohibitively expensive to establish a TV station. From any corner of the earth, one can enjoy lectures from world-renowned universities. In e-commerce, you can shop without going outside; online payment is very fast and convenient. The popularity of smart phones has only accelerated the speed of Internet penetration.

Although microcomputers have existed in the home for some time, in the past, one needed to study and master their usage to use them at all. Yet now, the operation of smart phones is very simple and can be done with your fingertips. There are two major systems in the field of smart phones. One is Apple and its application (app) store, and the other is Google's Android system and its apps. Each system had its own advantages.

In the development of Silicon Valley, some trends can be clearly found. First of all, manufacturing, the company is from vertical integration to horizontal integration, and then to vertical integration (to some extent). In the early days, IBM was vertically integrated, and it produced and developed both its own software and hardware. Later, with the development of microcomputers, the vertical integration method dissolved, and hardware and software became independent from vertically integrated firms. There are many hardware and semiconductor chips manufacturers. In terms of software, there are companies that develop operating systems and application software, such as databases and various application processing software. The market is refined and each company only produces part of it. Intel is the leading hardware company and Microsoft is the leading software company. The overall computer manufacturer has essentially become a supporting role. In an era of smart phones, Apple is vertically integrated to a certain extent. The hardware and software platforms are controlled by Apple, but the application software is open. In the Apple store, any software developed by individuals and companies can be used and traded; the Android system led by Google is similar.

2. The elements and characteristics of the success of Silicon Valley startups

Elements of Silicon Valley's Success:

A. Suitable products

A suitable product's prototype or idea can be developed quickly, has huge market potential, and has patent or other legal protection. New products and new ideas generally come from the company or university laboratories. People with new products and new technological ideas will become the founders of emerging companies.

B. The right team

A highly qualified and dedicated team not only includes technical experts, but also managers who have experience in sales, capital, market and operations. This was true of Apple's founders Wozniak and Jobs, for example—Jobs was more skilled in the market and creativity, while Wozniak was more technical.

C. Capital

a. Angel investment

b. Professional venture capitalist

c. Large industrial company

D. Basic system

a. Technical features

b. Social atmosphere

Allow failure and allow technical personnel to leave the original company to start a business.

c. Educational resources

Universities and related research institutions

There are similarities and differences in corporate management:

The management methods of Silicon Valley companies have some similarities and differences with traditional corporate management. For traditional companies, such as Carnegie Steel, Ford Motor, General Motors, etc., which we have discussed prior, the founders of the company had a certain amount of capital accumulation. Looking for investment partners, they needed bank loans. The founder acts as the general manager and chairman. The difference in the case of the Silicon Valley model is that the founders of the company are all engineers who have product prototypes or new product ideas, but no capital, management experience, or a management team—just like the eight physicists and engineers discussed. In the process of establishing the company, the bank did not intervene. Later, Noyce and Moore founded Intel; Jobs and Wozniak founded Apple; Jerry Chih-Yuan Yang and David Filo, Yahoo; and Larry Page and Sergey Brin, Google. These are all typical examples, based on creativity and business plans, and the engineer can obtain invest and start a business. Creativity is very important.

After a start-up company has passed the market test and survives and grows, its management method is not much different from that of a traditional company. Whether it is top or middle management, professional managers are hired and the company is divided into many departments by function; the scale of the company becomes larger. All of this is similar to traditional corporate management methods.

There are notable differences between traditional corporate management methods and those of these Silicon Valley startups in terms of labor relations. Traditional companies generally have strong labor unions to protect the rights and interests of their employees. For example, General Motors, where workers are known as worker nobles and have good benefits, employees are relatively stable in the company and can be promoted level by level. But companies like those in Silicon Valley are highly flexible. If an employee has a good idea and it is not accepted by the parent company, they are more willing to develop independently and create new companies, as was the case with Intel, AMD, and Microsoft. The high mobility of employees encourages entrepreneurship, and early employees involved in entrepreneurship were given stock options to encourage development within the company. Through the development of scientific management thought and practices, traditional large enterprises emphasized labor-management cooperation, provided workers with various benefits, and eased labor-management conflicts. In Silicon Valley companies, an employee could easily become the boss of another newly established company. If he or she were to succeed, the rewards would be greater, much more so than step-by-step development in large companies.

There are also differences between business ownership in the traditional model versus the Silicon Valley model. The founders of traditional enterprises had more shares. After the separation of ownership and control, the original major shareholders no longer participated in the management of the enterprise—e.g., the Rockefeller and DuPont families. After many rounds of investment by entrepreneurs in Silicon Valley, before a company went public, the founders of the company only held a small percentage of its shares. Some founders were even driven out of the company due to management differences, like Steve Jobs of Apple in its early years. Jobs had had a conflict with the management and left Apple, whereupon sold his shares.

Silicon Valley companies also have closer relationships with customers than traditional companies. Customers often enter the innovation process from the very beginning. There are several types of customers. Some are leading customers and are willing to spend time and create new products with entrepreneurs.

The social relations and social capital of Silicon Valley are also very different from traditional enterprises. In the social network of Silicon Valley, engineers central, in addition to universities, venture capitalists, managers, lawyers, accounting, seller, marketing… Because of the high turnover of employees in Silicon Valley, engineers are often more loyal to social relationships and technology than to any company. After work, employees often interact with each other, go to the same clubs, and exchange information. There is a wonderful example of this concerning Apple and Microsoft. When Jobs returned to find Apple in a state of crisis, he was invited to one of his employee's birthday parties. This employee was friendly with both Jobs and Gates, whom he also invited to his birthday. At the dinner, this engineer revealed Microsoft's latest tablet computer to Jobs, despite the fact that Gates was also present. That an engineer could introduce a new product developed by his company to a competing firm in the presence of his boss demonstrates how widespread this sharing was in Silicon Valley. This kind of social capital is not seen in the hierarchical companies in the eastern

United States, where engineers were more likely to believe in working alone. This can also be regarded as a sort of informal organization between enterprises.

In this set up, engineers can often obtain a lot of useful information and carry out a sort of cooperative production. This kind of cooperative production is not only between engineers, but also between enterprises and customers. This is the consumer participation or customer involvement and it is a question frequently analyzed and researched in consumer behavior.

Venture capital

Silicon Valley started with venture capital. Like Intel, Cisco, Apple, Yahoo, Google, etc., as mentioned earlier, the establishment of a traditional enterprise requires a certain amount of capital and relies upon mortgages and bank loans, in the event that the enterprise fails.

However, entrepreneurs in Silicon Valley companies are engineers who lack capital, and the enterprises they start are prone to failure. Therefore, this kind of investment is called *venture capital*. It is very risky, and so the returns on venture capital also tends to be quite high. This type of investment is closely associated with Silicon Valley. Some go so far as to say that the relationship between venture capital and Silicon Valley even closer than the relationship between husband and wife. However, it should also be noted that there are some companies that have little relationship with venture capital, such as HP and National Semiconductor.

Venture capital has several characteristics that should be noted

1.Venture capital is managed by experts. Many entrepreneurs and engineers, after they have work experience, often invest in venture capital.

2.Venture capital generally involves the coexistence of risks and returns. It is possible that only one or two of the ten projects are profitable, but these two profitable gains can far offset other loss-making projects.

3.Venture capital focuses on projects with great potential and requires a high rate of return on investment.

Venture capital is very different from traditional bank financing. Venture capital does not simply provide funds. Venture capitalists have a very close relationship with startups entrepreneurs. They are usually responsible for guiding the company through the early stages of development and controlling startups. Control over start-ups is stronger than traditional enterprises. The process of venture capital is generally divided into four stages: angel investment, seed investment, round A financing, and round B financing.

The composition of venture capital:

More than 80% of venture capital funds are private, independent funds. Ultimate investors include pension fund companies, foundations and endowments, families and institutions, and others. In addition, after many Silicon Valley companies have developed, they often set up a venture capital institution. American venture capital is mainly concentrated in the two areas, Silicon Valley and Boston 128 Highway.

In Silicon Valley and Boston area, there are one or several famous universities—Stanford University in the Silicon Valley area and Massachusetts Institute of Technology in the Boston area.

Universities are vital to the continued development of Silicon Valley. Every year, in universities there are many outstanding doctoral and master graduates. These students enter Silicon Valley companies directly after graduation. They often bring the latest research results from universities to enterprises and accelerate marketization of scientific research products. Although the founders of some Silicon Valley companies (such as Gates, Jerry Yang, Jobs, and Ellison, for instance) did not complete their degrees in universities, many of the employees they hire have doctoral and master's degrees. Those working in management in these companies often go to universities to teach and give lectures, attracting more college students to join technology companies—and some in management will return to universities to teach. Many prototypes come from universities or related laboratories, such as the man-machine graphical interface and object-oriented language first developed by the Xerox Palo Alto Research Center. The early development of Silicon Valley benefited from the large amount of land owned by Stanford University, which leased the land to start-up companies. But more importantly, the intellectual resources provided by Stanford University enabled Silicon Valley to flourish.

Case

The above compares the differences between Silicon Valley model companies and traditional corporate management methods, and summarizes some characteristics of them both. Because theory can be tiresome and difficult to follow, below we give an example, a real market case to illustrate the above concepts. This case is in the field of smart phones. The competition between Nokia and Apple is to analyze and compare the differences between traditional management companies and Silicon Valley model companies by analyzing the products, enterprise ownership, and management methods of the two companies in the market.

The mobile phone market, or cellular phone market, emerged in the United States in the 1980s. Motorola was the first to occupy an important market position in this field. In the middle and late 20th century, Motorola led the development trend of the world's mobile communication equipment. The world's first commercial mobile phone and the first GSM digital mobile phone were all developed by Motorola. Motorola was founded by Paul Galvin in 1928. It is one of the largest electronics companies in the United States and is still a leader in the global chip manufacturing and electronic communications industries. Motorola's wireless communication system was installed on the spacecraft in the American Apollo Moon Landing Program to transmit voice communications and television signals between the Earth and the Moon. In the 1980s, Motorola was the world's largest mobile phone manufacturer. When the mobile phone format changed from analog to digital in 1990s, Motorola failed to keep up with the market changes in the mobile phone field. Its mobile phone business was acquired by Google and China's Lenovo Group.

At this time, in the Nordic countries, Finland's Nokia Corporation began to take advantage of the market and replaced Motorola in the field of mobile phones. Nokia is a Finnish company with a long history, from the production of rubber boots, paper, to cables, tires, televisions, telephone switches, computers and mobile phones, involving many industries. In the early 1990s, Nokia gave up all its traditional basic industrial businesses and concentrated on the field of electronics. It gradually transformed into an enterprise, focusing on consumer electronics, computers and mobile phones. In the 1980s, most Finnish companies belonged to large banks and insurance companies. Managers of these institutions became members of a given company's board of directors, when the company often lacked the necessary professional expertise, decisions were made. Two large banks controlled most Finnish companies, including Nokia, but Nokia was ready to get rid of this restriction. From the mid-to-late 1980s, Nokia's leaders have adopted changes, on the one hand it appoints international talents, and on the other hand, in the management system, the separation of corporate ownership and control realize. The board of directors is composed of senior managers, and it sets up an executive committee to oversee Nokia's regular operations.

Leading Nokia's comprehensive transformation was a Jorma Ollila. Ollila was born in Western Finland in 1950 and had international work and education experience. In middle school, he studied at the United World College of the Atlantic, an international school with students from different countries, in South Wales, U.K. Ollila later studied Applied Physics at Helsinki University of Technology in Finland. After graduating, he studied at the London School of Economics and obtained his Ph.D. Upon completion, he then joined Citibank. Ollila worked for Citibank for 7 years. He came to Nokia in 1985, he had been CEO for 14 years. In 2012, he retired. Initially, Ollila was in charge of the company's international project plan before becoming the company's financial director. Then, in 1990, Ollila became the head of Nokia's mobile phone business department and in 1992, he became the president of Nokia.

In the mobile phone market in the early 1990s, Motorola was still the leader with a market share of approximately 22%, while Nokia's market share was 10%—however, in the Chinese market in the 1990s, Nokia took the first place with a market share of 31%. Nokia continued to introduce new models and was very successful, gradually replacing Motorola. However, Nokia's management model is still the traditional separation of corporate ownership and control. Managers run the company and managerial capitalism, this model being predominant in Finland in the 1980s and 1990s. So, from the 1990s to the first 10 years of the 21st century, before the emergence of Apple's mobile phones, Nokia obtained a dominant position in the mobile phone market. Nokia mobile phones were of good quality. The mobile phones later developed by Nokia initially appeared intelligent (they were early smart phones) and adopted the Symbian operating system which had a development platform on which programmers could develop software on Nokia mobile phones, such as browsers and mobile emails.

The emergence of the Apple mobile phone has changed everything in the mobile phone market. The smartphone represented by the Apple's phones can actually be regarded more as a sort of microcomputer. Compared with the traditional mobile phone, it is more convenient to use, more efficient, and has more functions. The basic functions of the computer, except for some professional application software limited by the screen size, other microcomputer functions are available in smart phones, such as internet, maps, videos, music, e-mail, and so on. The Nokia mobile phone is more like a traditional telephone device. Although its products also had some intelligence in the later period, like the N95 smartphone launched in 2006, the degree of innovation was not large, not the kind of disruptive innovation, and the innovation is far from today's this depth of smart phone.

The development of the smart phone has ensured that this new generation of mobile phones are more than just "mobile phones" - they are an entire ecosystem, containing hardware, software, chips, peripheral circuits, cameras, audio chips, display screens, etc., with each piece developed by a different company. The core of this "ecosystem" is software. Apple and Google provide basic software platforms and operating systems. Apple's mobile phones are designed and developed by Apple, but there are many manufacturers of mobile phone hardware for Android system, and any company can enter this market. In terms of application software (apps), there are software stores where a large number of programmers develop various apps. These programmers may belong to large companies or independent software companies. Application software can be traded in software stores, much like the field of microcomputers. After the changes in the vertically integrated organization, the field of software became independent, and a large number of software manufacturers appeared. The development of the smartphone parallels the development process of the microcomputer field.

From the perspective of management methods, Apple and Google are typical representatives of Silicon Valley companies, complete with venture capital, a focus on innovation, engineer - led corporate culture, etc. Meanwhile, Nokia's management achieved the separation of enterprise ownership and control. Most of Nokia's managers have financial backgrounds, but there is no software expert. Like Ollila, although he studied applied physics, his work experience is mainly in the banking sector. After serving as the head of Nokia's mobile phone department, he studied mobile phone design, production, and manufacturing. But Apple's Jobs has been in the computer industry from the initial establishment of Apple Computer, to the founding of NeXT (during the time he left Apple), continuing until his return to Apple. He had been in the computer industry, developed computer software and hardware, and understood technology. And for these reasons, he had a better understanding of the market, management, customers, sales, service design and marketing than general business managers.

Nokia achieved the separation of corporate ownership and control. It is a typical vertically-integrated firm, and their mobile phone software and hardware are produced by the company itself. Apple, meanwhile, is the representative of Silicon Valley's emerging high-tech companies. In the confrontation between these two systems, the Silicon Valley model has won. Today, in the field of smartphones, Apple and Android still dominate.

In the last chapter, when we talk about the law of market evolution, we focus on analyzing the process that this edge corporate challenge leading company. In new fields and markets, emerging edge companies develop brand-new products and eventually replace the original leading companies in the market. In new market, the most powerful and technical leading companies developed new products in the new environment, they recognized the new trend and made efforts, but made the wrong decision, and finally failed to the emerging edge companies. The emerging companies adopted new technologies and new ideas, and developed new products, to gradually gain an advantage in the market and become a new leading enterprise.

3. Summary

The most prominent feature of the Silicon Valley model is that it emphasizes loyalty to social relationships and technology, rather than loyalty to the organization, which is the biggest difference from traditional management methods. Whether it's organization theory researchers, Barnard and Simon, or behavioral scientists Mayo, Maslow, and McGregor, they all put a strong emphasis on authority. In Simon's "Administrative Behavior", we can see Simon emphasized that employees must be loyal to the organization; authority was emphasized. With the behavioral scientists Maslow and McGregor (Maslow's enlightened management, McGregor's X-Y theory) they did not deny authority; rather, they emphasized making up for the defects of authority. The management model of Silicon Valley has just broken through this point. Silicon Valley companies do not have so much hierarchy and are relatively egalitarian. Among Silicon Valley companies, the power of informal organizations is much stronger than that of traditional companies. Informal organizations include social networks composed of venture capital, lawyers, universities, clubs, etc. As long as the engineer is creative and has a business plan, it is easy to obtain venture capital, establish company, hire employees, form management teams, start business, research and develop products, and open up markets. This situation also leads to a fast change of enterprises. Anyone who has a good idea can start a business without having to have strong capital accumulation. There are constantly new companies appearing in the market. Enterprises with many management levels are slow to transform and cannot adapt to the market. The market evolution process of Silicon Valley enterprises is regular. In traditional management theories, informal organizations are only a supplement to formal organizations. Those eight physicists and engineers left Shockley with help of venture capitalist Lock and founded Fairchild Semiconductor. Ten years later, Noyce and Moore founded Intel with the help of Lock, who then became a famous venture capitalist. Engineers not only moved between companies in the same industry, they also moved from one industry to another, and moved back and forth between companies, venture capital institutions, universities, and others. Compared to traditional companies, engineers in Silicon Valley enterprises are flexible and have greater development space.

15 CHAPTER THE DEVELOPMENT OF THE COMPUTER AND THE REFORMATION

1.the Reformation

When it comes to cultural and social development, comparing scientific management thoughts with Chinese classical thoughts, ethics, one cannot avoid religious issues. Religious issues are also a key issue in the development of early capitalism; the Reformation has a great influence on the development of capitalism. On this issue, sociologist Max Weber wrote a very well-known book "The Protestant Ethic and the Spirit of Capitalism", which mainly elaborated on the relationship between religious ethics and social development, it belongs to the category of religious sociology. This chapter describes the role of religion and ethics in the social development, mainly viewed from the perspective of the religious sociology. The specific content of religious doctrines and ethics are not introduced. Another reason why the Reformation is mentioned in this book is that this movement is very similar to the history of the computer development; this is very interesting. The history of social development belongs to social science, and the computer is the invention and the creation of science and technology; its development and evolution are a result of constant innovation and change of technology, social science and natural science which have come together. The development of computers has brought a new situation to the management innovation of enterprises, and it will also contribute to the development of management and bring new changes. The development of the computer industry itself, the management of this industry and related industries is also different from the traditional corporate management, these have been summarized in the chapter 14; in here it compares the development process of the Reformation and the computer. Let me first introduce the Western Reformation.

In addition to its daily economic life and political system, any society is influenced by religion or morality on people's thinking. It can be found that since human being has written records, or since entering a civilized society, religion has followed human being like a shadow. From primitive religions, national religions to world religions, their development has some similar processes. Christianity later evolved into the Catholic Church and the Eastern Orthodox Church, and later Protestantism emerged from the Catholic Church. Buddhism also developed into Mahayana Buddhism and Hinayana Buddhism, and Zen Buddhism emerged from Mahayana Buddhism. The emergence of Christian Protestantism is inseparable from the development of capitalism and has a strong connection with it. Let me talk about the Reformation in Western history. European society first became the industrial society, leading the rest of the world; an analysis of the development process of European society can help understand the role of morality and religion in society. The Reformation is another major social movement in Western society after the Renaissance. If the Renaissance is only confined to the upper strata of Western society, then the Reformation involves everyone in Western society, especially the middle and lower strata in Western society and has a profound impact on social development. The Reformation involves religious doctrines and rituals, the ordinary reader will feel unfamiliar with these. The purely theoretical content is also relatively boring and generally not easy to understand. In here, we talk about the characters and stories of the Reformation in the development of Western society, more interesting than pure theoretical explanation.

In the Christian Reformation, Martin Luther appeared first.

Martin Luther was a German, born in Eisleben in 1483. He studied theology at the university. At the age of 22, he decided to become a monk. Later he entered St. Augustine's Monastery in Erfurt as a lecturer in logic and physics, and later a professor of theology. The Christian theology inherited the logic and physics of ancient Greece. It can be seen that religion and science are closely connected in ancient Europe. Martin Luther had been to Rome and understood the unethical behavior of the Holy See. After returning to Germany, he was promoted to be the preacher of the province; this was about 1512.

In 1517, Pope Leo X issued the indulgences, famous in history. Leo X belonged to the Florence Medici family, he was a scholar and poet himself, and his personal conduct was good, but he had a problem, as he was spending a lot of money, and was going to repair the old St. Peter's Basilica. In order to raise funds, he issued indulgences, which triggered the Reformation. Luther wrote "Disputation of Martin Luther on the Power and Efficacy of Indulgences". Luther's Protestant ideas included the appointment of priests to marry, the abolition of many rituals, including Eucharist, confirmation... His creed excludes the bishop's court and religious laws, and the salvation of God is by faith, not by good deeds.

At that time, many parts of Germany hated the Holy See; many people, faculty, students and the public agreed with Luther's ideas. In the 16th century Germany, there were many feudal kings, big and small, who were religiously subjects to the Pope and often accepted the Pope's apportionment; many aristocrats supported Luther. There were many sayings like "How dare you spend money on religion? In luxury, debauchery and pretense, let honest people suffer from hunger... Haven't you seen that the breath of freedom is stirring?" [59]

____

[59] Will Durant, The Story of Civilization: THE REFORMATION: A HISTORY OF EUROPEAN CIVILIZATION FROM WYCLIF TO CALVIN: 1300-1564, (Simon and Schuster, 1942)

The second appearance during the Reformation was John Calvin's. Calvin was born in Noyon, France in 1509. He studied at the University of Paris and then went to Orleans to study law. At that time, under the influence of Luther in France, many people talked about the Reformation; many of his friends were Protestant figures. As the environment in Paris was not conducive to Protestantism, Calvin later came to Geneva, at about 1536. At that time, Geneva was politically attached to the Duchy of Savoy, Italy, and the Bishop of Geneva was the main responsible figure for religion. Economically, Geneva is a commercial city, governed by a large assembly of 200 citizens, and a small assembly of 25 elected by the large assembly. The parliament fought against the bishop and the duke. In order to get rid of the control of the Duchy of Savoy, the parliament converted to Protestantism. Calvin established the dominant position of Protestantism in Geneva. Calvin's Protestantism in Geneva is relatively strict and morally strict, but Calvinism does not exclude industry and commerce. It supports the interests of the civilian class and encourages the development of the weaving industry in Geneva; then, Calvinism was established in the Netherlands and England, its popularity is not unreasonable. The Calvinists in France were the Huguenots; later, the Huguenot war broke out in France as a civil war. Compared with Britain, the French Catholicism was more powerful. The Calvinist sect in Britain is Puritanism, and later it dominated the bourgeois revolution in Britain. Some people say that the bourgeois revolution in Britain is a Puritan revolution and established Britain's Puritan status.

The third person to appear in the Reformation was the King of England—Henry VIII. His influence was even greater, his actions brought the Reformation to its peak and established Protestantism in a dominant position. This process is full of drama and accidental factors. It is said to be accidental, in fact it is inevitable; it contains many stories and is very readable.

Henry VIII was the pioneer of the Tudor dynasty—the son of Henry VII. He has beautiful delicate eyes, strong heroic spirit, is good at literary and martial arts, archery, wrestling, and hunting; he has a good study of theology, and has deep attainments in engineering, shipbuilding, fortification and artillery; he is also a composer, can sing, act, and compose. At the beginning of his ascension, everyone had high hopes for him, but everyone did not expect him to start the process of England Reformation, but the reason was that he was about to divorce.

When Henry VIII succeeded to the throne, he formed a military alliance with Spain because Spain was powerful at that time and Henry VIII also married the daughter of the King of Spain. At the same time, he also made good relations with France, and with the help of the minister Thomas Wolsey, everything went well. The English Church in Henry VIII's time had many ills, such as bad teachers and monks, concubines, adultery, and alcoholism. The Church was degenerate and corrupt; at that time, Churches in all countries were similar. The Pope himself had some illegitimate children, and he asked the kings of various countries to arrange titles and fiefdoms for these illegitimate children. The upper beam is not right and the lower beam is crooked. The parish collects chicken, eggs, milk, cheese and fruit from the people; some priests ask the people for service allowances. The people dare not resist these extortions because the Church holds the keys to Heaven. For the general public, it would be a big deal if they could not ascend to Heaven? The wealth of the Church of England accounts for 1/5 of the country. But at first Henry VIII had no interest in Martin Luther. In order to prevent the spread of heresy, he wrote an article "Assertion of the Seven Sacraments against Martin Luther", which slandered Martin Luther; Luther also did not show weakness, he wrote a reply article, hitting back at Henry VIII, the relationship between the two became very stale. But then one thing happened, and the king broke into a divorce.

Henry VIII's queen, Catherine of Aragon, was the daughter of the twin kings of Spain, Ferdinand and Isabella who sponsored the Columbus voyage. She first came to England and married Henry VIII's brother Arthur. She was only 16 years old that year, but just six months after the marriage, Arthur died. In order to maintain this political marriage and to keep the dowry of 200,000 ducats brought by Catherine, Henry VII suggested that Catherine marries Arthur's brother, who was later Henry VIII. Catherine and Henry VIII agreed. After Henry VIII came to the throne, Catherine gave birth to six children for him in a row. Only one girl survived, the later Queen Mary. The thinking of the British at that time was similar to Chinese' thoughts, they hoped that the king would have a male offspring, because Mary had been betrothed to the Crown Prince of France. If Henry VIII had no sons, Mary would become Queen of England, her husband would be the King of France, England would become a province of France. At that time, there was only one queen in power in British history, during which there was a lot of trouble. The House of Tudor had only been established for about 40 years, not far from the wars of the Roses in British history. Therefore, Henry VIII still wanted a son to inherit the throne, but Catherine never became pregnant. In this case, there is only one way out, and the king divorces and marries again.

Henry VIII has found a target, it is the daughter of a nobleman, named Anne Boleyn. He hopes to have a son as soon as possible and inherit the throne. At the same time, his minister Wolsey expressed that Henry desire to marry Renée, daughter of French King Louis XII, when he went to France. Some people would say that Catherine's failure to be pregnant was not her fault and it may also be Henry's problem. During this period, Henry had an illegitimate child, who was named the Duke of Richmond and Somerset, with a woman named Elizabeth, but this was an out of wedlock and not recognized by everyone. To have a legal heir, Henry can only divorce and then marry, and the Pope's approval is required to divorce, indicating that the previous marriage is invalid, then the problem is coming. At that time, the Pope was a captive of the Holy Roman Emperor Charles V, and Charles V was the nephew of Catherine. Charles V did not want Henry VIII to divorce Catherine, because if Henry VIII divorced, he would probably marry the daughter of the King of France, which would become a marriage between Britain and France; Charles did not want to see this situation. Henry VIII stepped up activities and sent people to get money to the Pope to lobby, but the Pope did not want to offend Charles, because the Pope Clement was born in the Medici family, and the Medici family was expelled from Florence at this time; Venice People also came to take away the Pope's fief. The Pope needed Charles to help the Medici family regain Florence and the Pope's fief. Charles asked the Pope not to declare Henry and Catherine's marriage invalid (unless Catherine herself agreed).

Henry could not obtain divorce approval from the Pope. At this time, the aristocracy and businessmen in England were worried about the Church's assets; the domestic sentiment was dissatisfied with the Church's greed, many people hoped that the king would confiscate the Church's property. In this case, Henry used many means to separate the Church of England from Rome and proclaim the birth of the Anglican Church. Then, the Archbishop of Canterbury declared that Henry's marriage to Catherine was invalid and crowned the new queen, Anne; the Pope declared Henry's new marriage invalid and his biological children were illegitimate children. After a while, the new queen Anne gave birth to Elizabeth, who would later become Elizabeth I. Then England Parliament passed a bill to transfer all income from the Pope to the King of England, and the right to appoint bishops belongs to the King. The Parliament passed another bill declaring the supremacy of kingship; the power of the former Pope over the Church in England belongs to the king. From now on, the power of the Pope will never exist in the UK; Henry VIII will become the leader of the unity of Church and state. Anyone who opposes Henry VIII will be thrown into prison and sentenced. Among them, there is a famous figure, Thomas More, who wrote "Utopia". More comes from a family of lawyers and is very religious. He was elected to Congress at the age of 26 and later served as Speaker of the House of Representatives. In 1516, More wrote the "Utopia", which is a household name in the European continent. More himself is a gentleman, a standard husband, a standard father, and a model councillor. In the Utopia written by More, everyone does his best and takes what he needs. There is a public cafeteria, property is shared; there is no shortage of food, everyone works, although there are laws, but rarely used; marriage is free, and the king is lifelong; religion is freedom. Later, many utopian socialists, such as the "New Harmonious Village" established by Robert Owen, could see Utopia as a model. More was later recruited into the Privy Council by Henry, because Henry appreciated his character and ability, more became grand minister in attendance, but More opposed Protestantism, he had ordered many Protestants to be burned. He could not tolerate heresy, and he found that Henry VIII's was the biggest heresy. When he was 54 years old, he resigned and went home, but he was soon put in prison because he refused to put an end to the Pope's authority over the Church of England. More was a martyr, although he was very talented, he walked on the opposite side of the times, he was finally convicted of treason, and later the Holy See made More a saint.

The new queen Anne went on to give birth, but gave birth to a stillbirth. Henry was disappointed, and later accused Anne of being unfaithful to him, and executed Anne. After ten days, Henry married Anne's maid, Jane Seymour. After more than a year, Jane gave birth to a son, later Edward VI. But Jane died 12 days later, and Henry finally had a legal male heir.

On the issue of the Church, Henry went a step further, dissolving monasteries and confiscating their property. Henry was short of money, at that time, there were not many economic growth points in Britain. The confiscation of monasteries property was very pleasant and without resistance. England people were dissatisfied with the priests and the king dismissed the monks, more than 8,000 people; the property of the Church fell into the hands of industrial and commercial people, the old nobles disintegrated, and new nobles appeared.

Henry later married three more times and married three queens, one of whom was guillotined by him. Henry was in power for 37 years. During these 37 years, the England Reformation was basically completed. During the reign of his children, Edward and Elizabeth I, they consolidated the achievements of the Reformation, and England experienced a repetition of Queen Mary in the middle. By the beginning of the 17th century, after Elizabeth I's reign ended,

England was not far from the bourgeois revolution. Looking at the history of England Reformation, one will find a very interesting feature. The direct cause of England Reformation is not how much England King loves Protestantism, opposes the Pope, and insists on supporting the Reformation, but only that the England King wants a male heir. It was originally the King's personal marriage problem, due to the involvement of religion and international politics, it eventually led to the England Reformation. In fact, Henry VIII did not have a good impression of Protestantism at the beginning. Behind these complex phenomena, what are the factors that dominate the development of society? Is it just because of the king's marriage? What kind of inspiration can we get from historical stories? What kind of experience and lessons we have been summed up?

2.the role of the Reformation

In ancient society, one wanted to develop and receive education. In Europe education was controlled in the hands of the Christian Church; in China, the main content of education is the Confucian classics. When people are grown up and live their life, they do business and become officials, they cannot get away from the control and influence of religion. They pay a tithe in the West; in China, officials at first need to pass the imperial examinations which check their familiarity with the Confucian classics; Confucianism and bureaucracy are combined. In everyday life, people cannot do without the rules and regulations of religion. Moral etiquette restrains individuals, each person's thinking must also be consistent with religious theory; otherwise, he or she will be regarded as heretic and be put into a place of religious judgment; social publications must also be religious reviews. It can be said that, in the past society, except for the kings and officials at all levels, religion is very important but it has different manifestations in different countries. In some countries, the religions are obviously dominant, the political ties are tighter, and the role of religions in other countries are recessive. So obviously, agricultural society, dynastic countries, are a combination of politics and religion; in Europe, Pope controls the king; in China, the emperor represents God; in Islamic countries, the religious and political union are more closely linked. The combination of Church and state does not happen just in the highest political class. In fact, this is true in any social unit or grass-roots social organization. Authority occupies an important position in any organization, authority not only plays a leading role in power control, but also ideologically dominates, subordinates, like a bureaucratic system, the ancient Christian Church and the ancient Chinese political system, modern vertically integrated firm... This bureaucratic system is from top to bottom and looks like a pyramid-like structure. The people in different levels have different privileges, the person in high level has more privilege, more wealth and higher rank. The bureaucratic system relies on religion, ethics and modern scientific management thought.

In Europe, before the Reformation, the lay faithful could not read the Bible and Gospels, they could look at the statues in the churches, paintings and listen to Bishops or rare knowledgeable priests to understand their religion. One reason is that the Catholic Church issued a Decree at that time, prohibiting ordinary people from translating and reading the Bible. The second reason is that the Bible is written by Latin or Greek, most people did not understand Latin or Greek. The third reason is that with the invention of printing press in 1456, many books could be printed including the Bible and Gospels and ordinary people can look the Bible. In the late of 13th century, there was the first English Bible and it was translated by John Wycliffe, this book was prohibited by the Church. In the Reformation, Luther translated into the German Bible and it was another important contribution for the Reformation. Later there were the French Bible, the Italian Bible, the Spanish Bible, the Portuguese Bible, the Dutch Bible, the Bohemian Bible, the Nordic Bible... The printing press and the Reformation make ordinary people can read the Bible and don't need the Church and the clergy to explain.

The clergy was ignorant and corrupt. So, the people started to make their own mind about their religion and Luther and others were disgusted by the corruption of the Pope and high clergy. The Church logic is that the indulgences were a kind of pardon/forgiveness of some sins and for people who were constantly menaced of damnation and going to Hell, it looked revolting that some could escape the punishment by paying, it increased the corruption of the Church. The method of spending money to eliminate disasters means God could accept bribes, if God receive money, individual sins will be eliminated. The practice of the Catholic Church naturally caused the honest man opposite and dissatisfied. Because according to this logic, if individuals get rich through proper channels, thrift in life, through business circulation, through starting a business, and through technological innovation, wouldn't it be better than bribing God? Isn't it better to get God's approval? Why there is the "original sin" in legitimate business success? There is a concept in Buddhism-"karma". Buddhism does not consider "bad karma", that is, bad deeds can be bought with money, and the elimination of "bad karma" depends on their own good action.

So, Reformation allowed people to study and criticise their religion, gave them responsibility for their own salvation. Individuals can talk directly with God, and churches and priests are no longer needed as intermediaries. The authority of the Church is questioned, and individuals get rid of the spiritual control of authority. Protestantism sees successful businessmen as rewarded by God for their good conduct, before all of the individuals success must be attributed to the Church. Now the developed countries in the world are basically Protestant countries. In modern history, although Spain made great achievements in the age of navigation, Spain discovered the Americas, established many colonies, and gained a lot of wealth, it is known as the world's first empire that sun never sets. However, in Spain the religion is still the Catholic tradition and there is no the Reformation. Until today, most people in Spain still believe in Catholicism. Compared with other European countries in the same period, Spain has no system innovation in economy and politics. After the 17th century, Spain slowly declined and is rarely seen on the international stage. Ancient Chinese thinker Mozi said, "So, the honoured and the rich cannot but obey the will of Heaven. He who obeys the will of Heaven, loving universally and benefiting others, will obtain rewards. He who opposes the will of Heaven, by being partial and unfriendly and harming others, will incur punishment."

In the history of Western countries, society first broke away from the control of religion and developed a new religious ethic --- Protestant ethics, which is conducive to the development of capitalism and is conducive to the progress of science. This stage is called the Reformation in the West. The importance of Reformation lies in the fact that Protestants opposed religious ceremonies; the individual broke away from the protection and guidance of the Churches and clergy, and the individual has autonomy. Many modern scientist and enlightenment scholars, such as Newton, Locke, Voltaire, Montesquieu, Rousseau, Kant, Fichte, Hegel ... engaged in research because of interest, hobbies and personal missions; no leader commanded them to do so. Scientific research can be combined with business. Individual can develop without relying on religion, the influence of religion is weakened.

Before Reformation, the Western Church possesses a large amount of fertile land, levying a tithe, levying interest on loans, and the Church class is corrupt and had departed far from the dedication of the early days of Christianity. Finally, the Reformation broke out because the Church sells indulgences. After the Reformation, the influence of religion shrank, scientific thought advanced and occupied the areas of religious control, so that people could devote their energies to scientific research. Protestant ethics views business achievements as the crystallization of a rational way of life, and wealth is an expression of individual ability. Some scholars, Talcott Parsons, who wrote "The Structure of Social Action", analysed that ancient China was superior to Europe in many conditions with fewer commercial restrictions, more free movement of personnel, more equal status, and less feudalization. The ethics of China also pursued the secular interests of the world and was more rationally as if China has been more able to develop capitalism long ago, but this is not the case. In ancient China, in fact, the protection of private property was lacking. The bureaucracy occupies an important position in social life, it is a typical bureaucratic society. This kind of social structure inhibits the development of commerce and further breakthroughs in commerce. The maturity of the ancient Chinese society and political system has prevented commerce from moving forward in overseas trade and joint stock management. Even if businessmen had the money, they could not use the funds for the expansion of reproduction. Instead, they were used to buy government officials positions or hoped future generations to enter government and could not complete the cycle of capital. It can say that the wealth of the East is mainly used for consumption, while the wealth of the West is more productive. Confucianism maintains the bureaucratic rule, it is traditional, but modern capitalism developed just after breaking the religion control.

It is a big topic why China did not take the lead in entering capitalism. Ancient China had some advantages. The previous chapters analysed it from an economic and political perspective. Economically, ancient China developed into a domestic system, but in terms of overseas trade, it is a laggard, there is no form of partnership and joint-stock company. Politically, the bureaucratic system is leading and mature in the agricultural society; in economic organizations, there were domestic system, in financial field, it invented paper money. This chapter analyses from the perspective of religion and ethics. Confucianism is conducive to maintaining the traditional social order. In a traditional agricultural society, politically, it is conducive to breaking blood ties and developing geographical factors, and it maintains the stability of traditional society, but it is not suitable for industrial society. It can be seen that religion or ethics in society and political systems are complementary, they adapt to each other, complement each other, and interact. From the history of the development of Chinese society for more than one hundred years, it can be seen that in the process of integrating Chinese society into the world industrial system, the Taiping Civil War, the Self-Strengthening Movement, Hundred Days' Reform in 1898, the Boxer Movement, 1911 Revolution, the rule of warlords, and the New Culture Movement, Lenin-style party, foreign war, civil war, socialist construction, cultural revolution, reform and opening up, constantly changing in the economic, political, and ideological fields, iterative cycle.

In the economic and commercial aspects of modern society, traditional ethics are still influential. Hong Kong, Macau and Taiwan, Southeast Asia, South Korea, Japan, these countries and regions were affected by Chinese civilization, or Confucian cultural areas, have developed modern enterprises. In East Asia, Hong Kong, Taiwan, Singapore, and South Korea have developed very well, they can be regarded as developed countries and regions. Japan is a member of the G7 countries; in economy, Japan is the world's third largest state. In the companies in East Asia and Southeast Asia, the family factor, blood relationship is more important, such as Toyota in Japan, Samsung Electronics in South Korea, Chinese family companies in Southeast Asia and so on. Traditional Chinese culture and ethics also pay great attention to family. Traditional ethics are not enough in business, there is not much content about industry and commerce. The traditional mainstream Confucianism emphasizes "value just above material gains", although one student of Confucius—Zigong is a big businessman; Mohist thought "multilateral benefiting" is conducive to the development of industry and commerce. From personal experience, thinkers in the Spring and Autumn Period and Warring States Period were born in declining aristocrats, bureaucrats, and handicraftsmen, but not many thinkers who were born or engaged in commerce. Laozi was the director of the library in the Zhou Dynasty and Confucius served as minister of justice in the Lu State; Zhuang Zhou was a small official; Mozi was born in a handicraft industry; and Han Fei was a nobleman. Ancient Chinese thought was lacking, especially in natural science. Thales of Miletus, the first philosopher in ancient Greece, was engaged in business, studied abroad, visited many countries, observed solar and lunar eclipses, and calculated the height of pyramids. There is a story about Thales. There was a time when Thales was relatively poor. At that time, the ordinary person laughed at Thales for being good at philosophy, but he was so poor that he could hardly support himself, and that ridicule philosophy was not the science of helping the poor. One year, Thales made climate predictions through astronomical observations, predicting that the olive trees would have a bumper harvest in the coming summer, so he rented oil pressing equipment in various oil mills in Miletus and Chios at a very low price. By the next year when the harvest season came, olives had a bumper harvest. Since the oil extraction equipment was controlled by Thales, those who needed oil extraction came to Thales, and they had to pay the rent for the equipment at Thales' high price. As a result, Thales made a fortune, which proved to the world that philosophers can become rich at any time as long as they have the will. Thales' experience is very different from that of ancient Chinese thinkers. Thinkers such as Laozi, Confucius, Mozi, Mencius, Zhuang Zhou, Xun Kuang, and Han Fei do not leave us stories about their survival in the market. They are more willing to interact with government of ancient countries and hope to be appreciated by the monarchs of various countries. When talking about the origin of civilization, I mentioned that Chinese civilization is relatively isolated in terms of environment. Chinese civilization emphasizes politics, neglects economy, and emphasizes agriculture and restrain business. Generally speaking, commercial development is not enough.

In chapter 16 and chapter 17, there will be a detailed analysis of Chinese classical thought, ethics and religion, analysis of the functions and roles of Confucianism, Taoism, and Buddhism in society.

3.the similarities and differences between the evolution of religion and the development of computer.

The above is the history of modern Western Christian Reform. We can combine this historical process with the history of computer development and we will find many similar characteristics.

The history of the development of computer science is actually similar to the evolution of the Church. I mentioned that Babbage invented the difference machine, but it was all mechanical. The invention of modern computers was realized on the basis of the invention of vacuum tube and transistor. During the World War II, aircraft have been widely used in warfare. In order to counter aircraft, ground artillery fire needs to calculate the trajectory of the aircraft and the flight trajectory of artillery shells and missiles. In terms of information warfare, Germany used an advanced encryption device-Enigma machine at that time. In order to decipher, various methods were used by the Allies of World War II. The first was from the perspective of linguistics, and then the password was deciphered by mathematical methods; this also required a lot of calculations. In this context, the United Kingdom first developed a computer (Colossus) for deciphering passwords, while the United States developed the world's first electronic technology computer—ENIAC (Electronic Numerical Integrator and Computer). This ENIAC has the size of a room, a total weight of 30 tons, is equipped with 18,000 vacuum tubes, 1,500 electromagnetic relays, 70,000 resistors, 18,000 capacitors, and costs 486,000 U.S. dollars. Such a behemoth! How is its computing power? It can perform ballistic calculations, weather forecasts, nuclear energy, cosmic rays, thermal ignition, wind tunnel test design and other tasks. It can say that the need of war has given birth to the emergence of computers.

The early computers were huge in size, they were all made up of vacuum tubes, and the memory was very few. They could not be compared with today's computers or even mobile phones. Early computer customers were mainly the military, government departments and large enterprises, and individuals rarely had the opportunity to use computers. Later, with the invention of the transistor, it was widely used in the manufacture of computers; and the next step was the invention of integrated circuits, so that computers could be made smaller and smaller, but in the 1960s and 1970s, computers were still very large, only large institutions, such as government departments, large enterprises, schools, and the military, can equip themselves and use computers. At that time, computers were used in this way. In institutions that used computers, the computers were stored in a separate computer room, and many computer terminals were provided for customers to use. The computer terminals did not have computing and storage capabilities and were mainly used by users to communicate with computer hosts. Each user gets a certain amount of time on the computer. Since there may be many users using the computer at the same time, the computer cannot process so many user requests at the same time, so it is necessary to process the requests of different users in different time, which is called time sharing; processing means that the computer processes a user's request during a certain period of time, and then processes other users' requests after this period of time. The user communicates with computer host through the display screen and keyboard, the user codes a program, submits the code, and the computer host processes the calculation and returns the result to the terminal or prints it out. I remember that Oracle Corporation later proposed the concept of a Network Computer (NC), which is actually an extension of this terminal. Now the cloud computing concept proposed is actually a subsequent concept of network computer. Although the mobile terminal now has strong computing and storage capabilities, it still needs to provide a large amount of information storage, processing and calculation functions on the server side. The simplest example is to query the weather forecast. The mobile terminal only makes this request, the database in the server query and can send the weather conditions of different cities every day or even every hour to the mobile terminal, and data like satellite maps are stored on the server.

The invention of integrated circuits made possible the appearance of central processing units (CPU) and random access memory (RAM). In this way, computers can be further miniaturized. As mentioned in the chapter 14, in the late 1970s, Apple computers appeared. It looks like a computer terminal; it is not big and the price is not too expensive. In this way, every family can have a computer to do financial statements and text editing at home. Every American must file taxes, accounting software has become an important application for the popularization of microcomputers. Later, after microcomputers had a graphical interface, they could do more and more work, such as computer graphics, graphics and image processing, and making videos. In the 1970s and 1980s, microcomputers were mainly working independently. At Xerox Palo Alto Research Center (PARC), some experts developed Ethernet to connect computers in a laboratory. At the same time, there is a network among various universities and research institutions in the United States, and their computers can also communicate. This network began to be called ARPA, which is mainly used for scientific research and military purposes and is not open to the public. It is composed of large computers distributed in various universities, and data are shared and distributed among computers. After the popularization of computer graphical interfaces in the 1980s, an English man, Berners Lee, invented hypertext in 1990, which is the file browsing format of today's World Wide Web, which can be run on different computer systems. ARPA later opened up to the society and formed the Internet today. Needless to say, the importance of the Internet is critical. After the appearance of the Internet, there was a great explosion of information, and various information and applications on the Internet were very rich. Information retrieval, web homepage, web blog, we media, online shopping, online payment, instant messaging, online video, downloading music, mobile navigation, map browsing, booking hotels, purchase air tickets and train tickets, smart phones have become people's daily necessities. These are all realized when mobile terminals have very powerful computing and storage capabilities. Mobile phones have not only entered the family, but also become a daily essential tool of everyone.

If you think computer terminals as living individuals, you will find that the development and evolution of religion and the development of computers have a lot in common. Individuals in the Middle Ages, like serfs, were tied to the land and depended on renting the land of the manor. They were religiously controlled by the Church. In the early days of computer development, computer terminals had simple functions and no computing power, and the processing of information was done by the computer host. The development of cities in the late Middle Ages promoted the revival of commerce. Individuals can have a lot of wealth by doing business, breaking the original social pattern. With the development of computers, terminals in the era of microcomputers have strong computing and storage capabilities, capable of completing many tasks independently, and are no longer restricted by the computer host. Similarly, the evolution of smart phones has similar characteristics. In the beginning, the mobile phone was just a mobile communication terminal; later, with the enhancement of functions, it was combined with the Internet and become a smart phone with many computer functions and intelligent terminals. We know that ancient societies were generally divided into slave owners and slaves; in the Middle Ages, they became lords and serfs. Slave owners and lords were the authority of the past era; slaves and serfs were the objects of oppression, but they were still different. The condition of serfs was better than slaves. Slaves did not have any property and belonged to slave owners; serfs rented the land of the lord and had a certain degree of personal freedom, but they had to perform military service and corvee. The reason why modern European society was able to enter the capitalism society ahead of other regions, after Reformation and political system changes, serfdom disintegrated, individuals gained more property and freedom, and gained more space for mobility. Serfdom was transformed into wage labor, and the economic center shifted from agriculture to industry and commerce, and from rural to urban areas. It provided more space for the development of businessmen and entrepreneurs. The religion was converted from Catholicism to Protestantism, and individuals were encouraged to engage in industry and commerce. The original social structure disintegrated and a new social order was created. In the Middle Ages, there were religious oppression and aristocratic rule; in the capitalism society, it has become materialism and workers' strikes, and the scientific management thought has also entered the stage of history as a way to solve strikes. The whole society has progressed and people have mastered more scientific knowledge. Today the development of computers has not been the structure of computer hosts and terminals in the past, but the structure of clients and servers, network intelligent terminals and large-scale network nodes. The terminals are more intelligent, and the computing ability of modern smart phones are better than the original computers. In computer networks, there are also large-scale network nodes, their computing power is much stronger than that of ordinary computers. They act as address decoding, distribute and transmit data, and provide mail services in the network; this structure replaces the previous structure of computer mainframes and terminals. The computer industry needs to develop in different products, like quantum computers; the development of robots will make terminals more intelligent and network speeds faster. The development of computers has a significant impact on business management and people's work and life. Some management experts, such as Simon, have realized that many new occupations and new ways of working have emerged in social life. At the same time, because of the development of computers in business management, a computer information management system has emerged, which integrates the company's person, finances, and materials. Based on information technology, it optimizes its resources, improves its business processes, and enhances its core competitiveness. The development of the Internet has provided people with lower-cost and easier-to-use tools for communication.

In short, any theory and doctrine cannot remain unchanged and has always been correct. Newton's classical physics in science later proved to be limited in space and time. When the speed of an object reaches the speed of light, it is necessary to use the theory of relativity to explain. The thinking of a society cannot be immutable. If a society wants to develop and progress, it must break the original situation, break through the original constraints, break the chains that restrict social development, break away from the unfavorable constraints and control of social development, and encourage innovation and new technologies, and encourages innovation in organization.

16 CHAPTER CHINESE CLASSICAL THOUGHT AND ETHICS

This topic is very big, and it's difficult to describe it thoroughly. Chinese classical thought, ethics and religion are part of the Chinese culture. The Chinese culture is broad and profound, with a long history, and accumulated countless experiences and knowledge, it cannot be expressed clearly in several paragraphs. From ancient times to the present, so many literati and scholars have studied the Chinese culture, about a certain part, aspect and writing of traditional thought and culture, they can write a lot of books. But since this book talks about the religion and the Reformation, the similarities between the Reformation and the development of computers, and the comparison of the modern scientific management thought, the vertically integrated firm with the Chinese classical philosophy and political systems, it is inevitable to talk about Chinese classical thought, culture and religion. According to the methods of the enterprise development and the scientific management mentioned above, when talking about the ancient Chinese thought, it can also be divided into the practice of politicians, the formation of the ancient bureaucratic government, the emergence of classical thought and the development and evolution of later thoughts, etc., Because this book still focuses on the content of economics and management, it is only a comparison of the classical thought with the scientific management. Therefore, there is no in-depth analysis of the Chinese classical thought and the ancient political system. I hope readers understand the shortcomings.

The Chinese classical thought is closely related to the people's level of knowledge, the mode of production, the scientific and technical level of the ancient society. Some content is not necessarily suitable for today's society, and it requires serious thinking, analysis, and judgment. I think spiritual things like culture and religion are not just a kind of knowledge, but also they need to be felt and experienced.

In this book, we can see that in the business management, the scientific management thought is closely related to the vertically integrated firm, and in political systems, religion, ethics are also closely related to political systems; their roles are similar, and they all rely on and interact with each other. The Chinese culture and religion are inextricably linked with the Chinese classical philosophy, ethics, and they are organically integrated. The content is all-encompassing, broad, profound and colorful, and contains all aspects of the society. In here, it is just to explain some of my views and experiences and I mainly talk about the ancient Chinese thought, ethics, and religion from the perspective of its function and the role played in society.

Regarding the ancient Chinese thought, ethics, and religion, this topic can be divided into two parts for discussion. According to the order of the historical development, we first talk about the Chinese classical thought, philosophy, and ethics, and then we talk about the ancient Chinese religion. How did the religion in ancient China come into being and how it is related to the classical thought? First, let's talk about the Chinese traditional and classical thinking and philosophy.

1.The background of the birth of the Chinese classical thought and its role in society

The Chinese classical thought is more regarded as a kind of ethics and a kind of philosophy, which is different from religion; it is quite different from the ancient India and somewhat similar to the ancient Greek philosophy. In the history of the human being development, from the 8th century BC to the 2nd century BC; in ancient Greece, ancient India, the Middle East and ancient China, many thinkers and philosophers appeared at the same time, and the phenomenon was called by historians as the historical "The Axial Age". The ancient Greek philosophy is a natural science, based on logic and mathematics, metaphysical thoughts, such as atomism, Euclidean geometry, Pythagoreanism and so on; the ancient India produced various types of religions, such as Brahmanism, Hinduism, Buddhism, Jainism, Sikhism, etc., with their methods of speculation, emphasis on the afterlife, and pursuit of transcendence; the ancient Chinese philosophy is regarded as a kind of ethics, focusing on the present world, focusing on how to deal with the relationship between people, the relationship between man and nature, and the relationship between man and society.

The Chinese classical thought is not only a doctrine and a theory, it is also a way of life and it includes philosophy and economics, politics, military, diplomacy, education, science and technology, medicine, life, etc. Before the emergence of the Chinese classical philosophy, in the society, the political systems were hereditary and aristocratic, birth determined fate, the society was organized according to blood relationship. After the emergence of the classical philosophy, it broke this limitation, individuals can receive various kinds of education, seek honour and rank and become officials. The society recruits talents according to their morality and personal abilities. Individuals have greater initiative than in the past, and the content of learning becomes more important. The world and the human being knowledge are endless, and it is impossible for a person in a short period of time to learn all the knowledge. The social education has its utilitarian nature, and what an individual learns in school is a knowledge that is helpful for personal career and development.

Now in society there is the primary education, secondary education or higher education, especially higher education, according to the division of majors, everyone learns their own knowledge of professional field; after graduation, they move to work positions and work according to their majors. After joining the world of work, according to the situation of the organization and company that an individual joins, the organization and company provide various benefits, such as pay, housing payment reserve fund, endowment insurance, medical insurance, vacation, and children's education. The organizations and companies also provide opportunities for continuing education, and this kind of education may be a kind of management education to provide preparation for personal promotion, and it belongs to category of vocational education. Such a functional division of labor certainly has its advantages. Individuals can concentrate their main energy on their own professional fields and the company business, and promote the development of the organization and the company. If the organization and the company develop well, they can provide more benefits and treatment for individuals; but at the same time, there are limitations. The personal vision and knowledge are limited and they are limited to the company's business. Only the company's management, middle managers and top managers are selected, and receive further education and training, they have more knowledge in management. Anyone in this model is generally confined to the fields and professions that he is familiar with; it is not easy to engage in other jobs across majors and fields, because they need to learn a new knowledge; it is still possible to learn similar knowledge. The way for an ordinary person to rise in society is like this: they first learn a professional knowledge in school, and then they start to work after graduation; they start to engage in grassroots work, and are gradually promoted to middle management positions, and gradually have more management skills and knowledge; a small number of people will be promoted to top management positions. The higher the management position, the fewer the positions and the higher the pay. In the end, only a few people can reach the top management position. This model exists in the ancient Chinese society or in the current vertically integrated firm. In this way, with the development of society and the progress of knowledge, on the one hand, the knowledge in society is enriched; but on the other hand, the knowledge that individuals can master is actually limited to a certain field. In the ancient society, it was limited to moral and ethical knowledge like Confucianism. In any organization and society, like the ancient China, the inventions and creations of natural science knowledge and technology will have a certain impact on the original system. In a stable society, there is always a kind of resistance to new things and new inventions and the new technological inventions and creations need to be incorporated into the original system. Therefore, the ancient Chinese society has been in a very stable state for a long time because there were no new thoughts and no technological innovation. From the first emperor of Qin Shi Huang in the Qin dynasty to the last dynasty-Qing dynasty, there is a continuous cycle of dynasties. The structure of each dynasty was similar. Politically, there was an imperial examination system, an official selection and a supervision system; economically it was a small-peasant economy in autarky; the handicraft industry remained at the stage of the domestic system, and the level of science and technology could not exceed the level of an agricultural society.

The same problem exists in the modern enterprise management. The management of the enterprise attaches a great importance to those talents who can directly and quickly bring benefits and profits to the enterprise. The performance of the enterprise stocks in the market is directly linked to the personal interests of the enterprise managers. Research directions that are inconsistent in the field of development or inconsistent with the company's development strategy, projects with high market risks will not be taken seriously by the company's management, and will not be subject to key training and capital allocation; new ideas and designs that want to become actual product require repeated approvals. Most people in the world are pursuing the interests directly related to them, promotion, gaining wealth, rising in social status, etc. In an organization or a company, if the organization and company cannot align with the interests of individuals; if the development goals of the organization and company is integrated into the personal interests of its managers, the development of the organization and the company will be limited. The so-called enterprise transformation is nothing more than transferring the enterprise from one strategic direction to another, and transferring the enterprise from a saturated market to another emerging market; however, this kind of transformation is not easy. It lies in entering from a familiar field to an unfamiliar field, new knowledge and skills must be learned, and innovation will have an impact on the original interest groups. If the organization and the company management system is not suitable for learning new skills or cannot innovate further, then the transformation will fail. What is expressed here is a simple model, the reality of the organization and enterprises is much more complicated. There will be various factors in the development of the enterprises, there will be nepotism in the immature stage of the enterprise development; after the management mechanism becomes mature, there will still be teacher-student relations, alumni relations, regional factors and interest groups, etc. There are emotional factors such as competition and jealousy, and it is difficult for a large company to completely get rid of so many complex factors and the company has to take care of various interest groups. While small companies are relatively in a more advantageous position in dealing with these problems, and they need to deal with fewer complex factors. The enterprise management can focus on product research and market development, and small businesses can transform quickly. If an organization and enterprise always focus a lot of attention and resources on certain parts or certain field, it will be much more difficult to shift to other areas.

During the Spring and Autumn period and the Warring States period, the original political system and values were disintegrated, social mobility was strengthened, individuals had more initiative, and a new social class emerged. At that time, it was said that "manners collapses and music is bad"(The old law and system were greatly destroyed). How to face new situation at that time? How to treat power and wealth? How to better survive in society? How to treat yourself? How to establish the goal an individual pursues? This is a problem that classical thought needed to face and solve in society at that time. The various Chinese classical thoughts came into being and put forward their own solutions and ideas. The birth of the Chinese classical thought can be regarded as the inevitable result of the development of the society and knowledge at that time. Productivity has increased, knowledge has increased, and the division of knowledge has appeared. Everyone can only engage in a knowledge field of a certain specialty and direction. In this field, those persons who break through are called experts and scholars. In the ancient China, especially before the Spring and Autumn and Warring States, during the Xia, Shang, and Zhou dynasty, witchcraft did play a great role in society, wizards or priests often possessed a lot of knowledge. In these ancient times, there was no distinction between the witchcraft and the medicine, witch and historian. These phenomena are recorded in many ancient books. During the Spring and Autumn and Warring States period, the emergence of the classical philosophy led to the development and differentiation of knowledge, and many specialized knowledge fields appeared, such as philosophy, administration, military, diplomacy, politics, economics, science, technology, medicine, etc. In each field, there are some representatives, from the perspective of the government, any government needs talents who are good at administration, politics, and diplomacy, and government gives these talents a certain social status, a certain amount of power, and various benefits and treatment. The ancient Chinese officials at all levels enjoyed different powers, benefits and treatment according to their ranks. If a person has status and better treatment in society, other problems can be solved easily, and he can enjoy various services provided by the government, according to different status. This is the same way that modern enterprises provide various benefits.

With the development and increase of knowledge, the content of knowledge learning and the attitude towards knowledge learning have become increasingly important. There is no end to knowledge in the world. The ancient Chinese thinkers recognized this, but their attitudes are different. Confucianism, like the motto of Confucius is "When I walk along with two others, they may serve me as my teachers", "learning without satiety and instructing others without being wearied", "Isn't it pleasant to learn with a constant perseverance and application?" Confucianism holds a positive attitude towards knowledge learning. But the attitude of Taoism, like Zhuang Zhou said, "There is a limit to our life, but to knowledge there is no limit. With what is limited to pursue after what is unlimited is a perilous thing." It puts life in a higher position and pays more attention to the value of life.

2.Confucianism

Confucianism is a mainstream thought and officially recognized in the ancient Chinese society. It is conducive to breaking the society of blood relationship organization, is conducive to the equality of education, and is conducive to social mobility. It can be seen that the scientific management thought plays a similar role in the current society. The scientific management thought is also a mainstream management thought and is recognized by the industrial society, which is conducive to the equalization of social opportunities, the popularization of education, and the upward and downward mobility of management positions in enterprises. The Confucian thought represented by Confucius and the scientific management thought represented by Taylor are both mainstream thoughts at a certain stage of society. As a representative of Confucianism, Confucius was the first person who started universal education. "Education without Distinction". There are 3,000 disciples and 72 famous persons in his students. Confucius was honored as the "model teacher of every ages" by later generations, all the China dynasties respected Confucius. The direct descendants of Confucius were appointed for "Duke Yansheng", the rank of nobility is hereditary. In the dynastic society, no matter how the dynasty changes, the status of the direct descendants of Confucius remained unchanged. There are data showing that the descendants of Confucius have reached a number of 3 million people. These are all well-founded and there are historical data available for query. It is said that Confucius once asked Laozi, a representative of Taoism, for courtesy and advice, but Laozi was not as influential as Confucius in teaching students and popularizing education. Confucius' thoughts may have a limited scope of application today, but Confucius' practice of propagating education has indeed had a very significant impact and significance on ancient society and even today. The great physicist Newton once said, "If I have seen further, it is by standing on the shoulders of giants." Newton's law of universal gravitation is based on Kepler's laws of planetary motion. Classical physics is applicable when the speed of objects is not fast; when studying atomic physics and particle physics, it has been replaced by relativity and quantum physics. Newton's greatness lies not in the permanent correctness of his physical theory, but the set of scientific experiment methods that Newton created is also the standard of scientific research today. Taylor, the founder of scientific management thought, is in a similar situation. Taylor's scientific management thoughts are mainly devoted to production management and many subjects of enterprise management are not included. However, the scientific management method that Taylor created can be practiced in enterprises and taught in schools. Taylor's students inherited Taylor's thoughts, further carried forward, gradually improved, and expanded their influence.

Confucianism stresses benevolence, righteousness, manners, wisdom, and trustworthiness, and emphasizes "harmony" and seeks common ground while reserving differences. In Chinese history, multiple religions can coexist, and the Chinese culture is also comprehensive and open-minded, and can continuously absorb the good points of other civilizations in the world, like Buddhism is a foreign religion for China. Confucianism talks about "Tao" (the way) and "Virtue", "What the great learning teaches, is to illustrate illustrious virtue." It talks about how to deal with interpersonal relationships and how to get along with people around you. Confucianism advocates saying less and doing more. "A gentleman wishes to be slow in his speech and earnest in his conduct.", while the Western loves to analyze and debate. The ancient Chinese bureaucracy dominated by Confucianism focused on literature rather than science and technology, and focused on poetry creation, not invention and creation. Officials and literati of successive dynasties in Chinese history spent a lot of their time on poetry creation. The Classic of Poetry in the Xia, Shang and Zhou

Dynasties, "Chu Ci" and prose of philosophers in the Spring and Autumn and Warring States, Han prose in Han dynasty, Yuefu poems in Wei-Jin-Northern and Southern period, and the poems of Tang dynasty, the verses of Song dynasty, Yuan songs and novels in Ming and Qing dynasty. Poetry, verses, songs have become the most brilliant part of the Chinese culture. Confucianism talks about the way of dealing with people. People always have to live in society, society is complicated, there are all kinds of people in society. Confucianism talks about how to get along with people, seek advantages and avoid disadvantages; but it does not talk about natural science. When talking about Maslow earlier, he mentioned that technological innovation will have an impact on the original situation; the people who are engaged in innovation are always different, and harmony and innovation are contradictory. Modern industrial civilization emphasizes science and technology, and is relatively weak in the handling of interpersonal relationships. A society that only emphasizes science and technology or only emphasizes interpersonal relationships is not comprehensive, and requires both. Innovation and development of science and technology, natural science knowledge and ethics, there is no problem which is important or unimportant. If you need technological innovation, you should learn natural science and technology; if you need to deal with interpersonal relationships, you should emphasize ethics. As Zen said, if you are hungry, you need to eat; if you are tired, you should go to sleep.

One era has the belief of one era. In the past, the ethics of agricultural society had to be changed to adapt to industrial society. In the future, higher-level society will have new changes in culture and beliefs. Only emphasizing science and technology will result in poor handling of interpersonal relationships and various social moral issues. People always have to live in society and there will be various contradictions. Significant scientific advances and inventions do not appear frequently, and have certain cycles. After the development of material civilization in modern society, the spiritual level is lacking. People are not completely satisfied with material aspects, modern people have this experience, too much material abundance can bring spiritual emptiness. The blind pursuit of material wealth sometimes affects the fulfilment of higher needs, peace of mind can enable individuals and teams to reach a higher stage. Everyone needs to have beliefs, whether they believe in a shaman, or God, Allah and others, there will be conflicts between different beliefs. Different religions or different sects of the same religion will have many contradictions. Therefore, ethics can play a reconciling role, which can reduce or avoid various contradictions caused by different beliefs. Therefore, the Chinese classical thought, like Confucianism, still has its value today.

Confucianism was the mainstream thought in Chinese society in the past, but with the development of the times and society, it can be seen that Confucianism has limitations. Confucianism emphasizes the relationship between people, and Confucianism does not include natural science. The content of Confucianism also has certain limitations on the understanding of life. It is only a part of Chinese classical thought, and it is a very influential part. Confucianism is very popular with the ancient Chinese rulers because Confucianism emphasizes hierarchy and order. Without great progress in science and technology, and under the condition that the mode of production and economic organization remain unchanged, Confucianism is very useful and can effectively maintain social stability.

Confucianism somewhat despises people engaged in natural science research. Mencius, the representative of Confucianism, once said, "Headworker ruled the people while the handworker ruled by the people"(officials are headworker). The main purpose of learning and believing in Confucianism is to be able to install government officials who have status and privileges, so that they can meet various needs, and the study of science and technology in ancient China can't achieve this goal, so the mainstream attitudes in ancient Chinese society somewhat despised science and technology. Science and technology were considered "diabolic tricks and wicked craft". People engaged in scientific and technological research were not valued by the ancient Chinese society and they had no status in society. Just as the managers dominate the engineers in modern enterprises, engineers cannot freely carry out scientific and technological research, and are restricted by the management in terms of research funding and personal status. In Silicon Valley, companies are all founded by creative engineers. Creative engineers receive venture capital and conduct research in the direction that they are interested in or think it has market potential. Engineers control the company. This is quite different from traditional corporate management. The bureaucratic system dominated by the Chinese classical thought can effectively maintain social stability without major technological breakthroughs and no foreign competitors. Just like the modern monopoly company, in the absence of major technological breakthroughs, or in the absence of disruptive innovation, existing management methods can maintain the monopoly of the company in the market. The most typical example of disruptive innovation is mobile phones. The emergence of smart phones on the phone market appeared under a completely market-oriented, competitive and exchange-filled condition, just like the microcomputer market in the 1980s and 1990s, and the international situation faced by the China Qing Dynasty in the 19th century; it is all in a competitive environment and full of exchanges, the original monopoly organizations face new challenges. IBM faced challenges from many compatible companies and many independent software companies, while the Qing Dynasty in the 19th century faced constant invasions by the Western countries. The original management system and the management thought are not suitable for the new situation, the rapidly changing market environment and society. In the 19th and 20th centuries, science and technology have made rapid developments in physics, chemistry, biology, medicine, and electric power, automobile, aviation, aerospace, energy and many other engineering fields are progressing rapidly.

3.Taoism

In addition to Confucianism, the Chinese classical thought also includes Taoism thought, Mohism thought, Legalism thought, military thought, Yin-Yang school thought, medical thought and political strategists thought, etc. These thoughts together with Confucian thought constituted the traditional Chinese thought. Talking about one aspect alone is not enough to fully explain traditional Chinese thought. Taoism includes natural sciences, and emphasizes the understanding of life. For instance, when the ancient Taoist looked for immortality medicine, in the process of alchemy, they invented gunpowder. Talking about the content of Taoism including natural science, I remember Dr. Joseph Needham in the United Kingdom. He started as an embryologist. Later, he was attracted by the Chinese culture and studied the history of science and technology in China and spent most of his life on this subject. He came to study ancient Chinese science and technology and wrote the book "Science and Civilization in China", which has a great influence. However, because Taoism also lacks metaphysical speculation, and lacks the formal logic of ancient Greece, the natural science is not integrated with handicraft and commerce; at the same time, the mainstream Confucianism despises natural science, and the traditional Chinese society is based on politics, so the traditional Chinese science and technology did not take the same path as in the Western world, but developed in certain technical fields; it is more some kind of accumulation of experience, and it did not form a complete natural science system that narrated in modern language. Like the ancient Chinese mathematics, it is more of a kind of algebra than geometry. The ancient Chinese society later accepted Buddhist thought with speculative content, which made up for the shortcomings of the traditional Chinese thought.

Taoism, including Chinese classical medicine, is explained by the theory of Yin-Yang and the theory of the five elements. The theory of Yin-Yang does have an application value in elaborating phenomena such as the evolution process. The theory of Yin-Yang is also an important part of the Chinese classical medicine theory. The traditional Chinese medicine thought was formed during the Spring and Autumn period and Warring States period, which is roughly the same as the period when the other Chinese classical thoughts emerged. The Chinese classical medicine is now called traditional Chinese medicine, its theories and Taoist thoughts have the same origin and are worthy to describe. The traditional Chinese medicine has always been the mainstream medicine in the ancient Chinese society, and it has been proved to be effective in practice. Its main theories are the theory of Yin-Yang, the theory of the five elements, the theory of visceral manifestations and the theory of meridian and collateral. The theory of Yin-Yang explains that Yin and Yang are the origin of life, and the evolution of everything in the world can be explained by the concept of Yin and Yang, including natural phenomena, climate changes and the characteristics of life. In the traditional Chinese medicine, the balance of Yin and Yang is used to explain the health status of the human body and the causes of diseases. The theory of Yin and Yang is also suitable for explaining the process of social evolution. The market evolution process discussed later can also be explained by the theory of Yin and Yang. The theory of Yin and Yang can also be used today to explain many physiological phenomena. For instance, the blood in the human body normally has two mechanisms. One is the hemolysis mechanism, which prevents blood clotting and promotes blood flow; the other is the blood coagulation mechanism, when a wound occurs in the body, the blood in the wound can be rapidly coagulating to prevent the blood from flowing out. This is the two processes that show that Yin and Yang exist at the same time, opposites and unified. There are also things like metabolism. Metabolism is one of the basic characteristics of life. Metabolism includes two processes: anabolism and catabolism. Anabolism means the process that organisms consume energy to absorb nutrients from the environment and synthesize the body's own substances to build and repair its own structure, and to store energy; catabolism refers to the process by which organisms use stored energy or decompose their own substances in the body to transform them into energy to maintain body temperature and perform various functional activities, such as physical exercise and blood activity, bioelectric activity and biomolecule synthesis, etc., these two metabolic processes occur concurrently.

This involves the question of how to look at the human body and life. Modern medicine, including biology, uses natural scientific methods to study the human body, decomposing the human body into cells, molecules, proteins, nucleic acids, DNA, bacteria, viruses, etc.; and the Chinese traditional medicine uses social science methods to study the human body. The traditional Chinese medicine treats the human body from a dynamic and balanced perspective. It treats the human body as a black box and studies its input and output. There were no modern scientific instruments in the ancient China. The human body cannot be broken down to the cellular level, but the human body can only be visually broken down into the five 'viscera' and the six 'bowels', heart, lungs, liver, kidneys, spleen, gallbladder, stomach, large intestines, small intestines, bladder, San Chiao the three foci (the three burning spaces). The diagnostic methods of the traditional Chinese medicine are observation, olfaction, inquiry, and palpation. In ancient times, the diseases of the human body were classified. Someone says that the Western medicine uses reductionist methods, while the traditional Chinese medicine uses systemic methods. The traditional Chinese medicine uses natural plants. China has a vast territory and diverse plants. Many countries have transplanted many plants from China; many species of China are also imported from abroad. The medical practice of the traditional Chinese medicine for thousands of years has accumulated a wealth of experience in the use of plants and drugs. People have a thorough understanding of the properties and effects of each plant and the interaction between plants and drugs. This is a rich and valuable experience. Some drugs and plant books still have an important reference value today, such as the book "Compendium of Materia Medica" by the famous doctor Li Shizhen in the Ming Dynasty.

The theory of meridian and collateral in the traditional Chinese medicine is different and unique. The meridian and collateral are not intuitively visible in anatomy. The meridian and collateral are related to the nervous system, but not exactly the same. Some meridian and collateral, and nerves have the same distribution, but now it does not appear that the direction of a certain nerve in the human body is consistent with the running route of the meridian and collateral; and the meridian and collateral are also related to the lymphatic system. The meridian and collateral are indeed effective in practice. At present, there are various explanations for meridian and collateral. There are phenomena such as the low resistance and the propagated sensation along the channels at the point of the meridian and collateral. Scientists have discovered that the meridian and collateral have the characteristics of sound, light, and electrical conduction. Someone believes that meridian and collateral are an energy exchange system in the human body; some believe that meridian and collateral are a comprehensive functional system including the body fluids and blood vessels, which is dominated by the nervous system; and some believe that meridian and collateral are the third balance system of the human body, etc. According to the ancient Chinese medicine books, meridian and collateral are channels for the circulation of "Qi" and blood. So, what is the relationship between meridian and collateral, and "Qi"? What is "Qi"? According to the Chinese medicine book, "Qi" should be a kind of energy. Some experience has confirmed that the human body will produce this kind of "Qi" during exercise, meditation, yoga, acupuncture and moxibustion, Tai Chi and Qigong, and will heal the sick of human body. The human body has the ability to heal itself. The human body has bio-electricity, and the application of bio-electricity is also very popular, such as electroencephalogram and electrocardiogram, the capacitive touch screen of smart phones, etc. Just like the electric current in the conductor generates a magnetic field, the human body's bioelectricity flows according to the meridian direction, and the flowing bio-electricity also produces a kind of field and a kind of energy. Is this kind of field "Qi" in traditional Chinese medicine? The traditional Chinese medicine says that "Qi reaches the diseased place", and every organ of the human body also contains bioelectricity; is "Qi" the field produced by bioelectricity?

Nowadays, in a fast-paced life and a consumer society, ordinary people face the temptation of various material interests and work for life. It is difficult for them to settle down, and they mainly rely on drugs and surgery to solve various diseases. There are also statistics showing that the average life expectancy of some ancient Chinese monks was relatively long. The founder of Buddhism, Siddharta Gautama, lived up to 80 years old. Buddhism prohibits killing and recommends eating vegetarian food. Buddhism emphasizes meditation, which is good for physical and mental health. Among the ancient Chinese thinkers, Confucius had a lifespan of 73 years and Mencius had a lifespan of 84 years. There is no record of the lifespan history of Taoist representatives Laozi and Zhuang Zhou, but later, many Taoist and Taoist figures had a longer life span. The modern British scholar Needham and the famous philosopher Bertrand Russell also admired Taoism. But we look at the representatives of the scientific management. For instance, Taylor's lifespan is 59 years, Weber's lifespan is 56 years, Fayol's lifespan is 85 years old. From this point of view, the ancient Eastern thinkers, their understanding about life, spirit and health is quite unique.

The treatment of the traditional Chinese medicine emphasizes the combined use of drugs and, acupuncture and moxibustion. Traditional Chinese medicine emphasizes the "homology of medicine and food" and pays attention to the combination of daily diet, many of our daily foods have medicinal value. Nowadays, drugs can be extracted from effective ingredients. Generalized acupuncture and moxibustion include these two methods, they have their own strengths. Acupuncture requires specialized learning and moxibustion method is relatively simple and can be operated by ordinary people. The theoretical basis of acupuncture and moxibustion is the theory of meridian and collateral, which is indeed effective in practice. With the further development of technology and society, a person will have a deeper understanding of the human body and nature. The development of the modern science and philosophy has evolved from Francis Bacon, Rene Descartes, Galileo Galilei and Isaac Newton to now, it's only a few hundred years and there are still many things unknown for us, human beings. Some things will be difficult to explain with science for a while, and further scientific development is needed to prove the existence and function of meridian and collateral. The traditional Chinese medicine still has its value today. At present, various countries in the world, especially developed countries, have generally high medical costs. A large number of new drugs need to be developed every year, which is costly and expensive. At the same time, various diseases and viruses will also produce various kinds of mutations, the human body will develop drug resistance, and it is necessary to continuously develop new drugs or new vaccines to deal with new diseases. The medicines of traditional Chinese medicine are natural plants, which are inexpensive, low-cost, and effective. In addition to drug treatment, modern medicine uses surgical procedures to remove or replace human organs, while traditional Chinese medicine emphasizes holistic medicine. It uses drugs, acupuncture and moxibustion, massage, scraping therapy, cupping therapy, and Qigong to solve problems, and causes little damage to the human body. In the modern society, people are plagued by various chronic diseases and mental illnesses, drug treatments have side effects. For some diseases, such as Alzheimer's disease, there is no effective medicine yet. Acupuncture and moxibustion have a unique effect in treating such diseases. The traditional Chinese medicine is currently applicable to diseases that include common colds, cervical spondylopathy, the protrusion of lumbar intervertebral disc, facial paralysis, diseases of the digestive system, allergic diseases and dermatosis (eczema, urticaria, allergic rhinitis, allergic asthma, herpes zoster), athlete's foot, hair loss, alopecia areata, pelvic inflammation, vaginitis, primary dysmenorrhea, menoxenia, insomnia, migraine, chronic nephritis, rheumatism, apoplectic sequel, tumours and suboptimal health, etc.; for these diseases, the effect of traditional Chinese medicine treatment is still good, compared with modern medicine, the side effects should be small. For some diseases, the modern medicine has a better therapeutic effect, such as the diseases of the cardiovascular system and cerebrovascular system, hypertension, heart disease, cerebral infarction in the acute onset, modern medicine can quickly control the symptoms, as well as gynecological infectious diseases; in the acute stage, modern medicine can treat the infection and the effect is good. (Above all, it is a personal opinion, if you are sick and you need to follow the doctor's advice)

The problem of the traditional Chinese medicine is that basic theories and doctrines are elaborated by the language of the past. In an era without scientific equipment, the language of observing natural phenomena was used to explain the causes of diseases, now it seems a bit outdated. For instance, the cause of diseases in the traditional Chinese medicine: wind, cold, heat, dampness, dryness, fire, evil Qi invading the human body and causing diseases, etc., which cannot be connected with modern medicine. The mechanism of the Chinese medicine treatment and the components of Chinese medicine need to be identified by modern technology. Just like the 2015 Nobel Prize winner in physiology, Chinese scientist Tu Youyou, her discovery was inspired by the writings of a Taoist scholar in ancient China. Artemisinin is extracted from plants, and the mechanism of the action of artemisinin is very clear. At present, the Chinese medicine is gradually recognized by the world, but there is still a lack of scientific diagnosis and clinical evidence, and its safety and effectiveness have been questioned. The theory of meridian and collateral in traditional Chinese medicine has not been fully clarified by modern scientific and technological means, and it is in the stage of scientific hypothesis. In the modern society, traditional Chinese medicine is currently valuable as an alternative medicine and is a supplement to modern medicine. It can be said that the modern medicine is yang and traditional Chinese medicine is yin. If one day, with the further development of science, the treatment of traditional Chinese medicine can use scientific language to explain its theories and guide practice. At that time, a new medical theory that incorporates the traditional Chinese medicine may emerge.

Taoism is derived from the historian's summary of the history of social development. It has been said before that in the four major civilized regions, the Chinese civilization was born relatively late, but the Chinese civilization has a characteristic, it has good continuity and a very detailed historical record. From the Oracle bone script of the Shang Dynasty to the inscriptions on the bronzes of the Zhou Dynasty, to the bamboo and wooden slips of the Spring and Autumn period and the Warring States period, paper was invented in the Han Dynasty and movable type printing was invented in the Song Dynasty, which was conducive to the publishing and printing of ancient books. The historian records the rise and fall of dynasties in history, sums up historical experience and lessons, like the Xia, Shang, and Zhou dynasties; the dynasty cycle is very regular, the traditional interpretation is from a moral point of view. The dynasty supported by people flourished and the dynasty that did not win the support of people died. When the dynasty is founded, the rulers were diligent and thrifty, the bureaucracy was small, the laborers were numerous; at the end of the dynasty, the rulers were corrupt and decadent, the bureaucracy was huge, the laborers were in reduced number, and the management failed. Nowadays, the capitalist society also has an economic cycle. The explanation of the economic cycle is the balance of supply and demand. Supply exceeds demand and overproduction leads to economic depression. If supply is less than demand, production will expand and economic prosperity will occur.

Taoism is a kind of analysis and summary of the process of social evolution. In "Tao Te Ching", it talks about "The movement of the Tao by contraries proceeds." When many things develop to extremes and peaks, they will transform in the opposite direction because the original impetus and factors which support and promote the development of things have decreased or disappeared. This phenomenon is very common in history. When the ancient dynasty reached its peak, it began to decline, with bureaucratic corruption and serious polarization. The enterprise development is similar. After reaching the peak of the industry, there will be challengers. For instance, after Nokia reached the peak, new technologies appeared on the market. Faced with the challenge of Apple Inc., Nokia at last lost the smartphone market. Another example is the prohibition of commerce during the Cultural Revolution in China, and the society went to extremes; after the reform and opening up, it focused on the development of the market and the economy, individuals could start business and issue stocks.

Society is an organism, in which economy, politics, religion, ideology, law, science, and technology are interrelated and exist together. The 19th century sociologist Herbert Spencer proposed the thought of social evolution, and believed that evolution is a universal law, society is an organism like biology. There are many similarities between the two organisms, he uses some theories in biology to study society. Taoism mainly focuses on analyzing the evolution of society from the perspective of history, politics, and morality. It also contains some content of natural science. Taoism is still rigorous in its research, but Taoism is looking for individual salvation. In fact, traditional Western universities and research institutes also exist as independent from governments. Universities emphasize independence and carry out research independently. The appointment and removal of personnel has nothing to do with the government. Until now, universities are often compared to ivory towers, as if universities are one place which is free from secular interference, universities should be an individual salvation. This is somewhat similar to Taoist concepts and attitudes. The Chinese traditional society is dominated by politics, and serving politics is the first thing. Because Taoism had an individual salvation aim, it has no influence in the government and a low status in society. Although some emperors in Chinese history believed in Taoism, one reason is to sum up historical experience and lessons and maintain the rule of the dynasty; the other reason is that the emperors want to live a healthy and long life after being in power. But for ordinary people, believing in Taoism means breaking away from society and a social system with Confucianism as the mainstream. Maslow has analyzed the five needs of people, people always go from low-level needs to high-level needs, they gradually meet. A person who believes in Taoism that means being separated from the mainstream of society, without status, without various benefits and treatment, and it is very reluctant to meet low-level needs, let alone high-level needs. Therefore, for ordinary people, in the past, Taoism was not a social mainstream thought, was not the object of government encouragement, nor was it the object of group imitation. Unlike Western societies, universities and research institutes exist independently and can receive various financial support from enterprises and governments. Basic research is independent, and the results of applied research can be marketed and gain commercial benefits. In this way, more people are willing to engage in scientific and technological research.

The basic Taoism thought is the concept of "Tao". According to "Tao Te Ching", "Man takes his law from the Earth; the Earth takes its law from Heaven; Heaven takes its law from the Tao. The law of the Tao is its being what it is.", "The Tao produced One; One produced Two; Two produced Three; Three produced all things." In addition to "Tao", Taoism also talked about "Nature". Xun Kuang once said that "Nature is governed by the law of its own. Neither does it exist for the judiciousness of king, nor does it perish for the inhumanity of the king." The concept of "trend (circumstances)" is also very important in the Taoism thought. "Tao Te Ching" writes "All things are produced by the Tao, and nourished by its outflowing operation. They receive their forms according to the nature of each, and are completed according to the circumstances of their condition." A person, a team and an organization can only show value by relying on the trend and taking advantage of the trend. In addition, Taoism does contain a lot of profound and beneficial content for society, life, individual and personal health, but it is at odds with mainstream social values. In society, most people pursue wealth, status, power, and they despise the poor and favor the rich, and cling to power and befriend nobles, etc., while Taoism says "clean heart and few desires", "Tao Te Ching" says "The highest excellence is like that of water, the excellence of water appears in its benefiting all things, and in its occupying, without striving(to the contrary)", emphasizing that the weak beats the strong, the strong is broken first, the weak can be preserved, just like the big tree and the grass, when the typhoon came, the big tree fell, but the grass was safe. In the ancient times of the earth, cold-blooded animals ruled the world like dinosaurs, mammals lived at the feet of dinosaurs; 65 million years ago, an asteroid hit Mexico's Yucatan Peninsula and caused major changes in the earth's environment. The dinosaurs could not adapt to the new environment and gradually became extinct and mammals gradually developed. Now most animals on the earth, including of humans, are mammals.

Taoism, later developed as a religion, and Buddhism are

somewhat mysterious. Confucianism does not talk about supernatural phenomena such as gods and weirdness. Like Confucius, "Confucius never talked about extraordinary things, feats of strength, disorder, and spiritual beings" and "Respect the gods and the devils but keep them at a distance". While Buddhism talks about supernatural powers and Taoism talks about immortals, they all have a mythological system. Taoism is somewhat mysterious, some of these mysteries are not taught publicly, and the audience is limited. The first reason is that there are some things in reality and they are not easy to explain in scientific language; in addition, it is like the craftsmanship of a company's products, which always has some skills and know-how. The know-how and skills are generally coming from some experience, which may be the company's technology patents, which are the advantages of this company in the market. The theory of the product is public, but each product is still somewhat different. Maybe this product functions are more diverse and that product quality is better, the principle here is similar. At the same time, Taoism talks about "the great way is always simple", but in the real society, people have a mentality that they like rare books and unique skill. They feel that as long as they read the rare books and master these unique skills, they can save time, take shortcuts, and become superior. The accumulation of long-term practice and experience of Taoism and Taoism teachers is valuable. For the mysterious things in Taoism, we need to use modern scientific methods to understand and judge, use scientific language to analyze and study unknown things, and study the laws of things. Today, Taoist thought is a reference value in many fields such as sociology, management, economics, medicine, physiology and personal health.

When talking about the Hawthorne studies, we mentioned that there are formal organizations and informal organizations in companies and enterprises, managers must maintain the balance between these social organizations. In an enterprise or organization, there are different levels according to the individual's ability. In the case of the same ability, the individual's treatment is not much different. If God, Allah, or the traditional Chinese "Heaven" exists, they may have to achieve various balances when arranging the layout of the world, and achieve a balance in power, wealth, personal life and health. In this sense, in the ancient Chinese society, Taoism existed in society as the opposite and supplement of Confucianism. But whether it is Confucianism or Taoism, they are all based on the natural economy of small peasants in the agricultural society and the ancient patriarchal system, and are closely integrated with the ancient bureaucratic system. The rule of the ancient Chinese society did not rely solely on Confucianism. "On surface Confucianism and in fact legalism", legalism also occupies a very important position in the management thought of the ancient government, and it has even more practical means. Those who study Confucianism have been selected and tested by the government, they are employed in the government, become officials, enjoy wealth and status, and are a privileged class. If an individual does not serve in the government, he believes in Taoism, retreats to the mountains and forests, and is self-sufficient.

Confucian scholars, Taoist scholars, and other representatives of the ancient Chinese thought are basically not involved in commerce, this is very different from the ancient Greek philosophers and there was little or no business knowledge in their writings. The ancient society in China also did not allow businessmen to serve in the government (in the later Chinese ancient society, it was different). Even if businessmen earned wealth, they had to let their offsprings enter the government to stabilize their position. They could not use wealth for expansion of investment and capital circulation. It is impossible to produce a combination of business and science and technology like the Western. The most typical example is the knowledge of geography. The ancient China believed the sky to be round and the earth square, while the Western believed that the earth was a round body regardless of the heliocentric theory and geocentric theory. Later, the compass was used to determine the latitude and longitude, which lay a foundation for the age of navigation and ocean trade on knowledge and technology. Many inventions in ancient China, such as papermaking, printing, gunpowder, and compasses, reached the Western world, opening the way for the Western society to disintegrate the feudal system and enter the capitalist system; these inventions did not play a similar rolè in the ancient China. The reason is that science and technology were not valued in the ancient Chinese society, were not integrated with commerce, and were restrained by the political system. The ancient Chinese history books are full of biographies of emperors, generals and literati, but there are few biographies of scientists and technological inventors. It can also be said that the ancient Chinese science and technology are compatible with the ancient Chinese political system and satisfy the conditions of the agricultural production methods and the agricultural economy.

We can compare the roles played by thoughts and religions of the Eastern and the Western ancient societies. The Eastern society, like China, has formed a cultural pattern dominated by Confucianism and supplemented by Taoism and Buddhism. In this cultural pattern, Taoism with its natural science content is suppressed and in a subordinate position. If this pattern is not broken, natural science would not develop. In the Western and European society, Christianity is the main ideology, but the government's role in controlling society is far less strict than China, and there is no bureaucratic system like China. It is the power of the kingship, the church, and the nobility. The religion and science in European society are closely related, and science and technology are also subordinate to religion. However, when the Reformation broke through the bondage of religion to society, the Western ancient governments themselves were without strong control over society, science and technology which can be combined with commerce and industry to promote each other. What we can often see is that commercial needs promote the advancement of science and technology, such as James Watt's invention of the steam engine, and many other inventions are in the same case. Therefore, the European social tradition does not emphasize the role of the government. As former president of U.S Ronald Reagan once said, "government is not the solution to our problems, government is the problem." John Maynard Keynes' contribution to modern economics lies in re-emphasizing the role of the government in social and economic life when workers' strikes and various economic crises continue to occur in the industrial society. The implementation of government projects, increasing government financial expenditure and improving the social security system solve various economic and social problems. The question often debated in modern economics is whether the government plays more or the market plays more, which is more important?

I want to emphasize one point in here. The traditional Chinese thought is secular and emphasizes the interests of the present world. These traditional Chinese thoughts, whether they are Confucianism, Taoism, Mohism, Legalism, etc., rarely talk about the afterlife, and they are quite different from religion. This is a characteristic of the Chinese traditional culture.

4.Exchange of thoughts between East and West

In the 16th and 17th centuries, after the opening of new shipping routes, Europeans could sail to India and China for trade and cultural exchanges. When the Eastern and the Western world began to come into contact, the Westerners admired ancient Chinese philosophy at the beginning, and thinkers in the age of enlightenment respected the ancient Chinese thought. Francois Quesnay was called "Confucius of Europe" and was the economist of the Physiocratic school; Voltaire said, "It is, in fact, in morality, in political economy, in agriculture, in the necessary arts of life, that the Chinese have made such advances towards perfection… a professor of mathematics in the university of Halls delivered once an excellent discourse in praise of the Chinese philosophy. He praised that ancient species of the human race, differing, as it does, in respect to the beard, the eyes, the nose, the ears, and even the reasoning powers themselves; he praised the Chinese, I say, for their adoration of a supreme God, and their love of virtue…the religion of their learned ones is admirable, and free from superstitions, from absurd legends, from dogmas insulting both to reason and nature."[60] The German philosopher, Gottfried Wilhelm Leibniz was inspired by the theory of Yin and Yang in "I Ching" and invented the binary number, which laid the foundation of mathematics for the computer science. In contrast to Europe at the same time, it was under religious oppression. In the ancient China society, the influence of religion was indeed not serious. The society was more tolerant of various religions, and there had been no religious wars like in Europe. But in the age of Enlightenment, thinkers are not monolithic, Montesquieu thought that the political system in the ancient China was very authoritarian; he was aware of the political system of the ancient Chinese society and wrote "But we may observe in general that all those dynasties began very well. Virtue, attention, and vigilance are necessary in China… It was natural that emperors trained up in military toil, who had compassed the dethroning of a family immersed in pleasure, should adhere to virtue, which they had found so advantageous, and be afraid of voluptuousness, which they knew had proved so fatal to the family dethroned. But after the three or four first princes, corruption, luxury, indolence, and pleasure possessed their successors… the family declined, the grandees rose up… a lazy set of people that dwelt there ruined the industrious part of the nation; a usurper founded a family, the third or fourth successor of which went and shut himself up in the very same place."[61]

Since the late Middle Ages, in European society happened the Renaissance, the Age of Discovery, the Reformation, the Scientific Revolution, the Enlightenment, and the Industrial Revolution. In the later 18th century, when the French Revolution broke out, huge changes were made in the political system, and the transformation of the traditional European society was basically completed. The Westerners realized that they not only overthrew the old feudal dynasties, but also made a breakthrough in social form and created a

---

[60] Voltaire, Dictionnaire philosophique, Chine

[61] Montesquieu, The Spirit of the Laws, chapter 7, para 7

new society, a society dominated by industry, which is completely different from the traditional agricultural society. Social political, economic, and cultural changes have led to rapid development of various sciences, inventions and creations. In 1687, Newton published "The Mathematical Principles of Natural Philosophy". In 1628, William Harvey established the theory of blood circulation. In 1665, Robert Hooke discovered the cell. In the 17th century, Newton and Leibniz invented the calculus. In 1799, Pierre-Simon Laplace published "Celestial Mechanics", Antoine Lavoisier published the first list of modern chemical elements in 1789, Andre-Marie Ampere discovered Ampere's law in 1822, Mendeleev published the periodic table of elements in 1869, Watt perfected the steam engine in 1769, and Fulton in 1807 invented the steamship, and in 1814 George Stephenson invented the train. These scientific discoveries and technological inventions are unprecedented in an agricultural society. They have a huge effect on people's understanding of nature, mastering the laws of science, and improving social productivity. The machine age has arrived, and the industrial age has arrived. At the same time, China, although leading the West at an early age and evolving into a bureaucratic society, and the development of various ancient political systems was very mature, but the society has not changed much in the past two thousand years, social development has stagnated, and it is still an agriculture society.

Many thinkers appeared in the European society during the rapid social change, such as Locke, Hobbes, Voltaire, Montesquieu, Rousseau, Tocqueville, Immanuel Kant, Schelling, Fichte, Hegel, Spencer, Comte, Marx, and Durkheim, Weber, etc. There has been a differentiation in knowledge, and many subjects were developed, the understanding of the laws of social development has been deepened, and political, economic and social thinking has been improved. They analyzed and compared Chinese classical thought, religion, and political system with the Western religious, ethics and systems. In this case, the analysis and evaluation of the ancient Chinese political system and classical thought have gone deeper.

Among the classical German philosophers, like G. W. F. Hegel, his evaluations of the ancient Chinese thought were quite pertinent. He realized that China is the only durable kingdom in the world. The Chinese history includes philosophy, administration, law, manner, religion and so on, recorded in detail and accuracy. China has a vast territory and a large population. The Chinese pay attention to family and have organized state-arrangements; no nobility, all are equal. For officials, China uses the wise and employs the capable. Social governance has been bureaucratized for a long time, mainly relying on morality, but it has not changed much in the past two thousand years, it is a monarchy. In China society, the emperor is center, it is mainly an administrative management model. It lacks the protection of private property rights. Individuals have no independence and freedom. Although everyone is equal, people are slaves and servile, the imperial power is supreme. The people depend on the emperor and the emperor depends on heaven.

In terms of thinking, the traditional Chinese philosophy is mainly a moral philosophy and a philosophy of life. Confucian thought does not include speculative content. The traditional Chinese thought has a speculative content, but the abstract consciousness does not go deep and only stays at a relatively low level. This shows that the Chinese pay more attention to pragmatism. Hegel has realized that there is a contrast between the deepest and most common things in the Chinese and the extremely external and completely accidental things, this is actually what Taoism say "the great way is always simple". The science appears pre-eminently honored and fostered in China, but the Chinese lack active scientific theoretical research, or lack scientific interest, and rely more on the accumulation of experience. The China mathematics, physics, and astronomy used to lead in history, but in modern times, it lags far behind Europe.

Technically, the China metal production and porcelain manufacturing are the world's leading. The Chinese are good at imitating. Although the Chinese invented gunpowder, the cannons were built with the help of the Portuguese. Medicine is studied empirically by the Chinese. The Chinese are too proud to learn anything from Europeans. Hegel concluded that there is no real science and art in China, Chinese obey authority, their individuality is suppressed, they have not been developed, and the society is in a static state without breakthroughs. Hegel realized that China would be invaded by the West after India.[62]

European thinkers have a higher evaluation of Taoism than Confucianism. After Western society entered the industrial society, the power of the government was limited, political parties were elected to power, religious status declined, individuals had freedom of speech, publication, and association, and their ideological and institutional authority was weakened, private property rights of individuals are protected. Individuals can devote more energy to natural science research and career development, without too much consideration and dealing with various complicated interpersonal and social relations, and can also achieve development in society.

The French thinker, Tocqueville said when talking about the centralization of government in "De la democratie en Amerique", "It is evident that a central government acquires immense power when united to administrative centralization. Thus combined, it accustoms men to set their own will habitually and completely aside; to submit, not only for once or upon one point, but in every respect, and at all times… Centralization imparts without difficulty an admirable regularity to the routine of business; rules the details of the social police with sagacity; represses the smallest disorder and the most petty misdemeanors; maintains society in a statu quo, alike secure from improvement and decline; and perpetuates a drowsy precision in the conduct of affairs, which is hailed by the heads of the administration as a sign of perfect order and public tranquillity; China appears to me to present the most perfect instance of that species of well being which a completely central administration may furnish to the nations among which it exists. Travellers assure us that the Chinese have peace without happiness, industry without improvement, stability without strength, and public order without public morality. The condition of society is always tolerable, never

---

[62] G. W. F Hegel, the philosophy of history, Part I, Section I

excellent. I am convinced that, when China is opened to European observation, it will be found to contain the most perfect model of a central administration which exists in the universe".[63] It actually reflected in the ancient Chinese society traditional thought and system were matured. Although there were also some capitalist production methods, but the society cannot allow large system innovation and breakthroughs, and cannot automatically enter capitalist society.

It must be mentioned here that the role of the Christian church at the beginning when the East and the West came into contact. The Society of Jesus was a branch of the Catholic Church and it was established in Paris in 1534. At the end of the Ming Dynasty and the early Qing Dynasty in China, the Society of Jesus sent many missionaries to China. Scholars, such as the famous Matteo Ricci, Johann Adam Schall von Bell, and Ferdinand Verbiest. They translated many classics of Chinese culture and spread these to Europe. They also translated many Western books and introduced Western astronomy, geography and mathematics to China. The introduction of such knowledge to China has made an indelible contribution to the advancement of the Chinese calendar and the promotion of Sino-Western cultural exchanges. When Western society was deeply influenced by Eastern thought in the 17th and 18th centuries, China knew nothing about Western countries, and did not understand Western countries' science and technology, thought, culture and religion, political systems, economic organizations, and urban systems. Only after the mid-nineteenth century, with the opening of the country, the exchange of trade, and the increasing exchanges between the East and the West, various aspects of the Western countries were introduced to China. This process is called "the West culture communication to China". The Christian Church has helped a lot in modern China's education and medical care and has achieved success in these two non-profit fields. It has established many famous mission universities and mission

---

[63] Tocqueville, Democracy in America, (Pratt, Woodford & Co, 1848), part 1, chapter 5, pp 88-93

hospitals, and spread Western advanced scientific and technological knowledge, like the famous Yenching University, Fu Jen Catholic University, Cheeloo University, St. John's University, Soochow University, Huachung University, Lingnan University, West China Union University, etc., there are also many missionary high schools. Missionary universities have played an exemplary role in the modernization of the Chinese education. These universities cultivated many talents in the fields of science and technology, engineering, politics, diplomacy and medicine. In the modern China, when the society accepted Christianity, many things happened. The time has not yet come for a correct evaluation. I remember the ruins of St. Paul's in Macau. It was originally a Roman Catholic church built by the Portuguese in Macau. After several fires, it was rebuilt after the fire. Finally, there was a fire in 1835 that burned the entire church to the front wall and it is today's the ruins of St. Paul's. The Protestant ethics produced in the Western society after the Reformation are very similar to the traditional Chinese ethics. This can also be seen in Carnegie's autobiography. Protestantism has played a greater role in modern Chinese education.

17 CHAPTER RELIGION OF THE CHINESE

1.Introduction

For the Chinese people, religion is a bit strange. The philosopher Bertrand Russell said, "China is practically destitute of religion, not only in the upper classes, but throughout the population".[64] Talcott Parsons wrote in "The Structure of Social Action", "In prudent care for the interests of this world and lack of interest in any other, perhaps no people has ever surpassed the Chinese". [65]

There are some things in any region and nation, and these things cannot be explained by science. With the development of the human being rationality, people believe more in science. The current world advocates science and atheism, but science is not omnipotent, and science cannot deny God. The sciences still face many problems. Is this world really as simple as atheism? How many factors are at work behind the various phenomena we know? The world can be simply divided into materialism and idealism? What is the role of religion? How have religions changed in different stages of society?

---

[64] Bertrand Russell, The Problem of China, chapter 11, pp 192

[65] Talcott Parsons, The Structure of Social Action, chapter 15, pp 546

There is no doubt that religion has played a considerable role in the development of the human history, and has had a considerable impact on philosophy, politics, culture, education, and art. In here, it is not possible to discuss religion and its influence from all angles, but only from a sociological perspective.

Generally, in China, there are Confucianism, Taoism and Buddhism. Now some professor think Confucianism is a religion, but the Chinese think Confucianism is a kind of moral or ethics. Simply put, the Confucian doctrine maintains a hierarchical system in which the monarch is monarch forever, minister is minister forever. The Confucian doctrine is traditional and conservative, emphasizing the traditional dynastic national order while the general religions emphasize equality. Confucianism emphasizes the present age, does not speak of the afterlife, does not speak of God; Confucianism is secular, religion is transcendental. From these aspects, there is a difference between Confucianism and religion. Relatively religious, the Chinese pay more attention to interpersonal relationships and ethics. Buddhism is an external religion for China, Taoism was produced later, Buddhism and Taoism are looking for individual salvation and Confucianism is searching for collective salvation. Buddhism, Taoism and Confucianism are complementary. The Chinese people do not have the religion of metaphysical theology and combined with politics; Buddhism is metaphysical, but Buddhism does not contain political thought; Confucianism contains political content, people who believe in Confucianism can become officials, but Confucianism lacks philosophical metaphysics and it is different from religion, Confucianism played a religious role in the ancient China society, Confucianism is the ideology of the dynastic countries. When China became a modern society, in the face of the impact of Western industrial civilization, the theory of Confucianism was somewhat outdated in political science. Confucianism affirms authority, and expounds theories from the perspective of authority, that is, from the perspective of the monarch. Confucianism praised the monarch and hoped the monarch would possess good morals, in order to safeguard the interests of the monarch. The communication between Confucius and the monarchs of some countries is also often reflected in Confucius' writings. But the two important movements in Western society before entering the industrial civilization, the Reformation and the political system revolution, negated authority in spirit and politics. Later the China social development denied Confucius thought, there was a "New Culture Movement".

The ancient Chinese thought, including Confucianism, also has a good side. Confucian thought is conducive to maintaining daily interpersonal relationships. Multi-ethnic groups live together in China, as long as foreigners and non-Chinese ethnic groups receive/understand the ethics of China and take part in and pass the imperial examination, they will be able to become officials without ethnic discrimination. As the Jews entered China in ancient times, later they were treated in the same way, there is no anti-Semitism in China. In Chinese history, the policy toward the Jewish people was "belong to China, abide by the ancestral customs, and leave behind Bianliang (capital of the Song dynasty)". Nowadays, in education in the Chinese society, schools seldom regard Confucianism as the golden rule as in the past, and natural science is much more important in the modern school education. As for religion, ordinary Chinese have started to travel abroad in the past twenty years and understand that in different countries of the world there are different religions. In addition to orthodox beliefs, Confucianism, Taoism and Buddhism in the ancient Chinese society, there are many folk polytheistic beliefs. Today, whether in some Chinese restaurants in China or overseas, you can often see the statue of the God of Wealth. People hope that the God of Wealth will bless the development of their business, as well as the God of Land, Guanyin (patroness of female fertility), etc., which actually reflects the secular nature of Chinese culture, the Chinese people still pursue the interests of the secular world.

On this land of China, the climate changes throughout the year are very regular. Winter goes and spring comes, cold and heat succeed each other, the four seasons are distinct, sow in spring, develop in summer, harvest in autumn, and store in winter, year after year, people can easily summarize the law of natural change, like the Chinese summed up 24 solar terms, every two solar terms differ by about 15 days. A year has 365 days, the solar terms are: Beginning of Spring, Rain Water, Insects Awakening, Spring Equinox, Fresh Green, Grain Rain, Beginning of Summer, Lesser Fullness, Grain in Ear, Summer Solstice, Lesser Heat, Greater Heat, Beginning of Autumn, End of Heat, White Dew, Autumnal Equinox, Cold Dew, First Frost, Beginning of Winter, Light Snow, Heavy Snow, Winter Solstice, Lesser Cold, and Greater Cold. In ancient society, agriculture is the foundation. Sowing and harvesting according to the season is the most important thing. When people master the laws of nature, the influence of other forces is weakened. In India, people are particularly easy to enter a state where they can feel a variety of revelations and there are many levels of this revelation. There are similar feelings in China, but it is not as obvious as in India. It can also say that in India intuition is stronger. Many people in developed countries and regions are willing to go to India and learn yoga. Steve Jobs insisted on sitting quietly and doing meditation after returning from India. Some things are beyond personal rationality and can only be felt by personal sense organs, this is not easy to form words and express it; everyone may have different feelings. There are so many religions in India for some reasons. A trip to India is more of a spiritual journey, and a completely different experience and culture.

The three elements or the four elements of the birth of civilization and the country are words, cities, etiquette systems, and bronzes. Among them, words are more important. How did humans live before words were formed? How did they accumulate knowledge? What is the function of intuition? Why is religion formed? These questions are also very interesting. The current world is progressing forward and becoming more and more modern. Computers, mobile phones, radio, television, Internet, cars, trains, airplanes, rockets, satellites, spacecraft are all available... Medical conditions are much better than in the ancient society, and people live longer. People grow longer and healthier, but with the development of industrialization, some aspects of mankind seem to have regressed, as if spiritual things were missing. The industrial age has the beliefs of the industrial age. Modern society emphasizes rationality and science. Science penetrates into all aspects of society. Natural science studies the universe and galaxies at a macro level, and studies atoms, quarks, cells, genes, etc. at a micro level. In social sciences, there are economics, anthropology, sociology, history, politics... Nowadays, scientists have a high status in society, but science is not a panacea. Modern science itself is also developing. There are still many unknown things in the world. Science cannot solve the problems of morality and belief, people need faith.

Confucianism was respected by the Chinese dynasties, respecting Confucius as a saint, using Confucius' books as classics, and combining them with the political system; the individuals relied on Confucian ethics to survive and develop in society. The Confucian ethics gradually evolved into religions, which were organized, have leaders and systems. Taoist thought later combined health preservation, medicine, astrology, book of prophecy, theology and so on, and later learned from Buddhism, established Taoist temples and various rituals, and formed the Taoism religion.

2.Buddhism

Buddhism was born in India. The reason why Buddhism was born in India, or in India why there are so many religions? I think it is also related to factors such as geography and climate. Between the Indian subcontinent and the Qinghai-Tibet Plateau in China is the world's highest mountain range --- the Himalayas. In India, the climate is very different from the climate in China. The Indian subcontinent is hotter throughout the year. The Indian Ocean generates monsoons every summer, and the Indian Ocean monsoon meets the Himalayas and is blocked, it will produce a lot of rainfall. It is the rainy season from June to September in the Indian subcontinent. In the Indian subcontinent, there are few mountains, many plains, and few deserts. It is also rich in agricultural products, rich in fruits, plants and crops such as mangoes, bananas, oranges, pomegranates, grapes, papaya, sugarcane, etc. In ancient times, productivity was underdeveloped and the population was relatively few. In the case of hot weather, people's food intake is limited. Worship of animals such as cows has led to a relatively developed dairy industry. For instance, in India, including other states of South Asia, there is a drink called lassi, which is similar to yogurt and is often seen on the market, and its price is very cheap. In hot weather conditions, drinking lassi can relieve hunger. In ancient India, it was easy for individuals to solve the problem of food and clothing. It did not require much effort and intensive cultivation in the farmland. After food and clothing needs were satisfied, individuals paid attention to their spiritual needs. As Maslow said, after low-level needs are met, people just pursue high-level needs. Siddhartha Gautama, the founder of Buddhism, was very weak after penance for six years. He took a bath in the Falgu River and recovered. At this time, a shepherdess came to him and give Siddhartha a bowl of milk porridge. After Siddhartha drank it, he felt much better. So, he crossed the Falgu River and came to Bodh Gaya. Under a bodhi tree, after seven days and seven nights of meditation, he finally realized fully enlightenment, created Buddhism. Under such material and climate conditions, many people are more willing to engage in spiritual exploration. Buddhist does not engage in production. If the material needs of society are easily met in the future, does it mean the revival of Buddhism? I think that in the future, people can focus more on creative work and spiritual pursuits; simple and repetitive work can be achieved with artificial intelligence and robots. At that time, people's main work is creative, artistic, and it gives rise to more discovery, invention and artistic creation, more spiritual and ideological thoughts, it solves more unknown problems, have more understanding and exploration of the human body, society, space, galaxies and the universe, and have more knowledge.

Buddhism was later spread to China through two routes, one was from Pakistan and Afghanistan today, to China's Xinjiang, and then to China's interior; the other route is from the sea to Southeast Asia and then to China. Buddhism is divided into Mahayana Buddhism and Hinayana Buddhism in the development. The Buddhism accepted in China is Mahayana Buddhism; Southeast Asia's is

Hinayana Buddhism. Buddhism in China is divided into Han Buddhism and Tibetan Buddhism. Han Buddhism has many branches, emptiness school, Tiantai school, Ritsu school, pure land Buddhism, Zen Buddhism, tantric Buddhism, Huayan Buddhism, Dharma character school, etc. Among them, Zen Buddhism has the greatest influence. In comparison, Taoism has 86 sects, and these Buddhism sects in China later spread to Korea Peninsula and Japan.

After Indian Buddhism spread to China, it encountered two problems. Economically, in China's land, there are four distinct seasons, and there is little or no harvest without labor. After the ancient government promoted Buddhism, many monks did not engage in production, which caused national economic problems. Therefore, in history, some emperors (Three Disasters of Wu) launched a campaign to suppress Buddhism, returned monks to secular life, increased the social labor force. In doctrinal terms, traditional Indian Buddhism speculates and debates; the debates in traditional Indian Buddhism are somewhat similar to the Western debates and both of them are logically rigorous. For instance, when monk Xuanzang of the Tang Dynasty in China went to India and studied, he often argued with other monks. There were also many debaters in the ancient Greek period. Western philosophy generally talked about subject, object, sign, logic, proposition, deduction, type, substance, consciousness, existence, representation, negation, syllogism, etc., and discussed these; Buddhism talks about concepts such as mind, nature, emptiness, karma, vipaka (maturation of karma), samsara (the concept of rebirth), higher virtue, higher mind, higher wisdom, prajna (insight, pro), paramita (perfection).

The traditional Chinese culture is a kind of imagery thinking, which emphasizes artistic conception. If you read ancient Chinese poems or listen to classical Chinese music, you will have pictures in your mind. Mountains, rivers, sea, flowers, and the moon are full of nature. The idyllic scenery gives people a sense of beauty. The artistic conception of well-written poems is very remote in time or space, like "The Yellow River rises to the white cloud; The lonely town is lost amid the mountains proud. Why should the Mongol flute complain no willows grow? Beyond the Gate of Jade no vernal wind will blow"; and "How long will the bright moon appear? Wine-cup in hand, I ask the sky. I do not know what time of year. It would be tonight in the palace on high"; "Wave on wave the long river eastward rolls away; Gone are all heroes with its spray on spray. Success or failure, right or wrong, all turn out vain; Only green mountains still remain; To see the setting sun's departing ray"; "A slanting stony path leads far to the cold hill; Where fleecy clouds are born, there appear cots and bowers. I stop my cab at maple woods to gaze my fill; Frost-bitten leaves look redder than early spring flowers"; "The desert sands look white as snow; The crescent moon hangs like a bow. When would the steed in golden gear, Gallop all night through autumn clear?"

The Chinese paintings and gardens are also similar. The Chinese traditional paintings are also based on aesthetic realm and focus on the likeness. "Paintings are silent poems, and poems are paintings with words." Many traditional Chinese paintings are landscape paintings, hazy, shrouded in mist and clouds, unlike the Western oil paintings that are realistic and following the laws of perspective. The Western modern abstract paintings, geometric patterns and colors are also incomprehensible for the ordinary Chinese, Chinese is good in mental image. The Chinese classical gardens pursue the unity of man and nature and reproduce nature. "Unnaturally natural", they imitate natural landscapes, rockery, pools and other things placed naturally, emphasizing the contrast between the small and the big, the virtual and the reality, the far and the near; the winding path leads to a secluded quiet place. The four classic gardens in China, the Summer Palace in Beijing, the Mountain Resort in Chengde, the Humble Administrator's Garden in Suzhou, and the Lingering Garden in Suzhou. The first two are imperial gardens and the latter two are private gardens. Many western gardens have geometric patterns, which form a sharp contrast, the Central Park in New York is square and rectangular. There is also the Chinese music, there is the famous ancient music "High Mountain and Running River". The Voyager 2 space probe launched by the United States in 1977 was aimed at flying out of the solar system. In 2018, it entered the interstellar medium. The probe carried copper records with the music "Higher Mountain and Running River".

After Buddhism entered China as a foreign religion and foreign thought, over a period of absorption and digestion, it has undergone a localization transformation, and an important sect, Zen Buddhism, has emerged and formed Chinese characteristics. China's Zen Buddhism is called localized Buddhism; economically, Zen is engaged in productive labor and is self-sufficient, "if one is not engaged in labour for a day, he will not eat for a day," and it can develop continuously. It is relatively less affected by government policies and has a very distinctive specialty. In terms of thought, Zen does not pursue pure theoretical speculation. It says "A special transmission, outside the teachings, does not depend on written words, directly points to the human mind, sees one's nature and becomes Buddha", and in Zen, there is no grand debate scene. Xuanzang founded Dharma character school after he returned from India, but the more theoretical Dharma character school has little influence in China. Zen Buddhism integrates practice into daily life and production labor and there are not many requirements for speculative theory; the practice method is relatively simple. It pays attention to Zen, "One flower, one world, one leaf and one bodhi". People should perceive and experience with their mind. There are many scientific discoveries and inventions in modern times, after a period of research, the scientists suddenly have inspirations in some chance coincidences. Sometimes in dreams, sometimes in conversation, sometimes in walking, they have new ideas. In meditation and contemplation, what will a person experience? Is it conducive to scientific and technological invention and discovery?

Zen Buddhism is full of stories, called Koan, which is also a feature of Chinese culture. For example, the four major Chinese literary masterpieces are "Journey to the West", "Water Margin", "Romance of the Three Kingdoms", and "Dream of the Red Chamber". The first three works, at the beginning, were many scripts for story-telling, and writers later summarized and formed novels. Many stories in Zen Buddhism are rich in philosophical rationality and are easy for people to remember and circulate. For instance, there is a story in Zen Buddhism that says that when a person is in the forest, suddenly a tiger pounce at him from behind. He ran hard and ran to the front of a steep mountain slope, when there was nowhere to go, he saw a tree vine, so he became wise and climbed up the tree vine. Just when he felt relieved that he could get rid of the tiger which was chasing after him, he suddenly noticed that a mouse was gnawing on the tree vine. At this time, neither is up nor down. A mouse bites the vine in front, and a tiger chase after it. At this moment, he suddenly found a berry on the steep wall and he forgot about the mouse and the tiger. He picked the berry, delivered it to his mouth, and tasted the sweet taste... The story stopped here. Some people will ask, what happened afterwards, did he go up or fall, and out of danger? You can think about why this story ends when that person tastes the berries? What is the meaning of the story?

There is also a story telling that there was a famous monk named Niutou Farong in the Tang Dynasty. It is said that when he was practicing in the cave, a flock of birds would carry flowers for him. Legend said that after he paid homage to Dayi Daoxin, the fourth Zen Buddhist Patriarch, there will be no more flowers. Someone asked other Zen masters, why did Niutou Farong get flowers before paying respect to the Fourth Zen Buddhist patriarch? Why did the flowers disappear after visiting Daoxin? A Zen master answered that we all envy wealth and nobility, and we all hate poverty and humbleness. The other answers are more interesting and both answers are "Niutou". Niutou is the name of the mountain. Fa Rong practiced in Niutou mountain and later founded Niutou Zen. These answers seem to say that in the world people are obsessed with difference, but there is no difference in the world.

In Taoism, there are also many stories; in "Chuang Tzu" there is a story. In Warring States period, there was a state "Wei", Wei state had a cook whose name was "Ding". One time, the cook was cutting up an ox for the king. His technique was very well and the sounds of cooking were all in regular cadence. The king said, "Ah! Admirable!

That your art should have become so perfect!", the cook said, "What your servant loves is the method of the Dao, something in advance of any art. When I first began to cut up an ox, I saw nothing but the (entire) carcass. After three years, I ceased to see it as a whole. Now I deal with it in a spirit-like manner, and I do not look at it with my eyes. Observing the natural lines, (my knife) slips through the great crevices and slides through the great cavities, taking advantage of the facilities thus presented. A good cook changes his knife every year; an ordinary cook changes his every month. Now my knife has been in use for nineteen years; it has cut up several thousand oxen, and yet its edge is as sharp as if it had newly come from the whetstone." The king said, "Excellent! I have heard the words of my cook, and learned from them the nourishment of life."

3.The spread of Zen in the world

Since then, Buddhism has Chinese characteristics, and Zen has become a part of Chinese traditional culture. Zen also has a great influence on modern Western society. It is more adaptable to the fast-paced life of modern society. After the modern management thought matures, the vertically integrated firm dominates all aspects of social life, and social development is orderly, but individuals are a little confused and found that this society is customized and programmed, and everyone's life trajectory is predictable; on the other hand, for modern people, they need to face all kinds of complicated changes and social phenomena in society, and they need to find spiritual sustenance. Now in society, the influence of traditional religion has weakened. Behind all kinds of complex phenomena, there are profound laws of things and social development, but many of these laws can only be understood and summarized after a period of time. The laws of science themselves also change and adapt to a certain space or a period of time. In modern society, people pursue material benefits, but blind pursuit of material benefits brings series of problems. Ordinary people cannot leave society, ordinary people rely on various treatments and benefits provided by organizations and enterprises; they have many relationship networks. Zen Buddhism does not require individuals to leave the family and society, so it is very attractive to modern people. Like the hippie movement in the 1960s in Western society, Zen became the spiritual pursuit of hippies, and the word "Zen" appeared in English. Gary Snyder, a famous American poet, graduated from Reed College and studied anthropology, and later turned to Oriental literature. He liked country life and practiced personally. He was deeply influenced by the Chinese culture. He has been to India and then to Japan to practice Zen culture. He lived in Japan for a long time and came to China in the 1980s. He published many collections of poems. In Europe, there is the famous Swiss German writer Hermann Hesse. He is the most read German writer in the 20th century. In the 1960s, he became the spiritual mentor of hippies. Hesse received the Nobel Prize in Literature in 1946. He loves Eastern culture and Chinese classical thought. His well-known works include "Siddhartha", "The Glass Ball Game", "Journey to the East" and so on.

The connection between Zen culture and the hippie movement is also a very interesting topic. The hippie movement and the "Beat Generation" in the West in the 1960s appeared as anti-traditions. After the maturity of various capitalism systems, for ordinary people, it is a common pursuit to receive a good education, find a good job in large companies and other institutions, gradually get promoted, and start a family. The hippies are contrary to this tradition, their behavior is not in line with the mainstream values of society, and they do not take an unusual path, but these hippies played a major role in the microcomputer revolution in the 1970s and 1980s. Steve Jobs is the most typical one. His family background is ordinary and he went to a good private university—Reed College, but dropped out and became a hippie. He went to India for a while. After returning, he found a job. Suddenly he was creative, got venture capital and founded Apple Inc with Steve Wozniak. He suddenly made a fortune and became a billionaire, an influential man, but later he encountered management disputes and left the company. After more than a decade, he became a figure influencing the world with Apple mobile phone. When Apple Inc first launched the Apple computer, it also produced an advertisement, "1984". The name was taken from George Orwell's novel of the same name, which has obvious anti-traditional meaning. This tradition refers to the traditional computer manufacturer represented by IBM. George Orwell is a famous British writer. His works include "Animal Farm" and "1984". At last on the market, the standard formed by Intel and Microsoft, many compatible computer companies and software companies together have shaken the position of IBM and formed the new pattern. Jobs' life experience is worth thinking about. As an ordinary person, he went up or step down several times, he was ordinary and was also wealthy. Finally, he died of illness at the age of 56. His fate is related to the great era. The Silicon Valley management model has provided him with a stage and development space, but we can think about it. Why aren't the people who develop systematically have made these careers? For instance, John Sculley, who later was hired by Apple; why are these anti-traditional people existing? Why are people who are different in the eyes of ordinary people existing?

In the field of science, Zen Buddhism has a great influence. In the 1970s, Fritjof Capra, a theoretical physicist, was also influenced by the hippies. He studied Eastern philosophy and religion, and published a book entitled "The Tao of Physics". The book explores and compares the connection between the concepts of modern physics and the basic thought of Eastern philosophy and religious traditions, reveals that the latest physics concepts are surprisingly similar to the ancient Eastern philosophy. This book has sold 1 million copies and has been translated into 23 languages. It has become a teaching reference book for many universities for quite some time.

These show that traditional Chinese culture is able to adapt to the modern industrialized society. In terms of how to treat work and life, and the attitude toward life, no matter how the mode of production changes, how the form of production organization changes, no matter how advanced the production tools, the traditional Chinese thought can still survive and develop in society. Now society is diversified and the exchange of diversified ideas can promote the birth of new thought. Bertrand Russell said, "The distinctive merit of our civilization, I should say, is the scientific method; the distinctive merit of the Chinese is a just conception of the ends of life. It is these two that one must hope to see gradually uniting."[66]

4.Tibetan Buddhism

Tibetan Buddhism is believed in Tibet. The Tubo dynasty in history was the first feudal dynasty in Tibet's history. During the Tubo dynasty, Buddhism was spread to Tibet from India through Nepal and China's inland in the 7th century. Mongolia also believed in Tibetan Buddhism in the 16th century, and later the Qing Dynasty further praised Tibetan Buddhism. The spread of Buddhism in Tibet has also undergone a process of localization, because there was a primitive religion in Tibet called Bon, which still exists today. Bon and Buddhism competed against each other. Finally, Tibet accepted Buddhism and formed Tibetan Buddhism. Tibet Buddhism is characterized by the reincarnation system of living Buddhas. Tibetan Buddhism is also divided into several factions, Nyingma, Sakya, Kagyu and Gelugpa. Now the Gelugpa, is the most influential in Tibetan Buddhism and the leaders are the Dalai Lama and the Panchen Lama. The Tibetan Buddhism is popular in Tibet and has formed theocracy regime. I think it should be analyzed from the political and economic perspectives of Tibet. The difference between Tibet and other areas of China, especially inland, is that Tibet has a noble system. The Chinese classical thoughts such as ethics thought have emerged in history. After the popularization of education, politics is a kind of civilian politics. Unlike in Tibet, it has been aristocratic politics until the 1950s. It can be observed that the Western medieval theocratic influence is also great. At the same

---

[66] Bertrand Russell, The Problem of China, chapter 11, pp 194

time, in the Western Middle Ages, it was also aristocratic politics, while Zen conformed to the characteristics of civilian politics. Tibet is a snow-covered plateau, where the altitude is high, the air is thin, and life is not easy. People mainly engage in agriculture and animal husbandry production; at the same time, there is basically no industry there. The environment is kept relatively pure and there is little pollution, it is a mysterious land. If some people have the opportunity to travel to Tibet, they could experience and feel, experience the traditional culture of Tibet, and feel the difference in Tibetan Buddhism.

5.the role of Buddhism in the modern society

Buddhism later disappeared in India. There are different explanations for the reasons of Buddhism disappearance in India. In the 8th century AD, after Adi Shankara reformed Brahmanism, he absorbed some theories and contents of Buddhism and produced Hinduism. Buddhism is regarded as a branch of Hinduism. Later Buddhism combined the content of Indian Shaktism. After the 10th century, Islam continued to invade India. Islam opposed idolatry and destroyed a large number of monasteries, all of which intensified the disappearance of Buddhism in India. The founder of Buddhism, Shakyamuni, said before his death that the Buddhism he founded was the era of Sad-Dharma in the next 500 years, and the era of idols in the next 1,500 years. After that, the Dharma will disappear. The development of Buddhism history seems to have verified his prophecy. But Buddhism was later introduced into East Asia and Southeast Asia, and it still has a great influence in these areas.

Buddhism is basically individual salvation and does not intervene in government affairs, but the development of Buddhism requires government support and sometimes conflicts with government policies. Buddhism is completely different from the traditional Chinese Confucianism and Taoism. Buddhism has a speculative thought, which is not available in the traditional Chinese Confucianism and Taoism. But Buddhism is also a religion and lacks the content of natural science. Therefore, in the beliefs of the ancient Chinese society, there is a lack of natural science, or natural science does not occupy the mainstream. Buddhism emphasizes meditation and emphasizes not pursuing material gains, abandoning desires, and even family. This is something that Confucianism and Taoism cannot do. Confucianism says, "There are three things which are unfilial, and to have no posterity is the greatest of them." Taoism does not require abstinence, but demands to be moderate. Buddhism does have its value today, it requires people to accumulate virtue, to do good, and not to do bad things. Moreover, it is not difficult to study Buddhism. Compared with Taoism, it has a wider spread and greater influence, especially today, in a material society, Buddhism emphasizes the power of spirit, thought, and meditation. Buddhism has led to a profound study of spirit and is of great value. Zen Buddhism is not only a religion, but also a representative of a culture and it represents a way of life and attitude towards life, gives people peace of mind, gives people a variety of enlightenments, can be integrated into people's daily life, people do not need to be separated from daily work, but it can also play a good role in daily work, it is beneficial to individuals, groups and society. Phil Jackson, a well-known coach in the American NBA League, has studied Zen very much and emphasized the power of spirit. He brought Zen practice methods into the training of the team. He was called a "Zen Master", and personally lead the team to eleven NBA championships.

Buddhism does have some mysticism. As we talked about before, it needs to be experienced by individuals. It is not easy to express this knowledge. It is a personal experience, and everyone's feelings may be different. Science is not omnipotent, many phenomena in the world cannot be explained by science. People in many countries and regions in the world still believe in religion. "Science cannot decide questions of value, they cannot be intellectually decided at all, and lie outside the realm of truth and falsehood. " [67]Religion is not science

---

[67] Bertrand Russell, Religion and Science, chapter 9

either; science seeks certainty, and what kind of results will be achieved when certain conditions are met. Life is full of various changes. Scientific knowledge is popular, universal and repeatable; scientific experiments can be achieved by anyone. Anyone with the same experimental conditions can repeat the results of other people's scientific experiments. Scientific experiments have no relationship with morality. The results of scientific experiments will not be affected by the level of personal morality, but religion generally talks about morality. The level of morality has a lot of relationship with personal practice. Religion is not only theoretical knowledge and religious doctrine, but it also needs to experiment, like Buddhism emphasizes meditation, and higher wisdom is born from higher mind.

Buddhism and Taoism have similarities. Buddhism not only talks about theory, but also about meditation. Taoism also emphasizes the "physical and mental practice." There is yoga in India. Yoga comes from meditation and is still very popular today. The capital of yoga in India, Rishikesh, is located in the upper reaches of the Ganges. It is a famous tourist city and a holy place in the hearts of yoga practitioners. In Indian religious tradition, it is believed that if one could bathe in the Ganges in one's life, he or she can eliminate karma (bad action) and wash away one's sins. In Rishikesh, there are many specialized yoga schools. Students come from all over the world. After graduation, they will be issued a yoga diploma, and they can return to their home country to teach yoga. Yoga is a good way to exercise and is beneficial to the body and the spirit. Yoga is very influential in the world. Similarly, Taoism also has a similar thing called Daoyin. The Mawangdui Han Tomb was excavated in Changsha in 1972, and it was confirmed that it was a tomb in the early Han Dynasty, the period was about 186 BC and Daoyin images were unearthed. At that time, there was Daoyin, and today there are still many people practicing in the society, such as Tai Chi and Qigong, the effect is similar to yoga.

6.Some thinking

Knowledge in the world is very broad, but it is impossible for individuals to master all of knowledge in a limited time, only master those knowledges that are most beneficial to their own development. In society, people pursue wealth, status, power, etc., and other needs rely on various services provided by the government and enterprises. In today's society, if some publicity says in a certain profession and a certain field, people can find a good job after they learn it well, a person can get a quick promotion in the workplace, and gain wealth and status. It is sure that people will go after and come in a continuous stream. But only learning a certain aspect of knowledge does not guarantee that all people's desires will be met. Everyone's needs and desires are many, hope to have a lot of power and wealth, want to be healthy, live longer, have a happy family, and everything. There is a story about someone who went to see Hades after he died. Hades opened the record and said: "You are a good person, and you will be a man in your next life, and enjoy the best blessings. What kind of person do you want to be?" This person said, "Thousand acres of fertile fields with enough water, the ten wives and concubines are all beautiful, the father is the prime minister, the son is Marquis, and I relax in the hall." After the Hades heard this, he stood up and said, "Man, if there are such good things in the world, you are Hades, I will be you!"

People's needs and desires cannot be fully met. There are always choices and trade-offs. I remember there is a saying in economics that economic growth, full employment, and inflation, these three goals cannot be well achieved at the same time. It says that it is difficult to achieve them at the same time. The economic growth rate is very high, the employment rate is high and inflation is low. It is quite good that two of the three goals may be achieved at the same time. We talk the emperor of China, the emperor in ancient China had the supreme status and unlimited power. Everyone dreamed of being an emperor. But in fact, being the emperor in Chinese history was a high-risk occupation. According to some scholars' statistics, there were total 559 emperors and kings (397 emperors and 162 kings) in Chinese history, the emperors in Chinese history have a poor life span. According to statistics, from the ancient Chinese Emperor Qin Shihuang to the end of the Qing Dynasty, only 6 emperors with a history of more than 2,000 years have lived beyond 80 years, and 12 have lived beyond 70 years. The emperor's average life expectancy is less than 40 years old. The treatment of the emperors is unmatched, and the medical conditions and safeguards in all aspects are the best, but why is the life generally not long? Because everyone wants to be an emperor, the incumbent emperor faces all kinds of conspiracies and tricks all the time. There are exceptions. The last feudal dynasty of China, the Qing Dynasty, produced an emperor, Qianlong Emperor. The emperor's political and military achievements was historically outstanding, he himself was also very diligent and very hardworking. During his time as emperor, the development of the ancient Chinese society reached its peak and the territory reached its largest surface (extension). At the same time, he himself had a very long life span, the longest-lived emperor in Chinese history. He lived to be 89 years old and claimed to be a perfect old man, he died at the later 18th century. Among the emperors in Chinese history, Qianlong emperor can be counted as a perfect figure in all aspects. Under his rule, the society was very stable and the economy was prosperous. The ancient Chinese society reached its peak, but the Opium War broke out shortly after his death. In 1792, the Macartney Mission of the United Kingdom visited China, hoping to expand trade with China and establish diplomatic relations, but also with the purpose of collecting intelligence. After the Macartney Mission arrived in China, the Qing government attached great importance to it and the mission was received by Qianlong Emperor, but the two sides had serious disputes over the etiquette to meet the Qianlong Emperor. In the ancient Chinese society, the degree of autocracy has gradually deepened. The status of the emperor was getting higher and higher, while the status of ordinary people, including ministers, was getting lower and lower; when the minister talked with the emperor, the minister in the beginning sat, stood, and at last talked on his knees. In the end, the purpose of the mission to visit China was not completed, and China also lost an opportunity to contact the modern industrial civilization.

Now there is a Nobel Memorial Prize in Economics Sciences in the Nobel Prize, which rewards economists who have made outstanding contributions. Economists, if they recognize the laws of economic development, can profit for themselves. There are indeed economists who have done so, like David Ricardo and John Maynard Keynes, who have made a lot of money in the market. For instance, Keynes was also the founder of modern economics. Since the establishment of the Nobel Prize in Economics Science, scholars who have made discoveries and breakthroughs in the academic field have basically been awarded. People who get profit in economic and politic field rarely win the Nobel Prize. For instance, we have introduced the Nobel Prize-winning economists Coase, Williams, North, Simon, etc., who are all scholars who teach in universities. Walt Whitman Rostow, a famous American economist, is also very accomplished in academics. He wrote the book "The Process of Economic Growth" and served as assistant to the US President for National Security Affairs, but he did not win the Nobel Prize in Economics. There is also the famous American economist John Kenneth Galbraith, who once served as the assistant to the office of the US Price Administration, and later as the US ambassador to India. He is a representative of the American neo-institutional school, and he also has not won the Nobel Prize in Economics Science. The well-known financier George Soros has very big influence in the financial market. In fact, he also has his own set of theories. Soros loves philosophy and he is different from ordinary business figures. He was heavily influenced by Karl Popper when he was young. Soros's theory is not recognized by today's academic discipline.

Let's talk about the Nobel Prize in Physics. I mentioned William Shockley when talking about the Silicon Valley Model. Shockley is an outstanding scientist and won the Nobel Prize in Physics, but he is not good at management and failed to start a business. The Intel Corporation's founder Robert Noyce is very successful in his career, with wealth, fame and achievements. Noyce and Jack Kilby independently invented the integrated circuit; Kilby worked in the company and taught in the university successively, Kilby's career is not as brilliant as Noyce and his reputation is not great; Kilby won the Nobel Prize in Physics in 2000; Noyce died of a heart attack in 1990 at the age of 62, Kilby died in 2005 at 82 years old.

There is such a story in the ancient Greek mythology. There was a prince in Troy called Paris, who later seduced Helen, wife of Priam and triggered the Trojan War. One day, Paris came to Mount Olympus and met three goddesses: Hera, Athena and Aphrodite; these three goddesses asked Paris which of them was the most beautiful. Hera is the wife of the Zeus, representing power, Athena is the daughter of Zeus, representing wisdom, and Aphrodite is the goddess of sexual desire, representing love. Hera said that if Paris thinks she is the most beautiful, she will give Paris power. Athena said that if Paris chooses her, she would give Paris wisdom. Of course, Aphrodite said she would give Paris love. At last, Paris chose Aphrodite and believed that she was the most beautiful, but Hera and Athena were all dissatisfied. In the end, Paris got love, but lost power and wisdom, it led to the Trojan War. This story actually says that power, wisdom and love, these three things cannot be satisfied at the same.

With the overall progress of society, some goals that were considered difficult to achieve in the past can now be easily achieved. Let's talk about the life span of people. The average life expectancy of people in ancient society was not very high. The average life expectancy may be more than 30 years old at the beginning of the 19th century. After the industrial society and the information society, the level of science and technology has raised, and the understanding of diseases is much higher than that in ancient times. Modern society has entered a welfare society, and medical security conditions are good in all aspects. In many developed countries, there are many elderly people and the population is ageing. Let's talk about wealth. A few decades ago, in China, for an individual to own two thousand US dollars, that was a big number. Now in society, many persons own a few million or tens millions of US dollars. Some rich men have billions and tens of billions of dollars wealth. At the beginning of 2021, the Forbes World's Billionaires announced that China entrepreneurs with one billion US dollars reached 1,058, surpassing the combined United States, India, and Germany. In China a few decades ago, ordinary households looked forward to buy watches, sewing machines, and bicycles. Then they started owning televisions, refrigerators, and washing machines. Later, their needs were air conditioners, stereos, and computers, and more recently, they want cars, housing, and savings. I do not know if there will be any new changes in the future?

In modern society, religion still exists and still has a great influence. This is indeed worth thinking. What exactly is religion? In the modern industrialized society, the era of the Internet, and the era of artificial intelligence, ordinary people can easily travel across continents. Human science and technology can send astronauts to the moon and will reach Mars in the future. But why in developed countries do many people believe in religion? It may also be another question. Why many people in the world do not believe in religion? Especially in those countries and regions with heavy religious traditions, religious beliefs may be taken for granted. Nowadays, society is a material society, everyone pursues wealth. Many people think that as long as they have wealth, they can own everything, power, official positions, status, cars, villas, dignity, even health and life, these can all be acquired with money. Like Maslow's analysis of the five needs of people, if a person think that these five needs can be exchanged for money, doesn't money become a religion?

Some sociologists believe that money are the new religions in today's society. Many people believe in this new religion and rely on this new religion to satisfy their various life and social needs. The famous American sociologist Talcott Parsons summarized the theories of many sociologists in the book "The Structure of Social Action," such as Emile Durkheim, Max Weber, Alfred Marshall, and Vilfredo Pareto, but he missed one person. It is the famous German sociologist, Georg Simmel, 1858-1918, who was a German sociologist, thinker and philosopher; Simmel's works include "The

Philosophy of Money" and "Sociology of Religion" and had a great influence on the subsequent development of sociology. Many sociologists were inspired by Simmel's thought and developed new content. Simmel believed that in modern society, money can buy more and more things, and money has become the core and absolute value. Currency has gradually changed from merely a means and tool of economic value exchange to the purpose of social life. The content of life becomes more and more expressible in money. Why is such a thoughtful sociologist ignored by Parsons? It is said that Parsons wrote a chapter about Simmel, and there is a manuscript, which is now stored in a library and can be consulted. In "The Structure of Social Action", at the end of the paperback preface, there is a note that Parsons said, "Along with the American social psychologists, notably Colley, Mead, and W. I. Thomas, the most important single figure neglected in the Structure of Social Action, and to an important degree in my subsequent writings, is probably Simmel. It may be of interest that I actually drafted a chapter on Simmel for the "Structure of Social Action", but partly for reasons of space finally I decided not to include it. Simmel was more a micro than a macro sociologist; moreover, he was not, in my opinion, a theorist on the same level as the others. He was much more a highly talented essayist in the tradition of Tocqueville than a theorist like Durkheim. Again, however, his influence on subsequent sociological thought has been a major one."[68]

What is a currency? In the book "Money Mischief" by the famous economist Milton Friedman, the story of a stone money island is told. In the Caroline Islands of Micronesia in the Pacific Ocean, there is a small island called Yap Island. The currency on the island is called "Rai". It is a huge and hard stone wheel, which is mined on other islands and shipped to Yap Island. This kind of stone currency is inconvenient to carry because of its large size, so after the transaction, only a mark is made on it to indicate the ownership of the currency. At the end of the 19th century, when Germany was

---

[68] Talcott Parsons, The Structure of Social Action, preface

administering the Caroline Islands, the government planned to repair the roads on the island. At first, the local residents were unwilling to do the work. Later, the managers thought of a way. They decided to impose a fine and how to collect it? The manager sends someone to draw a "+" in black ink on the most valuable stone wheel in each house or public place, and indicate that the stone wheel has been expropriated by the government. This method was very effective. Soon, the local residents repaired the road. Afterwards, the administrator erased the "+" on the stone wheel and indicated that the fine had been paid and the residents had regained their wealth.[69]

When society is about to progress to a higher stage, will the new religion of currency go through a similar process of reformation in history, and how to reform it in terms of ideology and system? What are the new ways of working? What is the new economic organization? How will new forms of work arise? What are the characteristics? How is it different from previous management methods? How will this organization change? Will the separation of ownership and control be adopted? We discuss these issues further in the next chapter.

---

[69] Milton Friedman, Money Mischief, chapter 1

18 CHAPTER CREATIVE WORK AND SERVICE SECTOR

In the development of the computer sector in the beginning, there was no distinction between software and hardware. Like in the large computers produced by IBM, both software and hardware were developed by IBM. A set of computer software could not be used on another computer. The concept of software compatibility was first proposed when the IBM System/360 computer was developed. The IBM 360 computer system has multiple models, and a set of software could run on computers of different models. Later, especially with the development of microcomputers, the establishment of computer hardware and software standards, and the emergence of a large number of compatible computers, the software became independent from the hardware, and many independent software companies emerged. The software developed by software companies can run on computers produced by different companies. The software system is divided into operating system software and application software. The operating system software is the basic software or platform software, responsible for the input and output of the system hardware, and the application software runs on it. Application software includes word processing, financial tables, graphics and image processing, databases, games and various industry application software, etc. Software development is basically a purely intellectual activity, it does not require large-scale production equipment, it only needs a computer. Now the computer is getting smaller and smaller, it is more and more convenient to carry, and the application on microcomputer are very popular. In many industries, a computer controls the operation of the equipment, such as the intelligent equipment and robots of the fully automated assembly line in automobile assembly, the dispatch of electricity, the daily signal control of the trains; the service sector also uses computer systems to provide user services, such as the sale of train tickets and airplane tickets, and the automatic registration system of hospitals, bank's self-service information service system, online store, e-commerce, etc., Daily household appliances, such as refrigerators, washing machines and rice cookers also contain many microprocessors, and are already intelligent. The work of software development is different from the traditional work in the factory. The main work of software development is to write codes, and intelligent equipment with computer codes can be applied to the factory.

The development of software is also a project. For example, the computer software in the Apollo Moon Landing Project is a very large project, which contains a lot of people. Software engineering first needs to analyze user needs, then it produces system design, including architectural design and detailed design, and division functional modules, it determines the tasks of the system modules, writes the software program, and then performs software testing, including user testing, etc.; sometimes in the development process, the above steps may be repeated, and if problems are found, code must be modified, modify the code or modify the design, user needs may also change.

Pure intellectual activities, like human thoughts, can change quickly. Software projects are much easier to modify and to perfect than traditional industrial projects. This is different from traditional industrial manufacturing. Traditional industrial products cannot be easily changed once the design is finalized, because it involves a whole set of systems, involves performance and quality of product, involves processing and manufacturing, and involves many parts and components and corresponding suppliers. Any design improvement and perfection can only be realized after the next model and next-generation product design. This difference in software work provides conditions for the development of creativity. We can see that computer products, whether it is hardware or software, are iterating very fast, and new products are constantly emerging. One product, which life is one to two years. may be outdated and replaced by new products. In comparison, the development cycle of a civil aircraft is 10 years or even longer. Therefore, in the computer sector, more attention is paid to innovation, which can be called creativity. We can expand the scope of discussion here and study creative work in a larger space. At the same time, the computer software sector can be regarded as an information service sector. We also need to study how the management of the service sector is different from the traditional industrial manufacturing management.

1. Creative work

About 20 years ago, the new British government came to power and launched a new initiative to encourage creative industries, mainly referring to advertising, architecture, art and antiques, arts & crafts, design, fashion design, film and photography, music and visual performing arts, publishing, software, computer games and electronic publishing, radio and television and many other fields; the government encouraged creative companies to use their imagination and stimulate creativity, thereby promoting economic development and driving new forms of employment. Later, a university professor, Richard Florida, also wrote a book "The Rise of the Creative Class", saying that there will be a large number of creative employees in society in the future, this creative group is different from another group of the capital class.

The work of a creative person is indeed different from ordinary work. Just like a writer, where and when the inspiration comes, there is no nine to five in the usual sense. No one knows when and where there will be any innovative ideas.

With the further development of society, the material will be more abundant, people's basic needs will be more easily satisfied, people can engage in more creative work; capitalist society undoubtedly creates more products and wealth than agricultural society, and the future society should be more creative. There is a prerequisite here. People who are engaged in invention and creation need a material foundation. Under certain material conditions, they can focus their energy on creativity. For an idea to become a product, a best-selling product on the market, it needs teamwork and the support of the financial system. In the current society, creations and inventions are mainly realized in enterprises, and enterprises will have a certain amount of research and development (R&D) investment, but there will also be changes in the R&D of enterprises. When the development of the company is mature, the company take care of the market of the current product, not of new products; the company is more willing to carry out micro-innovation of mature products rather than to invest in the development of disruptive products. So in such a society, there are many creative ideas, creativity exerts greater influence, creates a lot of wealth, and creates new forms of employment, then the corresponding management, work mode, various economic policies, including various social and economic policies must correspondingly change and have to adapt to the new situation. In the past, the traditional dichotomy divided society into two classes. In the dynasty country, there was the aristocracy and the peasant, and in the modern country there is the capitalist and the working class. According to this reasoning, in the future, society will be divided into creative and ordinary workers.

From a technical point of view, the development of artificial intelligence technology is now fast. According to the current trend, unmanned vehicles, unmanned aircraft, various smart devices, virtual reality glasses, smart clothes, artificial intelligence question answering systems, intelligent writing robot, robot doctors, robot secretaries, both robot lawyers and home service robots will appear. Some of these technologies have already been realized, and some will be used in the future. In 1997, IBM's Deep Blue Computer defeated the world chess champion Kasparov. In 2016, Google's computer program AlphaGo defeated the world Go champion Lee Sedol. In

2011, IBM's deep question-answering computer system Watson competed on the American game show "Jeopardy!" and won the championship and received a prize of $ 1 million. In the future, the Watson system may be applied to the medical field to assist doctors in disease diagnosis. The artificial intelligence expert system has been applied to the medical field. For example, in the future, image recognition and machine learning technology will be further developed, the popularization of home medical diagnostic equipment, combined with artificial intelligence question answering system; intelligent machines can screen and diagnose some diseases, and can effectively inhibit diseases in the initial stage of the disease development.

In the era of intelligence in the future, Chinese traditional medicine will also play a role. With the deepening of the study of meridian and collateral, and the deeper understanding of their functions, smart machines can perform acupuncture and moxibustion on people or use some modern electronic equipment, such as laser acupuncture apparatus for acupuncture and moxibustion treatment. Some chronic diseases can be treated at home to save medical costs and simplify medical procedures.

The artificial intelligence question answering system may also be applied to the education sector, for one-on-one teaching, tutoring, chatting with you, playing chess with you, telling jokes to you, and helping you learn foreign languages. Maybe the future smart phones will be voice-operated, just like Apple's Siri, Google's GoogleNow, Microsoft's Cortana. In november 2022, OpenAI company launched ChatGPT, it based on large language models. ChatGPT can answer question, translate language, search information, write paper, generate code, make picture and movie, it is a chatbot and virtual assistant.

In the manufacturing sector, such as the aircraft industry, civil aviation, and large aircraft with more than 100 seats, still have basically the traditional layout. In terms of military aircraft, flying-wing aircraft, also known as Blended Wing Body aircraft, are already practical, but this technology has not been applied to the field of civil aviation. The main technology of flying wing aircraft is the fly-by-wire operating system. At present, some companies are designing and developing it. I believe that in the near future, flying wing aircraft will also appear and be practical, as well as supersonic transport and electric planes and so on. In 2018, Massachusetts Institute of Technology (MIT) researched the first electroaerodynamic plane in the world. The plane has no propeller and jet thruster, it produces "ionic wind" through the collision of charged air molecules and provides dynamic force, the mechanical design is simple, no moving parts, no emission. In the future, other types of aircraft may also appear, such as the Skylon aerospace plane developed by the United Kingdom, which can take off from the airport, enter outer space, and reuse its push like an ordinary aircraft. In the aerospace field, chemical propulsion is currently used. Scientists have also envisaged many other propulsion methods, such as laser propulsion, nuclear propulsion, solar sail propulsion, magnetic sail, etc. The solar sail does not need to carry fuel and to spread a huge film in space to obtain light pressure, propelling the spacecraft. New things, new inventions and creations require new materials and technologies. Interstellar travel will also encounter problems such as loss of gravity and cosmic radiation. For these problems, experts envisage to provide artificial gravity and magnetic field shields.

When society has reached a new stage, simple labor may be replaced by intelligent machines. Humans are engaged in more advanced labor and creative labor. At that time, many machines will be intelligent, and intelligent machines will be much more complicated than current machines. There will be a lot of new job opportunities in the design, production, maintenance and sale of various intelligent machines. Nowadays, there is a term "smile curve" in enterprise production, which refers to the two ends of the product manufacturing process: the value of design, development and sales is increasing, while the value of the production process is decreasing.

The digital economy is characterized by the explosive growth of the amount of information. There will be a considerable number of people engaged in knowledge production, knowledge acquisition and maintenance, etc., like digital libraries; how to obtain useful information from a large amount of information will be a problem. People acquire knowledge not only in schools, but also on the Internet, anywhere on the earth, like the current Wikipedia. After Wikipedia has been popularized, it is very easy to inquire. The traditional encyclopedia stopped publishing the paper version and changed to the online version.

In the agricultural society, most people are engaged in agriculture. In the industrial society, agriculture is in a secondary position, because machines replace manpower. It can be speculated that in the future society, the number of workers engaged in more creative work will increase significantly, while the number of people engaged in simple labor will further decline. This kind of more creative work may be in various service sectors, innovative service sector, more technical service sector. The computer software can be regarded as a kind of service sector-information service sector, the production, processing of knowledge. Intelligent machines just solidify knowledge in the machine in the form of software, making it more convenient and easier for people to use. All kinds of intelligent robots that will appear in the future just turn knowledge in various industries into digital codes embedded in the robots.

In the agricultural society, the basic economic organization is the manorialism; in the industrial society the basic economic organization is the company system. In the future, which creativity organization will form? What kind of organization can bring out creativity? Workers employed in such organizations may be more flexible, they will not stay in one organization for their entire lives. They will go wherever they can realize their ideas. Which organization can quickly turn each idea into a marketable commodity? How to manage this type of new organization? How is it different from traditional management? What is the relationship between this type of organization and the enterprise? What is the relationship with the government? In service organizations, the importance of intellectual resources has become increasingly prominent. The most important resources in software companies are people. This is somewhat different from traditional capital accumulation. Now in society, capital is everywhere, and how to make good use of it is a big problem. This way of software work is also different from traditional ones. Traditional enterprises, factory systems, and personnel work are concentrated and use the same production line. Software is a line of code that can be written anywhere, and the production tool required is a computer. Sometimes, I think that a book can be written by several authors together, should these authors be together? Their cooperation only requires effective communication tools, allowing them to be in any different place. If there is an organization that concentrates people in different places and provides knowledge-based services, then the management of this organization is very different from traditional organizations. Traditional factories will still exist and will still use large mechanical equipment, machine tools, CNC machine tools... This equipment will be more intelligent, but due to the massive use of robots, the number of people employed by the factory will decrease. The digital nomadic tribe is a newly emerging group in society. The main feature is that the workplace and working hours are not fixed. Unlike traditional work methods, they work in the office all the year round from 9 to 5. The work of the digital nomad finishes in Internet, most creative work can be done online.

In the future, interdisciplinary and inter-professional learning will be more common for workers, and education will become more important. Not only learning in school, education will become more flexible. Maybe humans have landed on Mars and began to colonize at that time, transforming the Martian atmosphere and soil to make it suitable for human habitation. There are large space stations in outer space that can accommodate tens of thousands of people. At the same time, there are solar power plants in space that can transmit energy back to Earth and solve the problem of greenhouse effect. Titan has also been developed. Human beings have solved the problem of interstellar travel. Human beings step out of the solar system and to the galaxy. The scenes described in science fiction will become reality. Whether people will come into contact with aliens is another interesting topic. When it comes to aliens, I remember reading an article which said that in 1953 in Mexico, aliens visited a Mexican farm one day. The farmer was invited to visit the alien planet. The aliens were very polite and could speak Spanish and French. The aliens took the Mexicans to visit their planet for three or four days. After returning to Earth, the Mexicans gave the aliens some plant seeds and livestock. The scenery on the alien planet makes this Mexican feel very strange and curious, it is very different from the earth. There, food is rich in nutrients, everything is free, there is no currency, and the pattern of urban buildings is different from that of the earth; in the room, the light can be controlled freely. The transportation is a docking vehicle similar to a spaceship, point-to-point flight. The Mexican farmer described a lot of novelties. After reading what he described, I don't know if he really went to an outer planet. If there are intelligent life higher than the earth, if a person can go to the outer planet to explore and learn about the technological level, socio-economic development, and social hierarchy, class structure, personnel work and lifestyle, ideological, economic, cultural, and political systems, is there a market? Does religion exist? What is the organization of the economy? It's a good thing to be able to travel to alien planets. If there are aliens, are they as friendly as the ones mentioned above? In addition, if aliens exist, why are they not in open contact with us humans? For example, they can teach us some advanced technology, improve our material level, and promote social progress.

Today human science and technology methods, such as the Kepler Space Telescope, have detected thousands of exo planets outside the solar system. Some of them are not far away from the stars. They are similar to the earth and are in the habitable zone of life. They are known as terrestrial planets; some terrestrial planets also contain water as an important substance. In the search for terrestrial planets, scientists used machine learning technology to speed up the search process. In 2020, scientist find Kepler-1649c planet, it far from earth about 300 light year and it is in the habitable zone of life, it is about 1.06 times the size of Earth, the temperature is similar to the Earth's. In 2017, a scientist found TRAPPIST-1 star, it has seven planets that are the same size as the Earth. They all have water possibly, three planets that are in the habitable zone of life are the great possibility. Later more and more terrestrial planets will be discovered. In universe, stars generally have multiple planets, it is estimated that there are about 6 billion terrestrial planets in the Milky Way; in observed universe, there are about 200 billion galaxies at least. Many galaxies are bigger than the Milky Way and have more planets. Does life exist on these terrestrial planets? Or even advanced intelligent life? Is the earth the only home suitable for human being existence? Some scientists classify future civilizations. The first type of civilization can obtain the energy of the entire planet; the second type of civilization can obtain the energy of the sun itself and the third type of civilization can obtain the energy of the entire galaxy. At present, the civilization of our planet belongs to the zero civilization and is in the initial stage of the first type of civilization. Humans' current detection capabilities are limited. For example, is there any water on Mars? Are there living things?

2. Service sector

When it comes to the service sector, management in this field is indeed somewhat different from that of the industrial manufacturing sector. In the 1980s and 1990s, IBM took the lead in the field of microcomputers at the beginning, but then made some mistakes of decision and suffered serious losses. A manager, Louis V. Gerstner Jr, was hired to carry out service transformation. Under his leadership, IBM dusted themselves off, and started again in a new field.

Gerstner was born in Mineola, New York, USA in 1942. He came from an ordinary family. His father was a company dispatcher and his mother was administrator at a community college. He graduated from Dartmouth College with a bachelor of engineering and from Harvard University Business School with a master's degree. After graduation, he joined McKinsey & Company, worked for McKinsey

& Company for 9 years, and then came to American Express to be responsible for the company's travel services. In business, after 11 years of working in American Express, he became the CEO of RJR Nabisco. In 1993, Gerstner became the CEO of IBM. It can be seen from Gerstner's work experience and educational background that he is a typical professional manager who has been engaged in tourism services for 11 years and has a deep understanding of the service sector.

When summarizing and leading IBM's service transformation, Gerstner said, "The skills required in managing services processes are very different from those that drive successful product companies. We had no experience building a labor-based business inside an asset-intensive company. We were expert at managing factories and developing technologies. We understood cost of goods and inventory turns and manufacturing. But a human-intensive services business is entirely different. In services, you don't make a product and then sell it. You sell a capability. You sell knowledge. You create it at the same time you deliver it. The business model is different. The economics are entirely different." [70]

We can analyze an example of a service sector. This field is the healthcare sector. We analyze the healthcare sector from the perspective of management. The healthcare sector is a very important field in modern society, and it involves everyone. The more developed a country is, the more it will invest in medical care. This is very obvious in developed countries. The medical system affects people's health and family income, and social medical expenditures in developed countries reach a high proportion, generally reaching 10% of the country's GDP, and sometimes even higher.

The medical and health care system of any country is different, and must be affected by the country's history, economic development, politics, and society. The medical security system of

---

[70] Louis V. Gerstner, Jr. Who Says Elephants Can't Dance?, chapter 14

various countries can be divided into three types according to the government's role: 1. Market-oriented. Medical services are operated by the market, and the government does not intervene or intervenes very little. The government only provides medical services for a part of the population, such as government employees, military personnel and special groups, and other people purchase commercial insurance. The whole process is dominated by the market, and the United States is a typical example. 2. Social insurance type. The insured, the employer, and the government pay to form a medical fund, and the fund pays for the insured's medical expenses. Germany adopts this model. 3. Government arranged type. The government pays and the government runs hospitals to provide medical services for all citizens. The expenditure is paid by national taxes. The British National Health Service System (NHS) is of this type.

Each of these types has advantages and disadvantages. The payment mechanism and the government's role are different, and the effects are also different. Let us take the NHS, for example. According to information, the NHS in the UK is a planned economy with centralized management. Doctors and nurses are government employees. It is basically impossible to close any hospital. The cost of medical treatment is paid by government taxes. Hospitals are state-owned, and revenues belong to the government. Government expenditures return back to the government and become government revenue. The US model has the highest medical expenditure in the world, but the effect is not satisfactory. These models all face a common problem, that many countries hope to solve is the rising medical costs.

Regarding the problem of rising medical costs and a series of other problems brought about by society, relevant experts and scholars have analyzed many, from the professional field, from the management perspective, and from the economic level to analyze why the cost is rising and how to face it. For example, they analyze the high-tech characteristics of modern medical treatment: various advanced medical equipment, and various new drugs are effective and expensive. Technological progress has also brought some new problems, such as environmental pollution, chemical fertilizers, pesticides, antibiotics, various fast foods with high sugar, high salt, high fat, and high calories, plus unhealthy lifestyles, various chronic diseases, cardiovascular diseases, diabetes, etc., threaten people's health and cause medical expenses to rise.

From an economic perspective, the developed countries are all consumer-oriented countries, and the demand for medical and health services is increasing. In the form of third-party medical payment, when patients seek medical treatment, the proportion of self-payment is not high, which can easily lead to excessive medical treatment.

From a management perspective, the income of medical personnel is relatively high. As we all know, there are two industries whose employees have the highest income in the United States, one is a doctor and the other is a lawyer. So, some people suggest that doctors get a fixed salary. There are also issues about prescription drugs and drug prices, which have an impact on the rise of medical expenses. Another problem is the administrative cost of the healthcare system. This part of the cost is also very large, including the administrative expenses of insurance companies and hospitals, marketing and advertising expenses, here I want to mainly focus on the problem of rising medical expenses from management perspective and economic perspective.

Regarding the administrative costs of the medical system, some scholars suggest that it uses a single payer method to save this part of the expenditure, such as the United Kingdom, Canada, etc. However, the medical systems of these countries have problems such as long waiting time for medical services and low efficiency. The payment by patient or insurance is not the best solution either. What measures can be adopted to solve the increase in medical expenses and save administrative expenses? Should it be government-run or market-led? Why does the market-led US medical expenditure remain high, reaching 18%, but the effect is not satisfactory and the medical coverage rate is not high? These questions are not so easy to answer, we need to understand the origin of these questions.

First of all, I want to make it clear that this article mainly analyzes the problem of rising medical expenses when the market system is adopted in the medical care field and analyzes the role of vertically integrated firm in the medical system.

The modern manufacturing sector is basically dominated by vertically integrated firm. Vertical integration integrates the ownership of assets of various organizations within an enterprise; disputes arising from contracts are reduced. Vertical integration eliminates a large number of transaction costs and controls costs in the market. It will be competitive and have an advantage in the market. Now not only in the manufacturing field, but also in other fields, there is also a trend of vertical integration. It is worth noting that in the field of healthcare, the market-led United States has also experienced vertical integration, which is the development of the Integrated Delivery System (IDS), which consists of hospitals, physicians, outpatient clinics, family healthcare institutions, and nursing homes, they form vertically integrated organization. Health maintenance Organization (HMO) is a model of IDS. "Preferred Provider Organization" plan, by a larger insurance company or a third-party health care plan management company, and one or more by doctors, hospitals and other health care service providers (nursing homes, family health service agencies, rehabilitation agencies, etc.) form a "group" to sign contracts and provide services to policyholders. There are two types of medical insurance organizations in the United States. The first type of organization is a medical insurance organization licensed by the state government in accordance with the laws of the state, including commercial insurance companies, Blue Cross and Blue Shield insurance company, organizations, and health maintenance organizations (HMO). The second type of organization is "self-funded employee health care organization" governed by federal law is a medical insurance institution jointly funded by employers and employee organizations.

In service sector, include of the medical care industry, the customer satisfaction of large enterprises and organizations is not very good under the market leadership. People can think whether vertically integrated organizations are not necessarily suitable in the service sector. Then we need to think about the difference between the service economy and manufacturing in the service sector.

The modern service sector covers a wide range, including entertainment, hotels, tourism, wholesale and retail, banking, insurance, post and telecommunications, communications, medical services, and so on. The concept of service is defined as "a service is an intangible product or benefit provided by one party to the other." Services emphasize intangible characteristics. Compared with tangible goods, services are intangible, non-storable and inseparable. Services cannot be stored because they are intangible and the services provided to different customers are different. During the service process, service provision and consumption occur at the same time. During the service consumption process, customers will personally participate in the service process. The production and consumption processes of tangible products are separated from space and time. Tangible products have inventory and need capital turnover, while services are intangible and there is no inventory. The difference between the service process and production process of the general product shows that traditional management theories cannot be copied to the service field. In the aviation service sector, we can see that it is not necessarily large companies that can provide cheap, efficient, and high-quality services. For example, Southwest United Airlines and Virgin Airlines have good services and are not large in scale. Because once the scale is large, management costs will increase, it is not easy to provide low-cost services, and there is no competitive advantage.

The healthcare sector is a service sector, and it is a special service field. In addition to providing medical services, it also emphasizes public welfare and non-profitability (some groups of hospitals and insurance are also profit oriented). This is the biggest difference from the profit-oriented organization or the enterprise. This difference also leads to different management methods. Medical service access conditions are relatively high, requiring basic construction scale, necessary diagnostic and treatment equipment, and medical personnel with medical skills, who must provide all-weather services. Medical services are intangible, service provision and consumption are inseparable, patients are participants in the medical service process, and services are one-to-one services. Medical services are highly personalized and highly professional. At the same time, the information and knowledge of doctors and patients have is not equal.

The non-profit characteristics of hospitals are the most prominent feature that distinguishes the medical industry from other service industries. In modern society, non-profit organizations are becoming more and more influential and developing faster and faster. Political parties in some developed countries also have a deeper understanding of this. There are also a lot of research and discussion on the management of non-profit organizations. The modern scientific management is formed with the development of this organization of enterprises. It can also be considered that there is no mature management theory of non-profit organizations. The biggest characteristic of non-profit organization management is to rely on volunteers instead of professional managers. Corporate management talks about the functions of managers. Managers are the backbone of the enterprise. Enterprise development minimizes the loss of personnel, especially to avoid the migration of managers to other companies. Therefore, managers are given high salaries, equity and options, as well as various benefits, these are not seen in non-profit organizations (in some nonprofit, there is no profit because the employees benefits are so high). Non-profit organizations are not privately owned, and no one has the right to obtain profits. Non-profit organizations have no profit distribution. Among non-profit organizations, profit is not the first, and various cost control methods are not available. There are also non-profit organizations marketing. For an organization, whether it is a business or a non-profit organization, the larger the scale, the higher the management cost, and the more management levels and complexity. The greater the number of non-frontline staff such as managers, analysts, and planners, the greater the burden of management costs. The salary payment of middle managers is a considerable part. After an enterprise expands, it can offset the increase in management costs by increasing production capacity, expanding the market, and pursuing profit maximization. What medical care provides is services. Hospitals are non-profit in nature and cannot balance management costs through expansion like companies. If the hospital is large in scale and the management cost is high, then in order to balance the cost and daily operation, the only way to deal with it is to conduct excessive medical treatment, conduct too many medical tests or procedures, and prescribe more drugs. Because of the asymmetry of information between doctors and patients, this is not difficult to do. Then, because of third-party payment, it is easier. Hospitals cannot launch tangible products, and can only operate by increasing the number of services and increasing the price of a single service.

In service sector, medical care market, the organization with lower degree of vertical integration are more successful in market competition. It set up small-scale hospitals, like low-cost airlines. It reduces management levels and scale. Increasing supervision is important, increasing auditing is one method. In management, there are service marketing, non-profit organization marketing, and marketing auditing. It regular reviews of the organization's business activities and evaluation of the organization performance. Auditing is a profession, and the audit department is an independent institution in many countries, belonging to the parliament or the court of audit (there are also big accounting/auditing private companies KPMG…). Enterprises also have internal audits, mainly for accounting, finance and accounts to check for violations of laws and regulations. Marketing audit includes the organization's external environmental objectives, strategy, organization, system and function, which is quite a comprehensive physical examination of the organization. Marketing audits should be conducted by an independent third party to achieve fairness and should be independent of other departments of the company. Marketing audit is more suitable for non-profit organizations, suitable for such organizations as hospitals. Regarding the management of non-profit organizations, we will only mention personal views here. It may not be mature yet. We hope readers can write to us and discuss it.

Health cannot be simply analyzed by economic methods. Personal health is not necessarily proportional to wealth and status. The more medicine you take, the healthier your body cannot be guaranteed. Physical health is related to medical and health conditions, economic conditions, personal medical knowledge, diet and living habits, mental status, and personal moral level. The ancient Chinese classical medical book "The Yellow Emperor's Classic of Internal Medicine" (Huang Ti Nei Ching Su Wen) divides people into Spiritual man, Sapients, Sages, the Men of Excellent Virtue. Like Sages, "The Sages attained harmony with Heaven and Earth and followed closely the laws of the eight winds. They were able to adjust their desires to worldly affairs, and within their hearts there was neither hatred nor anger. They did not wish to separate their activities from the world; They could be indifferent to custom. They did not over-exert their bodies at physical labour and they did not over-exert their minds by strenuous meditation. They were not concerned about anything, they regarded inner happiness and peace as fundamental, and contentment as highest achievement. Their bodies could never be harmed and their mental faculties never be dissipated. Thus, they could reach the age of one hundred years or more."[71]

Ancient Chinese thinkers like Confucius and Mencius are Sages, in reality, it is impossible for everyone to be a sage, people always have many emotions and desires. "The Yellow Emperor's Classic of Internal Medicine" (Huang Ti Nei Ching Su Wen) also writes, " In ancient times those people who understood Tao (the way of self cultivation) patterned themselves upon the Yin and the Yang(the two principles in nature) and they lived in harmony with the arts of divination. There was temperance in eating and drinking. Their hours of rising and retiring were regular and not disorderly and

---

[71]Ilza Veith, The Yellow Emperor's Classic of Internal Medicine(Huang Ti Nei Ching Su Wen), (the Williams & Wilkins company, 1949), Chapter 1

wild. By these means the ancients kept their bodies united with their souls, so as to fulfill their allotted span completely, measuring unto a hundred years before they passed away. Nowadays people are not like this; they use wine as beverage and they adopt recklessness as usual behaviour. They enter the chamber (of love) in an intoxicated condition; their passions exhaust their vital forces; their cravings dissipate their true (essence); they do not know how to find contentment within themselves; they are not skilled in the control of their spirits. They devote all their attention to the amusement of their minds, thus cutting themselves off from the joys of long (life). Their rising and retiring is without regularity. For these reasons they reach only one half of the hundred years and then they degenerate." [72] Chinese old book has a tendency that thinks ancient society is better, a regular life is good for health, too much desire is not good.

In an organization or enterprise, capable individuals with high incomes, high responsibilities and work pressures, and more effort can enjoy relatively complete services; ordinary individuals have more free time and can concentrate on what they are interested in many things, they pay more attention to physical exercise and the quality of life.

Different individuals in the society, work status, education level, physical condition, family status, needs and desires are not the same, their status in society, personal income, benefits and treatments are also different. The society provides medical infrastructure and basic medical conditions, popularizes medical knowledge, invents new medical methods, and various types of organizations serve various types of customers and provide consumers with diversified services.

Nowadays, social products and services are diversified to meet the needs of different types of people. Just like the current smartphone market, there are distinctions between high-end, mid-range and low-

---

[72] Ilza Veith, The Yellow Emperor's Classic of Internal Medicine(Huang Ti Nei Ching Su Wen), (the Williams & Wilkins company, 1949), Chapter 1

end markets. Businessmen use high-end mobile phones with excellent performance, complete functions, and expensive price; middle-class and white-collar workers use mid-end mobile phones, which are cost-effective; low-income groups use low-end mobile phones, which are cheap and have basic functions; now key phones are available in many areas. There are many manufacturers of computers and mobile phones on the market, as well as many hardware and software manufacturers, competing with each other to promote technological upgrading. Different groups choose mobile phones of different performance and price according to their economic conditions and needs.

In the United States, there is another service sector that is completely different and very distinctive, and that is the higher education sector, American higher education, is world-famous, Ivy League colleges, Harvard, Yale, Princeton... Every year it attracts countless overseas students to study. After graduation, students are proud to graduate from these prestigious universities. These universities are the goals pursued by countless families. The quality of their education is also recognized worldwide. In these universities, many Nobel Prize winners, experts and scholars have been trained in various industries and fields. Harvard Business School and Yale Law School are also very famous. But we rarely see these famous universities, like supermarket chains, set up a chain institution, expand the scale of their schools, and expand all over the world (some start doing it, Yale/NUS, Essec in Singapore...). The number of students they enroll every year does not change much. There is also a market in the higher education sector in the United States, but it does not seem to be engaged vertical integration, although tuition is not cheap, people around the world also recognize the quality of education in American universities. This indicates that in the service sector, its management methods are different from those of vertically integrated firm.

3. Future work and organization

In the current society, the Silicon Valley mode occupies a leading position in the high-tech field. The society is going to develop. Will new management form emerge? How is it different from the current management form? The outstanding characteristics of the Silicon Valley mode, or the differences from the traditional management, are summarized as follows: 1. Loyalty to social relations and technology. 2. Focus on innovation. 3. Less management hierarchy. In the balance between creativity and capital, Silicon Valley puts more emphasis on creativity, and in the traditional management mode, banks are important. In the new management mode in the future, what kind of status will this balance maintain? Many experts and scholars have discussed the work mode of the future society. Here, we also talk about it from several aspects. In the society of the 20th century, with the maturity of scientific management thought, the increasingly perfect corporate management system, and vertically integrated firm occupy a dominant position in various industries; a series of characteristics emerged in society at this time. Ordinary workers had a job and had a certain number of years in the job, working in a company, companies not only provide wages, but also provide various benefits, some also provide living subsidies, housing subsidies, transportation subsidies, provide medical insurance and pension insurance, etc... Companies have retirement mechanisms, and individuals receive social pension after retirement. This is true of managers, employees in enterprises, including top management. With the advancement of science and technology, the development of society, and the improvement of various medical security conditions, the average life expectancy of people has increased. Many countries have become an aging society. A problem has arisen, that is, pensions cannot make ends meet. The solution is to postpone retirement and set up personal accounts for social pensions.

One feature is that with the continuous development of the information and communication industry, there are forms of mobile office and home office. Communication between people has become more and more convenient. For example, let's talk about the way meetings are held. Traditional corporate meetings require everyone to gather together to discuss in the same meeting room. Now with the popularization of the Internet, people living in different places can still participate in meetings at the same time, and telecommuting is becoming more and more used.

Another feature is the increase in mental labor in society. In the traditional repetitive mechanical labor, the number of employees is declining. Creative work and network are kind of mental work, and management work in an enterprise is also a kind of mental work. With the development of artificial intelligence, mental work will become more and more widespread in society. If this trend continues, then the difference between mental work and manual work will disappear, creative work and network will become the regular work of many people.

The above-mentioned characteristics will appear in the society at present and in the future. The first thing that may appear is the change of the retirement system. After people's life span is extended, many elderly people will still have the energy to engage in brainpower at the age of 60, 70, 80 or even 90. We can see that many managers are older and still energetic, hospital doctors, politicians and school teachers, many of whom can still engage in medical visits and teaching at a relatively high age. For these energetic elderly people, even if they are not working in the industry, if individuals are good at managing money, they can invest their funds to increase their wealth, they can still work, and they can work on a larger scale. Chile's pension system is this model that invests personal pension funds in the market in the form of a national system, and there is a supervision mechanism. The growth of people's average life expectancy in society is closely related to people's knowledge of nature and the human body, social systems, economic systems, business management, working methods, social security system, moral and ethical standards, public opinion, medical conditions, education and technological levels, etc. Changes in one aspect of society will affect other areas. There is a Chinese idiom, "pull one hair and the whole body moves" which illustrates this meaning. There is a "butterfly effect" in modern science, which means that small changes under initial conditions may cause a chain reaction of the system, which also illustrates this situation.

A person can continue to work after the current retirement age. The main discussion here is mental work, but not everyone can do so. It depends on the specific situation of each person. Just like not everyone in the world can become a national leader, not everyone can become a capitalist, and not everyone can become a scientist, university professor, or someone who has achieved something in a certain professional field. There is a lot of knowledge in society, and what to learn requires individual condition. In addition, it is different whether it is self-study by oneself or with a teacher. Learning also has a threshold. To enter a certain professional field requires some opportunities, and to make major discoveries in a certain field requires the preference of the Muse. The personal family environment also has a great influence on personal growth. People who grow up in a business family are better at business, and those who grow up in an artistic family are naturally interested in art. People who come from an engineer family are naturally more invested in science and technology. The words and education of the parents have a great influence on the children. The prolonged life expectancy and the increase in mental work in society have created such a trend. At the same time, we must also note that modern society is changing very fast. New concepts, new technologies and new ideas are emerging in an endless stream. Only people who are good at learning can in the future win in society.

Second, the management needs to changes to adapt to the situation dominated by mental work. At present, the Silicon Valley mode, management method where creativity and venture capital play a major role, is mainly concentrated in the Internet industry and the computer industry, and in those heavy industrial manufacturing fields, such as machine tools, automobiles, machinery manufacturing, chemicals, medicine, ships, aerospace, etc., The traditional management methods are still dominant. The Silicon Valley mode of enterprise creation and management has not been extended to other fields. This may mean that the Silicon Valley mode needs some changes before it can be applied to a wider range. Many experts and scholars have discussed some phenomena, such as knowledge workers, clover organizations, and so on. They believe that with the development of communication tools, organizational forms will become more flexible and major changes will take place. But this day, such major changes have not happened. Some companies give their employees flexible working methods, instead of the fixed work time of 9 am to 5 pm, some of the working time can be freely used, and even work at home. This phenomenon is more common in Silicon Valley companies. With the popularity of the Internet, many new professions have emerged, such as website design and maintenance engineers, self-media workers, bloggers, travel promoters, online store operators, and so on. However, the traditional corporate system and management methods still dominate the society. The kind of full-time, wage-receiving, and social pension work after retirement is still the goal pursued by most people. On the contrary, these new career opportunities are considered risky and unstable. Why is there such a situation? We need to think in details about the new model and what is the difference in the new way of working.

Why the Silicon Valley mode has not been extended to other industries and fields? It can be analyzed in detail. In this chapter, we mentioned the creative work and service sector. Individuals and groups who carry out creative work actually provide a knowledge-based service and sell knowledge, which is very similar to the law, education and medical field. Unlike traditional industrial product manufacturing, services are intangible and non-storable. In the service, the ownership system of an enterprise is different from that of the industrial field. The management form of the traditional industrial field is the separation of enterprise ownership and control, it can also be called the investor ownership system. Investors occupy a very important position in company, but in the service sector, such as law, accounting, investment banking, management consulting, advertising, architecture, engineering, medicine and service professions, the employee-owned firm is dominant, and the employee ownership is rare in the manufacturing. The employee ownership means that an enterprise is completely owned by employees. The firm's employees or some subset of them, share among themselves full rights to control the firm and to appropriate its net earnings. The employee ownership is sometimes called a partnership form. It is very common in the practice of law in developed countries. It is said that in the United States, employee ownership is explicitly required by law and employee ownership is presently the only available form for organizing the practice of law. Based on this reasoning, if the Silicon Valley model companies provide a kind of knowledge service, they should also adopt the form of employee ownership. As previously analyzed, in the ownership system of Fairchild Semiconductor-a pioneer in Silicon Valley, the New York Investment Bank, eight physicists and engineers jointly own the company. However, after the development and growth of Silicon Valley companies, they hire professional managers, who have considerable power, and the management mode has become traditional mode, which is the same as the traditional management, the separation of enterprise ownership and control.

Today's Silicon Valley companies, like Google and Facebook, adopt a two-tier or even a three-tier equity structure. The company's shares are divided into categories A and B. Class A shares are publicly sold, while Class B shares are not publicly traded. Class A shares stocks hold fewer voting rights, or even none, Class B stocks have more voting rights. This can ensure that after the company grows, even when the shares are diluted, the founders can have more voting rights by holding a large number of Class B stocks, continue to control the company, and avoid being driven out of the company like Steve Jobs. I think this two-tier ownership structure is actually an employee ownership system, but not every employee has controlled the company. The founders of the company are often one step ahead of the understanding of new technologies, and can control the company through the two-tier ownership structure. It is not only the amount of capital in hand that controls the fate of the company.

Silicon Valley companies rely on creativity. In the balance between creativity and capital, they tend to be creative. If Silicon Valley's corporate leaders can't keep up with the rapid changes in the market and technology, they are often prone to lose their advantage in the new market structure, and even cause companies to withdraw from the market and be merged and reorganized. There are many examples of this, such as Sun company, DEC company, Kodak company, etc... The next chapter will talk about the evolution of high-tech companies in the market, the phenomenon of mutual transformation between leading companies and edge companies in the market.

So far, we have not seen traditional manufacturing companies adopt a management mode similar to Silicon Valley companies, and basically adopt traditional management methods. If manufacturing companies cannot break away from the traditional mode of separation of corporate ownership and control, knowledge services cannot take an important position in corporate management, the creative-dominated management approach of the Silicon Valley mode cannot be applied to manufacturing companies.

This book has been talking about organization, whether it is a shareholding system or a factory system, it is an autonomous organization directly oriented to the market. Modern capitalism is also born out of an autonomous city in the Middle Ages in Europe. Therefore, the future economic organization may also be an autonomous organization. In the future, the autonomous organization will provide knowledge services, it is a service-oriented organization, and adopt an employee ownership system instead of a mode of the separation of ownership and control. How big is this autonomous organization? What is the relationship between the future autonomous organization and the enterprise? It is still a business in itself, just like the current law firm and accounting firm. Enterprises are pursuing profits, and autonomous organizations are also pursuing profits, but profit is not the main goal, the main goal is new ideas and new products. If an organization cannot see the changes in the market, but only maintains the micro-innovation stage of existing products, with profit as the main purpose, and the main means of expanding the current product market share, when disruptive innovation appears in the market, the organization will go downhill and face difficulties. Therefore, in the future, such autonomous organizations, organizations that provide knowledge-based services, and organizations that adopt employee ownership system will be very different from today's enterprises in management and other aspects. They will focus on innovation instead of market, and they will be able to change quickly to adapt market. How does this type of organization survive? Do they need financing? What is the relationship with the financial system? How to develop products? What services are provided? What will happen to the financial system? Now that digital currency, Bitcoin, block chain and other technologies are developing rapidly, after the emergence of digital currency, what will happen to the currency and the financial system? What is difference between digital bank and traditional bank? Can the company or autonomous organizations issue currency? Where does their credit come from? Does the central bank still have the right to issue currency? Is the issuance of currency still controlled by the state? What impact will the global penetration of the Internet have on the financial system? In 2020, Facebook launched the Libra digital (2021 It was renamed to Diem), which is currently mainly used for cross-border remittances and will develop into a global payment system in the future.

In the future of corporate management, will there be a market within vertically integrated firms? Can the firms issue currency? Will there be an election method in management? The leaders of large vertically integrated firms are comprehensively selected through shareholder appointments, supervisory and employee elections. One leader is selected from several candidates to be the company's manager. The manager has limited powers and has time in office, it can be re-elected. In firm, there is supervision, the supervision can be composed of creative, autonomous organizations and shareholder representatives. The management is subject to the internal supervision of the enterprise. There is no subordinate relationship between department managers and senior managers.

Perhaps this method of electing managers is very different from traditional administrative methods. This method of election is similar to the political system. The election has a similar place, democratic management of enterprises.

The vertically integrated organization is established by administrative means, which saves transaction costs and has high efficiency. It is a pyramid-shaped structure, which establishes many levels of authority, and is interdependent on an education system, which is beneficial to personnel flow, gives full play to the talents of personnel, and maintains organizational stability. The market-oriented structure is a flat organization centered on the market with few management levels, which is conducive to creativity and encourages the emergence of new technologies. There is functional differentiation, separation of legislation, justice and administration, separation of politics and economy, and the emergence of autonomous organizations, it can create more products and wealth.

The current capitalist society is based on the market and has a series of institutions and systems such as banking, insurance, family partnerships, shareholding systems, and credit systems. It is a more advanced than an agricultural society, whether it is aristocratic government or bureaucratic government. So, we can reason, the current evolution of such large vertically integrated firm will also have a different structure centered on the internal market, based on the current network communication methods, digital currency, digital finance, autonomous organizations, etc. New forms will have further differentiation in function, reduce management levels, and encourage the emergence of new technologies and new products.

Under the vertical integration model, if an individual wants to make new inventions and creations, he must first obtain authoritative approval, obtain authoritative funding and personnel support, and coordinate with the internal departments of the enterprise. There are many personal factors, emotional factors, irrational factors. In a market-centric structure, individuals have greater independence. Anyone or any group with new ideas and new inventions can obtain financial support, establish autonomous organizations, develop products, provide services, transact in the market and encourage individual. Autonomous organizations are engaged in a certain function, have a say in large organizations, and have representatives of different interests.

If we look at vertically integrated firm, like Ford Motor Company, Ford is interested in cars and wants to invent new cars. He needs to start a business, raise funds, hire people, buy equipment, prepare factories, contact parts suppliers, establish sales networks, and form a vertically integrated firm. In the era of mainframe computers, companies like IBM are dominant. Computers are developed by IBM's internal engineers. The development of large computers takes a long time. For the development of IBM360 mainframes, 2,000 software engineers worked on the project. For individuals, mainframe computers are not easy.

With market-oriented structure, standardization of product internal structure, modularization, platformization, the company produces diversification of products and services, there are market expansion, market refinement, and many suppliers. After the appearance of microcomputers, individuals, whoever wants to improve computers do not need to establish a company like IBM. Individuals can have a new invention in hardware or software, and then they can transact in the market. The era of microcomputers and the Internet is also considered to be a platform economy. The software platforms of microcomputers are operating systems, Unix, DOS, Windows... the programmers develop application software on these platforms; software platforms for smartphones include Apple iOS and Android systems; Internet platforms, like videos, are YouTube, social media platforms are Facebook, Twitter, Instagram... Users publish their content on these platforms. The difference between the platform economy and the vertically integrated firm is that the platform economy is characterized by openness, and any enterprise and individual can participate, with greater freedom, fiercer competition, richer products and content, and faster upgrades.

So far, in terms of corporate management methods, we have

talked about the family business, vertically integrated firm, the Silicon Valley model, and the internal marketization of enterprises. These corporate management models may coexist in the future society. In different industries, they have different advantages. Just like in nature, biology is diverse. There are mammals, oviparous animals, marsupials, insects, various plants and microorganisms, terrestrial animals, marine animals, amphibians, reptiles, and flying animals, spore plants, gymnosperms, ferns, single-celled organisms, multi-celled organisms... and intelligent creatures --- human being.

19 CHAPTER EVOLUTIONARY PROCESSES OF SILICON VALLEY MODE

A few years ago, I wrote an article analyzing the laws of market evolution of high-tech companies. Here I have slightly modified and added some content to compare the market evolution process with the traditional Chinese philosophy --- Yin and Yang theory. This chapter quotes some articles and more professionals.

In management, the concept of the product life cycle is often used to describe the stages of the product changes in the market. In fact, the evolution of the market is far more complicated than the concept of the product life cycle. The process of market evolution is a complex process involving many aspects, such as product competition among different companies, decision-making mechanisms for internal management of the company, competition for the market by new companies and companies occupying market leadership positions, product innovation, and new product development and proliferation, consumer participation, joint development of enterprises and supply chain organizations, etc.

The concept of the path dependence refers to the influence of events in the past on future decisions. In fact, it considers the role of history and how history affects the present and the future. Path dependence was first used to explain the self-reinforcing phenomenon in the process of technological evolution, that is, the "positive feedback" phenomenon, and was later introduced into the study of economic history to analyze the institutional changes of economic organizations and to establish the path dependence theory of institutional changes. Introducing the concept of path dependence in the market evolution theory can lead to better understand the process of market evolution and better understand where the concept of product life cycle can be improved.

What role does history play in the evolution of the market? How does it work? What are the effects on the market of those factors? In the process of market evolution, how do companies interact with their environment? How do companies interact with consumers? How did the corporate organization itself evolve? How does the role of corporate managers change? In the new market, how do the original leading companies rely on the past market methods? Which companies have led the innovation and diffusion of new technologies and new products, and what kind of interactions do these companies have? This article attempts to establish a theoretical framework to understand the evolution of the market from the perspective of path dependence.

1.Review of path dependence

Path dependence means that the system can't get rid of the influence of the things that happened in the past, the asymptotic distribution is a function of its own history. In economics, political science, and sociology, history is very important; in the German economics history, there was once a German historical school of thought; in the American economics history, the institutional school is under the influence of the German historical school; in management science, history is also important, market evolution is a historical process and the process could last several years, more than ten years and decades. In the process, it includes technological changes, system evolution and the diffusion of innovation. The history is a process of change.

Initially, the path dependence is used to analyze the self-reinforcing phenomena in the process of technological change---"the positive feedback", Arthur and his colleagues in the late 1970s and early 1980s(Arthur 1989,1994; Arthur, Ermoliev, and Kaniovski, 1987) had discussed the ways of technological change, they had researched the phenomenon of increasing returns in the economic life. In late 1980s, David (David, 1985, 1986) presented the results of a serie of historical studies of the typewriter keyboard; QWERTY keyboard was regarded as a symbol of the phenomenon of path dependence.

Later economist Douglass North (North, 1983) had researched the institutional change with path dependence, he researched how to carry out system innovation, change the economic structure, found the modern economic and political system, and he opened a new direction of economic history research.

This article analyzes the market evolution from the angle of process, history, and change. The growth of the market, the expansion of the enterprise is the result of the structure, the institutional change. In this process, the technology innovation is very important. The process of market evolution is also the process of the technology innovation. Technology innovation can be divided into continuous innovation and disruptive innovation. Continuous innovation is on the basis of existing technology improvements and upgrades; disruptive innovation is the leap of existing technology, for example, smart mobile phone is disruptive innovation for traditional mobile phone; disruptive innovation challenges the status of the existing enterprise.

2.The process of the market evolution

About the process of the market evolution, there are many articles that analyzed it, the product life cycle theory is popular. The theory divides the product shape of its market into early, growth period, mature period and recession period; the theory pretends that the life of a product is limited, like the life of organisms, it has a process of growth and recession, but the product life cycle theory is limited (Lambkin, Mary and George S.Day, 1989). The theory doesn't point out the problem of the enterprise strategy, it also doesn't involve the spread of technology and the creation of product. Lambkin, Mary and George S. Day (Lambkin, Mary and George S.Day, 1989) tried to find a model of market process with the view of ecology; a lot of discussion is needed to check if the method is suitable for the analysis of a social organization

2.1 The structure of the market

This article tries to explain the process of the market evolution with the view of history, of path dependence. At first, we need to understand the subject that participates in the market. Now, in the theory of the market, the enterprise is the subject; in the market, there are many enterprises. Some scholars (Raghu Garud, Peter Karnoe, 2001) point that the main body of the development should be divided into two parts in the Silicon Valley. They think that the regional economics is divided into enterprises and a loosely network of entrepreneurs. The article shows that the market should divided into two parts, one part includes formal organizations and entities, enterprises, including manufacturing vendors, sellers, and various existing enterprises engaged in manufacturing and sales, upstream and downstream enterprises, these companies compete or cooperate; they engage in design, produce, manufacture, sell; another part includes informal organizations; the part isn't a substance, and it is the association and relationship between these people engaged in enterprise related activities and the social network between various people, such as venture capital, universities, lawyers, consultants, clubs, communities, and communication platform. The people in the social network are engaged in the joint production of knowledge, such as product design, management consulting, marketing and other service activities. These informal networks expand to include peripheral companies with high-tech ties: law firms and commercial companies specializing in intellectual property, venture capitalists, suppliers and so on. This non-profit network organization helps to strengthen any aspect of the public/ private cooperation, from taxation to intellectual property licensing (Dara Elizabeth Menashi, 1997).

Some sociologists put forward the concept of "social capital", Robert D. Putnam (Putnam, 2000) points that "social capital" is a relationship of mutual benefit in the society. The people who want to help other people can get good return from other people. In the Silicon Valley, the birthplace of the microcomputer industry, under the leadership of a small group of computer entrepreneurs and, at the same time, being assisted by a resource-rich university community, the Silicon Valley emerged as the world's high-tech development and manufacturing center. Much of its success is due to the region's horizontal information network and formal partnerships developed between start-up companies (Putnam, 2000).

According to Putnam's view, getting good social attention and relying on social relationships is a necessary condition for social prosperity. The "social capital" is a concept of sociology. In the article we will use the concept ---"relationship network". We think that "relationship network" can explain the role of this relationship. "Relationship network" is a combination of people, it is a group of interconnected, communicating with each other, sharing knowledge, producing knowledge together; they exchange ideas and design, stimulate creativity; they offer creative thoughts and produce knowledge together for the enterprise. Richard Florida discussed the role of creativity in regional economic development.

Formal organization and informal organization constitute the whole market; market evolution is the result of the two parts together. The group of manufacturing vendors includes many enterprises, they produce and sell commodity, their purpose is profit and it is tangible; the relationship networks offer many services for manufacturing vendors, they are the source of sellers and manufacturers growth, they offer knowledge, creativity, design, consultation services, ideas, methods for manufacturer, they offer a reserve of talented persons, and technical force. The joint production of knowledge is a service activity, it is invisible. The relationship network is an autonomy team in the production of common knowledge, the joint production of knowledge beyond the boundaries of enterprise. It is a distributed knowledge production system(Gibbons, et al, 1994). The role of manufacturing vendors is to produce/realize creativity, produce commodity, they create value. Manufacturers create tangible commodity, the relationship network is the initial market, it offers invisible services. These two parts are interdependent, mutually inclusive, they are contradictory. The two parts aren't static, they are mutually complementary, perfected, related to each other. They will mutually transform under certain conditions.

The theory of Yin and Yang

Some readers, or those who have some knowledge of Chinese culture, will find this dichotomy here, which divides the entire market process into two groups, formal organizations and informal organizations, manufacturers, entrepreneurial groups, and social relationship networks. This dichotomy is very similar to a theory, the traditional Chinese theory of Yin and Yang. We can explain the Yin-Yang theory here, compare and contrast it with the situation of formal and informal organizations.

The theory of Yin and Yang comes from the ancient Chinese classic "I Ching". The book "I Ching" is really interesting. There are so many books in ancient China, countless books. Some books have been preserved, and some books have been lost, there will be different editions of the same book. The Book "I Ching" was written very early and has been retained until today, it records many historical experiences since the birth of the Chinese civilization; it contains many aspects of life and is the crystallization of the wisdom accumulated by people. It is not only a philosophical work, but it has also practical value. Later, the theory of Yin and Yang was gradually integrated into various traditional Chinese thoughts and doctrines, and is reflected in the theories of Confucianism, Taoism, Yin and Yang, and medicine. "I Ching" says that "The Yang and the

Yin of the Universe are called Tao". Confucianists include "I Ching" in classic works. The Taoist book "Tao Te Ching" says that "all things bear the shades on their backs and the sun in their arms". The Chinese medical theories of traditional Chinese medicine are also based on the theory of Yin and Yang. "The Yellow Emperor's Classic of Internal Medicine" (Huang Ti Nei Ching Su Wen) says, "The principle of Yin and Yang (the male and female elements in nature) is the basic principle of the entire universe. It is the principle of everything in creation. It brings about the transformation to parenthood; it is the root and source of life and death; and it is also found within the temples of the gods." [73]

The theory of Yin and Yang is a theory and method that the ancient Chinese people summarized as they observed many phenomena such as nature and society. There are two sides to everything in the world, there are good and bad sides. A person must look at things comprehensively in order to correctly understand the law of the development of things. As mentioned earlier, the traditional Chinese philosophy is formed by summing up the experience of the historical development. The process of the historical development is constantly alternating and repeated. There are often similar phenomena in history. Yin-Yang theory is an important part of the traditional Chinese philosophy. It is very valuable when used to analyze the development process of things. It can also be said that the traditional Chinese philosophy is a philosophy of process.

Yin and Yang are a pair of categories. Generally speaking, the sun is Yang, the moon is Yin, men are Yang, women are Yin, fire is Yang, water is Yin, the day is Yang, and the night is Yin. The static, the inwardly guarded, the descending, the cold, the tangible, the dull, and the restrained all belong to Yin; the sporty, outgoing, ascending, warm, invisible, bright, and excited all belong to Yang. Yin and Yang are integrated; Yin and Yang are opposed; Yin and Yang are

---

[73] Ilza Veith, The Yellow Emperor's Classic of Internal Medicine(Huang Ti Nei Ching Su Wen), (the Williams & Wilkins company, 1949), Chapter 5

mutually rooted; Yin and Yang are ebb and flow; Yin and Yang are transformed and there are five aspects. Yin and Yang are opposite and unified, representing two aspects that are mutually opposed and connected. The ancient people used the theory of Yin and Yang to explain everything, thunder and lightning, rain and dew, etc. Yin and Yang are in eternal movement. When in a state of harmony, sympathetic interaction occurs. Either one of the two sides of Yin and Yang contains the other. There is Yang inside Yin and there is Yin inside Yang. Yin and Yang oppose each other, inhibit each other, restrict each other, ebb and flow each other, and achieve unity. Yin and Yang are interdependent, there is no Yang if there is no Yin, and no Yin if there is no Yang. Just like if there is no cold, there is no heat, if there is no up, there is no down, lone Yin does not grow, and lone Yang does not grow. Under certain conditions, Yin and Yang transform in opposite directions. Night ends in day, and after day is night. After winter, it will gradually come to summer, the end of summer will gradually transition to winter.

Yin and Yang are always in constant movement and change, one will increase and the other will decrease. During the year, the Yin increases and the Yang decreases in winter. After the winter solstice, the Yang increases and the Yin decreases, and it gradually comes to spring. In spring and summer, the Yang has been increasing and the Yin has been decreasing. After the summer solstice, the Yin has been increasing and the Yang has been decreasing, and gradually it has come to fall and winter again and again. The temperature changes similarly throughout the day.

In market activities, formal organizations and informal organizations are just like Yin and Yang, forming two aspects of the unity of opposites. Who is Yang in formal and informal organizations? Who is Yin again? Formal organizations are tangible, produced tangible goods and it should belong to Yin. Informal organizations are intangible and provide intangible services, which should belong to Yang.

1. Mutual acting and containing between Yin and Yang

Formal organizations interact with informal organizations. Informal organizations provide financial support, managers, and technical staff. Formal organizations establish company, develop products, form a market, and sell on the market. This can be seen as the interaction of Yin and Yang, mutual interaction.

2. Yin and Yang are opposed and restrict each other.

Formal organizations and informal organizations are opposed to each other, restrict each other, and ebb and flow. The venture capital in the relationship network controls the management of the manufacturer's enterprise, the personnel employed by the enterprise is from the university and social relationship network. At the same time, the growth and shares of manufacturers is directly related to the profitability of venture capital.

3. Yin and Yang are interdependent and based on each other.

Formal organizations and informal organizations are interdependent, based on and prerequisite for each other. If the Silicon Valley companies left venture capital, and the social relationship networks such as universities and clubs, they would have a difficult development. In the social relationship network, without companies absorbing capital and personnel, it is difficult to maintain mutual relations. This is that lone Yin does not grow, and lone Yang does not grow.

4. Yin and Yang are mutually balanced.

The growth and decline of formal and informal organizations are balanced. In the growth stage of the Silicon Valley manufacturers, a large amount of venture capital is required, round after round of venture capital. Capital is increasing, and at the same time the number of staff employed by enterprises is also increasing. Professional managers are hired to form a mature management team. Capital and personnel are consumed in large quantities, and the company is growing rapidly. After the company goes public, the venture capital will recover its investment and search new targets. After the company expands, it has its own capital, which can also be used to invest in other emerging companies. The demand for investment and employment will no longer expand rapidly, and the capital consumption will decrease. The personnel tend to be stable and the market reaches a point of balance. Market activities have reached a relatively static balance from the initial movement, and in this relative stillness, there are new movements.

5. Interchange between Yin and Yang

Formal organizations and informal organizations transform each other. The Yin and Yang shift in the opposite direction under certain conditions. The founders and managers of the company will leave the company, enter the venture capital field, or return to the university to teach after their experiences. Members of the social relationship network, university graduates, and engineers in various fields leave the relationship network and become corporate managers.

From the above comparison, we can find that the situation of the formal organizations and informal organizations is very consistent with the theory of Yin and Yang. The theory of Yin and Yang can be used to illustrate this market evolution process. This seems to indicate that the traditional theory of Yin and Yang is not outdated and today can still be used to explain many social and economic phenomena, including corporate management, market evolution, and so on.

2.2 The stage of market evolution

The process of market evolution is a process in three stages, early market, developing market and mature market. The three stages evolution is a dynamic process; when a new technology appears, it will experience the three stages until the technology is mature. The new technology should be a breakthrough in the industry, it is called a disruptive innovation (Christensen, 1997), it isn't a micro innovation, and micro innovation is a continuous innovation on the basis of existing technology. The disruptive innovation has a characteristic that subverts the industry structure, it often gets restructuring the enterprises on the market position. The market change that is caused by a disruptive innovation will experience three stages, then it waits for the emergence of the next disruptive innovation technology. It causes a new market evolution; it is a cycle of evolution.

In the article, the enterprises in the market are classified into two kinds of enterprises. One kind of enterprise is the leading enterprise in the market, another kind of enterprise is the marginal enterprise. We analyze the process of market evolution from the management of enterprise, the strategic adjustment, the joint production of knowledge.

Early market

Before a new technology appears, the pattern of the market is stable, balanced. There are a few technical standards in the market. Around these few technical standards, several leading enterprises are respectively established in the market place. Each leading enterprise has some associated enterprises and the composition of an industrial chain, they occupy different positions in the industrial chain, and there are many related services for developers. At this time, the product and technology are mature, the market is stable, the client is clear: leading enterprises engaged in the micro-innovation, they improve the existing, mature, dominant products in the market, at the same time, they perfect sales channels and after-sales service. Before the emergence of new technologies, the market is in the silent period.

New technologies tend to be born in the "relationship network", sometimes new technologies are creative, they need a process for prototyping and commercialization; it may be a new project of a professor at the university, it may be a new idea of college students, it also may be a new thought of an enterprise staff(Freeman, 1982), it also may be the creative idea of customer confronted to the old products. At this moment, the relationship network has a certain size, the people in the relationship network communicate with each other. When the enterprise gets creative, it becomes a prototype, then it becomes a product and enters the market. The initial product may not be good, but the size of market isn't big, the relationship network is initial market. The reaction of the market to a new technology keeps calm, it doesn't exist in the fierce competition, because the outlook for the market isn't clear, the new technology is not perfect.

In the face of such situation, different enterprises have different coping strategies, old leading enterprises assess risk for the new technology, it has to go through a long time because of the size of leading enterprises, this is decided by each enterprise's decision-making mechanism and hierarchical. By being submitted to the management, the new technology usually can't attract the attention of enterprise top decision-makers, because leading enterprises mainly focus on the market share of existing products. Their existing products reap big profits and mature market; unless the top decision-makers are aware of the value of the new technology, they won't allocate manpower, material resources and financial resources for the development of new products. At this moment, the enterprise management is perfectly functioning, bureaucratic management tends to form a barrier to the emergence of new technology, because of past dependence, their dependence on existing product that is a success in the market and depends on the large amount of investment in the mature technology and long-term capital investment. In a large leading enterprise, the best way of professional manager promotion is to sale company's mature products in the market. It represents a risk to develop a new product that isn't clear in the market. No one will risk his position to do this kind of gambling, unless the leader orders him to do so.

In large-scale leading enterprises, the role of authority cannot be ignored. Traditional corporate management emphasizes authority and the role of authority. The main characteristic of subordinates is loyalty, and innovation is secondary. In the development process, the leading enterprise will form a level-by-level management structure led by each level of authority. In this way, major corporate management and operation decisions require the approval of the top management, which often leads to the dominant company's response to new changes in the market, a slow response and missed market opportunities. Leading companies are more willing to carry out micro-innovation on existing and mature products on the market, so that they have to use less investment, they get quick results, low market risk, and easy access to the company's management's approval, while research and development of new products with large differences require large investment; the cycle is long, the market risk is high, the dominant enterprise is unwilling to proceed.

On the other hand, some marginal enterprises, small enterprises in order to survive and develop will use less resources to promote the development of a new technology; in marginal enterprise, due to fewer personnel, management cost is low; this type of enterprise only needs a smaller market and can maintain their survival and development, the marginal enterprise needs less resources because of its moderate scale, it decides quickly; the new product cost is small for the marginal enterprise, the marginal enterprise's founders or management may come from the relationship network, and from groups who have a clear understanding of new technology; it may also be a leading enterprise internal staff who seek a development outside the enterprise. The marginal enterprise is unable to ensure that each one can survive, there are many results of many factors; the reason of the failure is probably the lack of funds, the management confusion, and that the product is not mature, and so on. After some market development, some marginal enterprises survive in the market.

Developing market

At this stage and acceptance of new products to win the market, there are more and more consumers of the new products, new technology to expand the market, the market does not have a balanced development, the market competition intensified; as the scale and advantage of marginal enterprises are growing, more and more people realize the value of the new technology. Leading enterprises are faced with the problem which is technical transformation, they are aware of the threat of new technology, they also realized that the arrival of the new market, ready to invest in the enterprise internal resources, with the development of corresponding products. But they would have difficulty, because more competitive products can be formed in the enterprise. The manufacturing of the original products in the enterprise has formed a series of chains from design, development, production and sales, involving many suppliers of supporting products in the supply chain. The development of new products will involve the adjustment of internal and external interests of the enterprise, which means the division of internal resources of an enterprise; internal competition is no less difficult to beat than external market competition.

There are several possible results: one kind is stillborn, new product development is not listed, enterprise transformation failure; Another possible result is that the new product development gets successful in the market, and gets profitable but the product development success does not guarantee the smooth transition of the enterprise. Some leading enterprises couldn't get the first round, launch new products, as the original product market is shrinking, enterprise profits decline, exit the market gradually. When the market grows and expands, marginal enterprises increase the number of their employees, the enterprise management gradually is matured, hierarchical, they gradually become a new leading enterprise.

At this stage, the market is not balanced, a "positive feedback" is an accelerating stage. This is the stage where technological innovation accelerates diffusion, and market competition speeds up this process(Robertson. Thomas S and Hubert Gatignon, 1986). The marginal enterprise accelerates the development, improves the new technology and expands the scale of the enterprise, by recruiting many new employees who came from the relationship network, and marginal enterprises which also accelerated get support from the relationship network to obtain all kinds of resources. This is the mutual transformation between manufacturer and relationship network; the relationship network promotes the rapid development of manufacturing vendors. The creations at early market evolve into the joint production of knowledge. During this period, the functions of the product are becoming more and more, new products technical standards are gradually established, the new technology is also gradually getting complicated, the new technology production and dissemination of knowledge are no longer contained only in a limited time in a particular area, by the specific research institutions or private research laboratory, they are actually created in common about some problems by members of the relationship network. Faulkner and Jaqueline (Faulkner and Jaqueline, 1995) found that the research project has a strong extensionality, involves the professional knowledge outside, engineers and researchers need to create a personal relationship with external partners and strong connection, though they do not belong to the same research institution.

Mature market

New technology is increasingly perfected, the market scale and pattern established, the market goes from unbalance to a new equilibrium. Several marginal enterprises establish monopoly, they grow up to be new leading enterprises, around them, and they established a new industry chain. The original leading enterprise missed the right time to enter the market, there were internal benefit disputes, the strategic adjustment of error, relying on outdated technology, are responsible for the result that the original leading enterprise did not occupy a certain position in the new market, then relevant enterprises exit the market continuously, even collapse, restructuring. And the developed marginal enterprises through mergers and acquisitions ensure their market leader position, become the new leading enterprises, they control the new technical standards, dominate the market around the new technical standard;

the new leading enterprises with vertical integration and symbiotic way to occupy the market with upstream and downstream enterprises, they are also likely to form strategic alliances with partner enterprises, they establish benefit from the relationship network who controls the market. New entrants have difficulties to enter the market, new leading enterprises improve the threshold at this moment, they deposit patents and establish higher technical standards to prevent other companies to enter, they have a lot of investment in new technology; the product is perfected and it needs to add micro-innovation. The new leading enterprises improve the sales channels, through scale and price to edge out all their opponents, the new leading enterprises use their own money, sufficient, on products to provide high quality service, the other enterprises have a hard time to do it. In short, the new leading enterprises established the technical standards, market leadership, their management is perfectly adapted, they have mature marketing and quality service, and they have completed a smooth transition from the marginal enterprise, or from a small enterprise in the market to a leading enterprise.

During this period, the market gradually evolves towards a new equilibrium, new leading enterprises developing in a mature way, reached their peak, fully get many supports of aspects from the relationship network, a lot of personnel in the relationship network start a business. In this period, the market completed a cycle of mutual transformation between the two groups. The market gestates a new technology, it is ready to open a new round of mutual influence and mutual conversion cycle between manufacturing vendors and relationship network.

3.The model summary

In the product life cycle theory, it is difficult to explain why the new technology has not been adopted by leading enterprises in the market? Why there is the replacement of the organization? Why will appear constantly the phenomenon of mutual transformation between leading enterprise and marginal enterprise in the process of appearance of new technologies?

Path dependence as a concept provides a different perspective from economics to explain the market evolution process. The view of simple economics is limited, some sociological concepts, such as social capital, the relationship network, the creative capital concept are used to explain the economic growth, the market evolution.

Early market, developing market and mature market, the three stages show the circulation of products from the creative prototype, goods, when the old and new enterprises compete, the market pattern is changed. Market positions were restructured, the market develops from the initial imbalance caused by the new technology to enter the new equilibrium, the market waits for the emergence of a new technology, and begins the next round of a new market evolution cycle.

REFERENCES

Arthur, W. B (1989). Competing technologies, increasing returns, and locking-in by historical events. The Economic Journal, 99, 116-131

Arthur, W. B. Increasing returns and path dependence in the economy. Ann Arbor: The University of Michigan Press

Arthur, W. B., Ermoliev, Y. M., & Kaniovski, Y. M. (1987). Path dependence process and the emergence of macro-structure. European Journal of Operational Research, 30, 294-303

Clayton Christensen(1997), "The innovator's dilemma", President and Fellows of Harvard College

Dara Elizabeth Menashi(1997), Making Public/Private Collaboration Productive: Lessons for Creating Social Capital, unpublished doctoral dissertation, John F.Kennedy School of Government, Harvard University

D. North(1983), "Structure and Change in Economic History," New Haven: Yale University Press

David, P. A. (1985). Clio and the economics of QWERTY. American Economic Review, 76, 332-337

David, P. A. (1986). Understanding the Economics of QWERTY: The necessary of history. In W. N. Parker, (Ed.), Economic history and the modern economist (pp.). New York: Basil Blackwell

Faulkner Wendy and Jaqueline Senker (1995), knowledge Frontiers, (Oxford: Clarendon Press)

Freeman, John(1982), "Organizational Life Cycles and Natural Selection Process", Research in Organizational Behavior, B.M.Staw and L.L.Cummings, eds., 4, 1-32

Gibbons, Michael, Cambining Limoges, Helga Nowotny, Simon Schwartsman, Peter Scott and Martin Trow(1994), The New Production of Knowledge, (London: Sage)

Lambkin, Mary and George S.Day(1989), Evolutionary Processes in Competitive Markets: Beyond the Product Life Cycle, Vol.53 (July '89), pp.4—20. Reprinted from the Journal of Marketing, published by American Marketing Association.

Levitt, Theodore(1965), "Exploit the Product life Cycle" , Harvard Business Review, 43(November---December), 81-94

Raghu Garud, Peter Karnoe(2001), "Path dependence and Creation", Lawrence Erlbaum Associates, Inc,

Richard Florida(2002), "The rise of creative class", Susan Schulman literary agency, Inc, 317-326

Robert Cushing, "Creative, Capital, Diversity and Urban Growth", Unpublished manuscript, Austin, Texas, December 2001

Robert Putnam(2000), "Bowling Alone", New York: Simon and Schuster, 376-379

Robertson. Thomas S and Hubert Gatignon(1986), "Competitive Effect on Technology Piffusion" , Vol.50(July '86), pp.1-12, Reprinted from Journal of Marking, published by the American Marketing Association.

APPENDIX:

中国历史朝代表 eras of Chinese history

中国历史 History of China

1.　　先秦时期 Pre-Qin Period〔221 BC〕

夏 Xia Dynasty (2070 BC–1600 BC)

商 Shang Dynasty (1600 BC–1046 BC)

周 Zhou Dynasty (1046 BC–256 BC)

春秋战国时期 Spring and Autumn Period / Warring States Period (770 BC–221 BC)

中国古典思想诞生时期 the birth period of Chinese classic thought

2.　　秦 Qin Dynasty (221 BC–207 BC)

3.　　汉 Han Dynasty (202 BC–AD 220)

4.　　三国时期 Three Kingdoms (AD 220–280)

5.　　魏晋南北朝时期 Wei Jin and the Southern and Northern Dynasties〔AD 266-589〕

晋 Jin Dynasty (AD 266–420)

南北朝 Northern and Southern Dynasties (AD 420–589)

6.　　隋唐 Sui and Tang Dynasties (AD 581-907〕

隋 Sui Dynasty (AD 581–618)

唐 Tang Dynasty (AD 618–907)

7.　　五代十国 Five Dynasties and Ten Kingdoms (AD 907–960)

8.　　宋 辽 金 西夏 Song, Liao, Jin, and Western Xia Dynasties (AD 960–1234)

北宋 Bei Song Dynasty (AD 960－1127)

南宋 Nan Song Dynasty (AD 1127-1279)

9.　　元 Yuan Dynasty (AD 1271–1368)

10.　　明 Ming Dynasty (AD 1368–1644)

11.　　清 Qing Dynasty (AD 1644–1911)

12.　　民国时期 Republic of China (1912-1949)

13.　　中华人民共和国 People's Republic of China (Since 1949)

ABOUT THE AUTHOR

I studied computer science at university. After graduation, I worked in engineering and technology fields in the army. I accumulated management experience and for a period of time I worked in some local governments. For economics, sociology, culture and history, it is an interesting hobby for me. I think that the family environment does have a significant impact on the formation of a person's thoughts. According to the Western understanding. I grew up in the environment of a manager's family in a large state-owned enterprise in the aerospace field in Beijing, the capital of China. Although I did not work long in the enterprise, this family background is unusual among the Chinese especially, a few decades ago, compared with the Western society, the degree of China industrialization was not high, this makes me have a deep understanding of enterprises, especially large vertically integrated firms. Beijing is the capital and cultural center of China, and there are many exchanges with other countries, all of which have a great influence on my growth. Traveling also enriched my personal knowledge and experiences and gave me a new perspective on life. There are many unknown things in the world and people are looking forward to exploring and discovering them. Due to my limited personal knowledge and ability, there must be imperfections within the content of this book. I hope readers can understand and tolerate it. I also hope that this book can arouse more readers, thinking and putting forward different opinions. My email: wang570468@gmail.com